# Guilty M'Lud!

Six convicted thieves of 1870 and 1871. Taken from the 'Register of Convicted Criminals' held at the Northamptonshire Police Museum.

# GUILTY M'LUD!

**The criminal history of Northamptonshire**

RICHARD COWLEY

PEG AND WHISTLE BOOKS
KETTERING, NORTHAMPTONSHIRE
1998

First published 1998



ISBN 0 9534095 0 3

Published by
Peg and Whistle Books
147 Russell Street
KETTERING
Northamptonshire NN16 0EW

Printed and Bound in Great Britain by Woolnough Bookbinding,
Irthlingborough, Northants NN9 5SE

For
VALERIE
For all her constant encouragement

# ACKNOWLEDGEMENTS

I wish to thank everyone who has helped me by giving the use of their time, and allowing me to inspect, read, photograph, copy and ultimately publish, all the records, original or otherwise, that they hold in their care. Especially, I wish to thank Mr Edward Crew QPM, former Chief Constable of Northamptonshire, in giving me full use of all the records kept at force headquarters, more especially in allowing the photographs of 'The Register of Convicted Criminals' to be used. Also to former Inspector Graham Rogers, curator of the force museum, whose never-failing humour, cheery banter, and deep pocket for canteen coffee, brightened my every visit to force headquarters.

Likewise my thanks go to Miss Rachel Watson and her staff at the Northamptonshire County Record Office; Miss M. Arnold and her staff at the Northampton General Library in Abington Street; Mr N. Ward and Mr T. Bracher of the Northamptonshire Libraries Service; Mrs I. Thompson of the Northampton Borough Council Cemeteries Department; and to the staff at the Kettering Central Library.

I would also like to thank Mrs Maureen Chalker for her editorial skills. Her prowess in freeing my manuscript of grammatical misdemeanours and "policeman's jargon", was most welcome; as also were her suggestions as to the contents of some of the chapters. I am most grateful.

The source for each photograph and illustration is given in brackets after the captions: NP = Northamptonshire Police; NRO = Northamptonshire County Record Office; NL = Northamptonshire Libraries and Information service and Popperfoto. Where no acknowledgement is given, the illustration is from the author's own collection.

# FOREWORD

EDWARD CREW, QPM

## CHIEF CONSTABLE OF NORTHAMPTONSHIRE POLICE 1993-96

I am delighted to be asked to write the foreword for this book about the History of Crime and Punishment in the County. The book charts the most serious crimes committed between 1202 and 1945, and follows the cases right through from the initial investigation to the court room. The volume is the fruit of painstaking research, conducted by one of my retired colleagues and he is to be commended for producing a work that I am sure will be compulsive reading for all who have an interest in local history.

# LIST OF SUBSCRIBERS

Mr L. Allday, Kettering
Mr P. Anderson, Barkingside, Essex
Mrs M. Bailey (2), Kettering
Mr D. Belgum, Northampton
Mr A. Booth, Desborough
Mr K. Birch, Aberdyfi, Gwynedd
Mr A. Black, Barnsey, Isle of Man
Ms D. Burch, Brackley
Mrs M. Button, Northampton
Miss H. Cameron, Thrapston
Mr P. Chambers, East Hagbourne, Oxfordshire
Mr R. Coverdale, Sidcup, Kent
Mr T. Finbow, Collompton, Devonshire
Mr T. Gardner, Leamington Spa, Warwickshire
Mr R. Gould, Goodmayes, Essex
Mr W. Gregg, Ruislip, Middlesex
Mr J. Griffiths, Wethorden, Suffolk
Mr D. Giese, United States of America
Mrs G. Horan, Moston, Manchester
Dr D. King, Thornton Heath, Surrey
Mr S. Knatt, Great Billing
Mr T. Madigan, Luton, Bedfordshire
Mrs A. Malin, Hartwell
Mr S. Morris, Stoke on Trent, Staffordshire
Mrs D. Oakensen, Seaford, East Sussex
Mrs P. Parsons, Sidcup, Kent
Mr K. Renew, Dagenham, Essex
Mr K. Sayner, North Humberside
Mr D. Sevkett, Plumstead, London
Mr F. Spokes, Wellingborough
Mr M. Stallion, Leigh on Sea, Essex
Mr V. Tambling, Great Barr, Birmingham
Mr D. Taylor, Huddersfield, West Yorkshire
Mr A. Toseland, Kettering
Mrs D. Tyson, Great Grimsby, NE Lincolnshire
Mr M. Vince, Buckingham, Buckinghamshire
Mrs R. Walker, Honley, West Yorkshire
Mr F. Wilkinson, Holborn, London
Mr K. Williams, Eglwysbach, North Wales
Mr R. Williams, Corby

# LIST OF CONTENTS

# INTRODUCTION

## 'THERE IS NO EXPLANATION FOR EVIL'

"There is no explanation for evil. It must be looked upon as a necessary part of the order of the universe. To ignore it is childish, to bewail it, senseless".
*The Summing Up* W. Somerset Maugham (1874-1965).

CRIME, it is sad to say, has been an attribute of the human species ever since time began: since Eve stole from the tree of knowledge and Cain killed Abel. And nobody has yet come up with an explanation why. Everywhere mankind goes, crime, it seems, is never very far away, so even in this apparently tranquil corner of the universe we call Northamptonshire, we have not been free of it. Indeed, throughout history, Northamptonshire has probably had more than its fair share of criminal activity, from the foulest of murders, robberies and rapes, through to the cheekiest of thefts, and to some which are reflections of more turbulent social times than ours, witchcraft, treason and heresy.

Thus it seems strange, that given the apparent significance of crime in human history, studies of historical crime, especially of one locality, are so very hard to come by. Northamptonshire is no exception. No attempt has ever been made to examine the county's criminal past, and therefore published information is non existent.

The realisation that nothing had been published on this subject was brought home to me when I was undertaking research for a degree where I was examining the origins of the police in Northamptonshire. To want to examine the crime rates of the early 19th century was therefore a natural progression. But I searched in vain. Nowhere could I find out any published information at all. I therefore had to start completely from scratch and research it all myself.

Although at first I was only interested in the 19th century, the subject was so fascinating that eventually I broadened out to include all the written documents I could find, which took me back to the 13th century. Northamptonshire, I found, was rich in documents in which criminal activity is recorded, and from which a fairly comprehensive picture of the course of crime in the county could be charted.

Firstly therefore, this book has a serious purpose, which is to examine the historical incidence of crime in Northamptonshire, along with the way it was dealt with by the criminal justice system. For by considering crime, we cannot ignore society's attempts to control it, in the shape of the policing arrangements, the courts system, and then the punishment which was given.

However, it would be foolish to assume that everybody who reads this book will do so for this reason, for it is a fact that crime (especially the murders), and the murkier doings of our fellow men, does hold a fascination for all of us, as evidenced by the large number of fictional 'whodunits' and 'true crime' books written and sold every year. So although the serious side of the book is there if you look for it, the general reader will also find a catalogue of crimes, some of which are so fantastic that no fiction writer could ever have made them up.

# CHAPTER 1

## 'THE REGISTER OF THE CRIMES' THE HISTORICAL OVERVIEW OF CRIME IN NORTHAMPTONSHIRE

"History ... is little more than the register of the crimes, follies and misfortunes of mankind"
*The Decline and Fall of the Roman Empire*: Edward Gibbon (1737-1794)

NORTHAMPTONSHIRE is rich in criminal activity, and the documents that record it. So a fairly comprehensive picture can easily be built up of the murkier doings of our county ancestors.

Homicides, obviously, figure largely, and although in the medieval period details are somewhat hazy, as we come nearer our own times, information is easier to come by, and from about the year 1800, a *complete* list can be made of every murder or manslaughter that has occurred within the county. Although space does not permit a description of every single one, nevertheless a good cross section is described, from Northamptonshire's 13th century triple murderer, to the GI murder of 1945; from the case of seven year old Arthur Pittam, the youngest ever person to be tried for manslaughter in the county, to the incredibly ghoulish murderers, Thomas Morris, James Shaw and Alex Claydon, who left their victims horribly mutilated.

The traditional punishment for murder is death, and hanging, beheading, burning and pressing are the four ways that the death sentence has been carried out in Northamptonshire. Each one, contrary to popular opinion, was used only in specific circumstances. Pressing, for instance, when great weights were placed on top of a man lying flat on the ground, was not done indiscriminately, but for a specific charge. Only one person has been pressed to death in Northamptonshire, in 1630.

Likewise, burning was a very specific punishment reserved for very specific offences, and beheading was only used for those of noble blood. In contrast, the criminal from the common herd was launched into eternity by being hung. These hangings, which before 1837 could also be for crimes other than murder, were public affairs, and were great social occasions.

We shall read of the public hanging of Meadows, Gent and Middleton found guilty of rape in 1822, and of the last hanging in Northamptonshire of a woman, Elizabeth Pinckard in 1852 for murder, which incidentally, was the last *public* hanging in the county as well. After that, hangings were in private, but the press were invited, and every detail was freely published in local newspapers and broadsheets, from where we get the description of the hanging of the 'monstrous' Thomas Chamberlain in 1874, whose only motive for the murder of a defenceless old man of 72, was to 'see what it felt like'.

The taking of human life by another human being is quite obviously of such seriousness (remember the Ten Commandments: 'Thou shalt not kill'?) that society cannot tolerate it, and condemns such 'criminal' activity. Other 'crimes', although less serious than homicide, nevertheless still demand society's displeasure. The activities of theft, robbery and burglary, for example, have *always* been considered as criminal, and we shall see that they have not changed much over the centuries, although there have been subtle twists along the way. What, for instance, did the medieval thief steal the most often? What did the 18th century thief steal? Are they different, and if so, what does this tell us?

The crimes of robbery and burglary have tended to be confused over the years, with robberies being described as burglary and vice versa, but they are totally different criminal concepts, and both have always been prevalent. Robberies and burglaries can be found in 13th century documents, as well as last week's court reports in the local newspaper.

Never changing also, are the offences of arson, assault, damage and drunkenness. These crimes are with us today, as much as they were in medieval times, in Tudor times, in Commonwealth times, and in Victorian times. Endless numbers of these are described in the records, and some are given here, including the last person to be hanged for a non-homicide offence in Northamptonshire, Thomas Gee for arson in 1834.

The sexual urge is one of the three great driving forces of humanity (together with eating and finding shelter) so we should not wonder when sometimes this innate urge is combined with criminality. The rape of Helewisa and Christina in 13th century Northamptonshire, was as traumatic to them as it was to ten year old Ann Swannell in 1830, for which Thomas White was hanged. George James also found that the law was just as harsh following his indecent assault on 11 year old Charlotte Coleman at Glendon in 1868.

But all the above crimes are still being committed today, as they have always been. There are, however, some practises which have declined markedly. Organised criminal gangs, for instance, roamed the countryside from medieval times right up until the county constabularies started appearing in the mid 1840s. Northamptonshire has had its fair share of these gangs, from the county's 13th century equivalent of Robin Hood, to the 'Captain Slash' gang of the 1820s, including that most notorious bunch of all, the Culworth Gang of the 1780s. We shall read of these gangs, their crimes, and of their demise following the hanging of their leaders.

Vagrancy is also not a problem nowadays. Or at least not the problem that it was in the past, when law abiding men had a fear almost bordering on paranoia of travelling vagrants, and went to great lengths to control them. Begging and sleeping rough, were regarded as vagrancy, and we can judge what society thought of these two activities when we see what sentences were given to Edward Vann and Thomas Wragby, who were convicted of doing just that.

Riots do not happen much now either, but they did in the past, sometimes with admirable social reasons. Joseph Clapham when he was involved in the 'Captain Swing' riot at Finedon in 1830, was trying to improve his social lot, and that of his family around him, rather than just drunkenly destroying property. The 1852 Wellingborough Election rioters, on the other hand, just wanted a good 'punch-up', which they got, but which left a policeman so badly injured that he never worked again.

And what of the 'crimes' that have disappeared altogether, in these enlightened, thoughtful and non-superstitious times of ours? We never hear of witchcraft any more, but Northamptonshire was a hotbed of it. In fact, the last two women to be executed as witches in the whole of England, both came from Oundle, and were hanged at Northampton in 1705. We shall read of their execution, together with the other poor souls of earlier times, who also suffered at the hands of a substantially more intolerant society.

If crime is to be described, then so also must the criminal justice system, or the way in which society tried to curb the criminality of its more unruly members. So the policing, the courts system and the punishments used, have all been given separate chapters. We shall learn how the English system of policing (the 'old' system) evolved and lasted for nearly 500 years, but how by the early 1800s, society had changed so much that the 'old' system just could not cope anymore. The revolution of policing (the 'new' system) which occurred in London in 1829, was actually adopted quite speedily in Northamptonshire in 1835 and 1840, making this county one of the pioneers of the 'new' provincial policing in England.

This, however, proved the death knell for that other great law-and-order idea connected with the 18th century, the private prosecution associations (otherwise called catch-criminal societies or felons' associations) which in Northamptonshire will be shown not to have been very effective in fighting crime. Consequently, the associations declined quite rapidly after the county constabulary came on the scene in 1840.

Nowadays, only imprisonment is used as the ultimate deterrent for crime. But throughout the centuries, stocks, pillories, whipping and birching, branding and fining have all been used as punishment. All these have their place in the criminal history of the county, and so deserve a mention, even though they have since dropped out of the armoury for combatting criminal behaviour.

## *The Register of the Crimes*

The old saying about statistics may be true, but they do have their place. So wherever possible, statistics have been deduced to indicate the 'trend' of certain offences. It must be stressed however, that these figures are unsophisticated because they are based only on the extremely scanty evidence which has survived. Nevertheless, some of these figures can still be surprising and eye opening.

# CHAPTER 2

## 'OF VIOLENT DEATH': CRIMINAL HOMICIDE IN NORTHAMPTONSHIRE

"No arts; no letters; no society; and what is worst of all, continual fear and danger of violent death; and the life of man, solitary, poor, nasty, brutish and short."
*Leviathan:* Thomas Hobbes (1588-1679)

WHEN studying criminal homicide (the unlawful killing of one human being by another) Northamptonshire is one of the better served counties in the number of written records that have survived. For the medieval period, the roll (in other words, the written record, so called because the parchments on which the court proceedings were written were sewn together end to end and then rolled up) for the county Assizes of 1202 and 1203 has survived together with the Supervisors' Rolls of 1314 to 1320, and the Coroners' Rolls for 70 complete years during the period 1290 to 1420.

Nearer our own time, we can read the reports in one of the world's oldest newspapers, the *Northampton Mercury*, continuously published from 1720; and from the turn of the 18th and 19th centuries, a continuous series of the Assize Calendars (the printed list of cases being tried at each Assize session) is preserved.

Using all these sources, a formidable record of the murders that have occurred within Northamptonshire can be compiled. Although patchy during the early years, from 1800 onwards, every single case of criminal homicide is known, and there are literally hundreds of them. Most of them make repetitive (and boring) reading, but occasionally a case stands out by its sheer unusualness either in the motive, the age of the offender, the weapons used, the ferocity of the attack, or in some other way.

The earliest recorded murders are the eight reported in the 1202 Assizes. As the population for the county can be estimated (from published figures) at 20,000 at that time, then eight murders, gives a rate per 1,000 population of .4. Today, in these supposedly violent times, we have nothing like approaching this rate. In 1993 there were six murders from a population of approximately

575,000, a rate of per 1,000 population of .01.

In only one instance of the eight 1202 murders is the murderer actually caught and punished. Godfrey of Warkton had murdered Roger the Reaper in Warkton sometime during the year, and was caught, tried and hanged, with his worldly goods valued at 12s being forfeited to the Crown. This was a very rare occurrence, as in those days there was no official authority who would actually do the 'detective' work to investigate crime and murder. England had to wait for over 500 years before it got any sort of detective/investigative police force ('The Bow Street Runners'), and even then, this was started by a private individual and not by central government.

The Coroners' Rolls from Northamptonshire are preserved at the Public Record Office. They record inquests for 70 years, the first starting in 1290 and the last in 1420. The office of Coroner is an ancient one, probably starting sometime during the twelfth century, with each county, generally, having four Coroners at one given time, and every borough having just one.

As they still do, the function of the medieval Coroner was to enquire into all sudden or unexplained deaths; that is, homicide, suicide or accident. When a body was discovered, and the murderer was thought to be nearby, the first on the scene was to raise the 'Hue and Cry' (see Chapter 4).

The Coroner would then be summoned, and he would attend with a jury and view the body still in situ. The jury would be 12 free-men of the locality who had been quickly gathered together.

The Coroner would examine the body for marks of violence, and would record the date, place and time of death as far as he could. The jurors were then asked to identify the body, determine the cause of death, and if possible, the circumstances surrounding it; and in the case of a homicide, try to name the suspects.

The arrest of any suspect would be ordered, his possessions confiscated, and he would be sent to gaol to await trial. If the accused had fled the scene, which most obviously had, the Coroner would direct the local law enforcement officer (the sheriff or his bailiff or the parish constable) to arrest the person as soon as possible.

All this Inquest information would then be copied onto rolls of parchment and await further examination by the professional judges, the king's justices, on their periodic visits to the county, as distinct from the Assizes. These periodic visits were called 'Eyres'.

Not to put too fine a point on it, the Eyres were more about filling the king's coffers than the administration of justice. As with the Assizes, each offence could (and was) punished by a fine. It is perfectly understandable therefore, to see the Eyre examine the Coroners' Rolls of the previous few years to see how much money they could extract from it in the shape of fines.

In 1327, Edward III on coming to the throne, found himself short of money, and so a general Eyre was ordered. The Northamptonshire Eyre took place in 1329 to 1330, where the Coroners' Rolls of the previous 40 years were looked at.

This explains why so many Coroners' Rolls have been preserved. At the Public Record Office, the county of Northamptonshire has one of the best series preserved. In all, rolls for 70 of the 130 years between 1290 and 1420 have been preserved. In a study of these rolls, Dr Barbara Hanawalt of Indiana State University, has analysed all the homicides that are recorded.

In those 70 years, there were 1307 inquests into sudden deaths; 16 suicides, 716 fatal accidents, and 575 criminal homicides. Again, this is an incredible number — 575 in 70 years — an average of just over eight per year, every year. The Coroners' Rolls therefore confirm the high number of homicides that the Assize Rolls indicate happened every year in Northamptonshire.

Using these rolls, Dr Hanawalt constructed a 'profile of the average medieval murderer. He (99% of murderers were men) will be a man of middle means in the peasant society. ... He is most likely to attack a man over 40 who is a neighbour or an acquaintance rather than a family member, and he will kill with a knife or a staff. He would also kill during the evenings or after dark on Sundays during the summer months. The killing will be done after an argument, and will either be in the fields, or in the victim's own home'.

**Northamptonshire's first serial killer?**

1291 *Victim:* Geoffrey, son of Alexander Broun of Bradden:
sometime during 1291
Chipping Warden

1305 *Victim:* William de Hynton, clerk of Woodford Halse
Wednesday 8 September 1305
Woodford Halse

1323 *Victim:* Geoffrey of Warden
sometime during 1323
Chipping Warden

*Offender in all three:* Martin of Littlebury

The triple murderer, Martin of Littlebury, must have been quite a character. One dark night in the year 1291, he met up with Geoffrey, son of Alexander Broun, on the banks of the Cherwell at a place called 'le Mede' in Chipping Warden. Martin then shot Geoffrey with a bow and arrow, killing Geoffrey instantly. Martin fled, but before he could gain sanctuary was arrested and gaoled at Northampton castle to await trial. All his goods were confiscated, and amounted to 54s 6d, indicating that he was a man of substantial means.

At his trial, it was found that Martin shot Geoffrey in self defence. In those days, there was no difference between murder and manslaughter, those were not differentiated until 100 years later. Martin was therefore imprisoned to await sentence by the king's justices. However, he apparently escaped and managed to avoid capture for a number of years before he surfaced again.

On Wednesday 8 September 1305, Martin struck again. This time it was the parish priest of Woodford Halse, William de Hynton. There are no exact details of this murder, but Martin fled to sanctuary in Chipping Warden church. He confessed his crime and abjured (was banished from) the realm. This time his goods were worth only 10½d .

Eighteen years were to go by before Martin of Littlebury came to light again. In 1323 he suddenly turned up at Chipping Warden alleging that he had a charter of pardon from the king. No doubt a few old scores needed to be settled, and Martin finished up in a fight with Geoffrey of Warden, and in which Martin murdered Geoffrey by stabbing him with a knife.

Instead of seeking sanctuary, Martin fled, and because of this was declared an outlaw. There is no record of his capture or his subsequent career; perhaps men did not want to tangle with a fiery tempered character with at least three killings to his name.

It is at this point that history draws a veil over Martin of Littlebury. Perhaps it is just as well. For the meanings of Sanctuary and Outlawry, see Appendix 1.

**One law for the rich and ...?**

1301 *Victim:* John of Weldon
Saturday 13 May 1301
Polebrook
*Offenders:* Reginald Porthors of Polebrook
Ralph le Chapman

On the evening of Saturday 13 May 1301, Reginald Porthors and Ralph le Chapman, acting on orders from Lord Ralph Porthors, Lord of the Manor of Polebrook, went to John of Weldon's house in Polebrook, either to arrest him or to kill him. What the Lord of the Manor wanted John for is unknown, or whether he had the legal power to arrest him anyway.

Ralph and Reginald (a kinsman of the Lord of the Manor?) went to John's house, but he was asleep. Apparently without even waking him, Reginald hit John on the head with a blunt instrument which spilled his brains out; and then Ralph split his back open with a hatchet.

They returned to Lord Ralph's with 10s they had taken from John's body. The parish constable and men of Polebrook in the meantime, having learned of the murder, followed the two criminals back to Lord Ralph's. Lord Ralph, however refused them entry, and allowed Ralph and Reginald to escape.

Whether Ralph and Reginald were ever captured, we are not told, and their subsequent fate is unknown. This case shows that men of noble birth had no need to murder, as they could order their servants to do it for them. Obviously, there had been some dispute between Lord Porthors and John of Weldon, hence the return of the two servants with 10s.

Although Lord Porthors had instigated and conspired in the murder, and had assisted in the escape of the criminals (which in modern legal eyes would make him just as culpable), in medieval times he was deemed innocent purely by his noble birth. Even if a noble such as Lord Porthors were indicted for murder, he would have immediately received a pardon from the king. Truly in those days, there really was one law for the rich and one for the poor, which is exactly as everyone thought anyway.

**The Reluctant soldiers**

1322 *Victim:* John Roberd of Cold Ashby
Saturday 13 March 1322
Cold Ashby
*Offenders:* Richard, son of William le Clerk of Crick
John, son of Richard of Ashby

In 1322, a two year truce with Scotland ended, and the Scottish army under Robert the Bruce invaded England. They got as far as Preston, spreading alarm and despondency, before having to return northwards. To counter this, Edward II ordered an army to assemble at Newcastle, and so started the nearest thing to conscription, and it fell upon the shoulders of each parish constable throughout the land, to chose men for the army.

John Roberd was the parish constable of Cold Ashby, and the two men he picked, Richard, son of William le Clerk of Crick, and John, son of Richard of Ashby obviously did not want to go. They sought out the unfortunate parish constable, and told him exactly what they thought of him. John was obviously frightened and ran away through the village of Cold Ashby, hotly pursued by the two 'soldiers'.

They finally caught up with him in the porch of a house in the village, and there Richard, ran him straight through the middle with his lance. John took two days to die.

In the meantime, Richard and John fled to Cold Ashby church for sanctuary. But in this case, the sanctuary machinery did not work, because before the two could confess to the Coroner, the other recruits on their way to join the army, dragged them out of the church, and forced them to go with them to Scotland. A case of 'if we have to go, then you do too'. Whatever happened to our reluctant soldiers, history tells us nothing.

**The wrong side at the wrong time**

1450 *Victim:* William Tresham
Wednesday 23 September 1450
Moulton
*Offender:* Evan ap Rice

William Tresham was a very important man, not only in Northamptonshire, but in all England as well. He was a lawyer in the Crown service and on several occasions had been appointed to Royal Commissions empowered to gather money to finance Henry V's French expeditions. It is probable that he was also Attorney-General to Henry V.

Between the years 1423 and 1450 as a Member of Parliament for Northamptonshire, he had been elected Speaker four times, an important and powerful position. He was also very influential within the Royal administration, and had gradually increased his position until in 1449, he was appointed Chancellor to the Duchy of Lancaster.

To be suspected of collaborating with the exiled Duke of York was therefore remarkably undiplomatic, not to say foolish, of him. And when it was discovered that the two intended meeting at Northampton after the Duke had invaded the country, powerful enemies plotted to remove him, by force if necessary.

Edmund, Lord Grey of Ruthyn had large estates in Northamptonshire, and was a passionate Lancastrian, and it is generally thought that it was Lord Grey's servants who carried out Tresham's murder. On the evening of Tuesday 22 September 1450, the time of Tresham's departure for Northampton was obtained by trickery, and using this information, a gang of about 150 armed men laid an ambush at Thorpelands in Moulton on the road between Kettering and Northampton.

Early on the next day, Tresham, together with his son Thomas, came riding by. William was murdered by a Welshman, Evan ap Rice, by being run through with a lance. His body was stripped of a collar of the royal livery, a gold chain, his signet ring and other jewellery, and about £20 in money. Evan ap Rice was then alleged to have continued to keep and ride Tresham's horse for some time afterwards.

Thomas Tresham was severely injured, but survived. The body of William Tresham was taken to Northampton by his servants who had been some distance behind when the murder had taken place. His murderers, although well known, and despite appeals by Isabel Tresham, were never brought to trial.

**The butcher of Wappenham**

1685 *Victim*: The 'Reverend' Theophilus Hart (65)
Tuesday 23 January 1685
Wappenham
*Offender*: George Tarry, Butcher

The Wallop family were Lords of the Manor of Wappenham, near to Towcester. When Sir Henry Wallop died, the Manor passed to his son, Robert, who obviously then fell on hard times. This was during the English Commonwealth under Lord Protector Cromwell.

Robert Wallop's chaplain was the 'Reverend' Theophilus Hart, although there is some doubt as to whether he was an ordained priest or not. These were reli-

A

# Kalendar *of the* PRISONERS

## (*Whether for* Felony *or* Miſdemeanors)

Now in Cuſtody of HIS MAJESTY's Goaler for the County of *NORTHAMPTON*,

To be Try'd on *Tueſday* the 15th Day of *JULY*, 1735.

### William Hunt,

Condemn'd, but Repriev'd 'till further Orders.

### William Blinman,

Continued for Want of Security.

### Frances Goodman,

(*Committed by* Thomas Hawley, *Eſq*; March 15.)

Charged upon Oath to have feloniouſly ſtolen one Sheet, one Table-Cloth, one Pillow Drawer, Value Five Shillings, the Property of *William Hart* of *Earl's-Barton.*

### Elizabeth Wilkinſon, Hanged

(*Committed by* Thomas Hawley, *Eſq*; April 9.)

Charged upon Oath of *William Hicks*, for feloniouſly picking his Pocket, and taking thereout One Pound Seventeen Shillings and Ten-pence, the Property of the ſaid *William Hicks.*

### Robert Pittam,

(*Committed by* Smith Fleetwood, *Eſq*; April 11.)

Charged upon Oath to have in an unlawful Manner defrauded *Richard Slatter* of Two Blacks Filleys, the Property of *John Slatter.*

### Elizabeth Ward,

(*Committed by* John Freeman, *M.D.* April 18.)

Charged upon Oath to have in an unlawful Manner defrauded *Suſannah Collins* of Two Guineas in Gold and Thirteen Shillings and Sixpence in Silver, the Property of the ſaid *Collins.*

### Thomas Winpreſs,

(*Committed by* Robert Dextor, *Coroner*, April 25.)

Charged upon an Inqueſt, found Guilty of Manſlaughter.

### Elizabeth Fawſon, Burnt

(*Committed by* Nathaniel Humphreys, *L. L. D.* and Thomas Richards, *Coroner*, June 26)

Charged with a violent Suſpicion of feloniouſly poiſoning her Husband, *Thomas Fawſon*; and alſo upon an Inqueſt charged with a violent Suſpicion of poiſoning the ſaid *Thomas Fawſon*, the Younger, by giving him a Quantity of White Mercury on the 18th Day of *June*, of which he languiſhed 'till the 21ſt of the ſame Month, and then died.

### William Clarke,

(*Committed by* Thomas Richards, *Coroner*, July 9.)

Charged, on an Inqueſt, with murdering, on the 9th of *May* laſt, *Henry Wright* of *Grendon*, in this County, Plaiſterer, by violently and cruelly beating and bruiſing him.

Thomas Bassett of Keysoe Committed by John Orlebar Esq and [illegible] moved by [illegible] Corpus for Horse Stealing from Bedford

Northamptonshire Summer Assize Calendar 1735, when three people were tried for homicide offences Elizabeth Fawson was burnt in August for 'Petty Treason' (see Chapter 3). Winpress and Clarke were imprisoned. (NRO)

giously troubled times, and on Robert Wallop's presentment, Hart was sequestered to the parish of Wappenham after the rightful incumbent, the Reverend Caesar Williamson, had been ejected because he had fought on the Royalist side at the battle of Edgehill.

Eventually, Hart brought all Wallop's property in Wappenham making himself Lord of the Manor. In this position he made himself very unpopular by bringing lawsuits against many of his parishioners.

With the Restoration of the Monarchy in 1660, the inevitable backlash happened, and all the incumbents who were forced out of their parishes by the Commonwealth were allowed to return. Hart, however, remained at Wappenham, by bribing the Bishop of Peterborough's secretary. And not only that, but he also became the Vicar of Blakesley as well, and so had two salaries coming in. Because he could afford it therefore, he employed curates to do all the ecclesiastical work for him, thus disguising his lack of spirituality and vocation.

So the years ticked by, with Hart forever scandalising his parishioners. But his come-uppance was soon at hand.

On Tuesday 23 January 1685, the local Wappenham butcher George Tarry, decided to call at Wappenham rectory. Whether he knew what he would find, or whether he had been ignorant of such things, we can only now guess at. But in bed with the Rector, he found his own wife.

Showing much nimbleness for a man of 65, Theophilus Hart fled naked from his house being pursued over the field by the irate George Tarry, equipped with the tools of his trade. Eventually the chase ended, and then Tarry proceeded to practise his trade on the unfortunate Rector. Theophilus Hart died instantly when his brains were expertly extracted by the raging cuckolded husband.

George Tarry was found guilty of murder at the Northamptonshire Assizes, and was hanged at Northampton on Tuesday 27 May 1685.

**A ghostly sequel**

1763 *Victim*: Thomas Corey
Sometime between Thursday 29 September 1763 and
Tuesday 18 October 1763
Guilsborough
*Offenders*: Richard Butlin (Breeches maker)
John Croxford (Tailor)
Benjamin Deacon (Carpenter)

Croxford, Butlin and Deacon and another man called Thomas Seamark formed a band of villains living in the Guilsborough area. They were addicted to gambling and drinking, and rather than do an honest day's work, would turn to crime to gain money. So much so, that in April 1764, Seamark was caught and hung for highway robbery. However, in the summer of 1764 another crime came to light in which Seamark had been implicated, and which resulted in Croxford, Butlin and Deacon standing trial for murder at the Northamptonshire Assizes.

Sometime in 1763 (the exact date is unknown) a travelling Scottish pedlar, Thomas Corey, called on Seamark's house in Guilsborough. Inside the house drinking were the four ruffians. They refused to buy any of his wares and sent him away. But they followed him, overpowered him and dragged him back to Seamark's garden where Croxford murdered him by slitting his throat.

The four then shared out all the pedlar's goods and clothes, and buried the naked body in a plot of disused land. But a few days later they learnt that the land was to be ploughed up. Fearing that their crime would be discovered, they were then faced with ridding themselves of the decomposing body.

The body was duly dug up, and all the entrails were fed to the pigs and dogs. The flesh was burnt off in the household fires, and hammers were used to smash the bones into dust and tiny pieces, which was then buried in the garden. The whole grisly deed took them three days to complete.

Unfortunately, however, despite all their endeavours at covering up, they had been witnessed. The day after the actual murder, one of Seamark's children said to his brother, 'If you give me a marble I will show you the place where daddy and Croxford killed the man and buried him near the cucumber patch'. Croxford then threatened Seamark's wife, Ann, with death if ever this story leaked out. But children will be children, and soon tales of the murder were common knowledge, despite Ann Seamark's attempts to keep her children quiet.

Obviously, this soon came to the ears of John Bateman, the local squire and magistrate. The details of the investigation are too complicated to list, but a walking cane belonging to the murdered man was produced as evidence. The apprehension of the criminals was easy: by that time Seamark had been hanged anyway; Croxford and Deacon were already in the County Gaol for further highway robberies, and Butlin was arrested at Brackley.

At the trial at the Northamptonshire Assizes in August 1764, Ann Seamark gave prosecution evidence, and Seamark's ten year old son testified that he had spied on all four men through a crack in the floorboards from the room above, and had actually seen a human hand hanging out of the oven and a human leg burning in the fire.

Croxford, Butlin and Deacon were all hanged at Northampton on Saturday 4 August 1764. But that is not the last that was heard from John Croxford. Soon after he was hanged, a pamphlet was printed in Northampton written by an anonymous clergyman who claimed that he had had a meeting with Croxford's ghost on Sunday 12 August 1764.

Appearing to the reverend gentleman whilst he was alone in his study after Sunday Evensong, the ghost confessed to the murder but explained their continued protestations of innocence by saying that all four had entered into a 'sacramental obligation which they sealed with dipping their fingers in the blood of the deceased and licking the same; by which they bound themselves in the penalty of eternal damnation never to betray the fact themselves; or confess if condemned to die for it on the evidence of others'.

The ghost also stated there was no motive, they only murdered out of 'continued habit of wickedness' rather than for necessity, as they were in no need of money at the time. The ghost explained that the clergyman had been chosen deliberately so as to acquaint the world with this deterrent to others.

The clergyman was then told of the pedlar's gold ring. It had been buried by Croxford because he was afraid of the inscription on the ring which said 'Hang'd he'll be who Steals me 1745'.

The ghost disappeared as quickly as it had come. The very next day, the clergyman went to the indicated spot, and unearthed the gold ring, exactly as the ghost said he would.

### When soldiers fall out — I

1812 *Victim*: Samuel Lees, Drummer, 2nd Battalion Northamptonshire Regiment
Weedon Barracks
Wednesday 18 December 1811
*Offender*: William Jones, Sergeant, 2nd Battalion Northamptonshire Regiment

Returning from the Peninsular War, the remnants of the 2nd Battalion of The Northamptonshire Regiment, arrived back at their Depot at Weedon Barracks in August 1811. The battalion had been decimated at the battle of Albuhera, and not surprisingly, after having experienced that, nerves were still on a raw edge even several months later. On the night of Wednesday 18 December 1811, a fight developed between Lees and Jones, which was calmed down.

But the fight flared up again in the barrack yard just before midnight, neither man gaining much advantage. Lees went back to his room, but Jones went to fetch the Sergeant of the Guard.

Following the Sergeant to Lees' room, Jones stood behind the Sergeant as he knocked on the door. The door was opened by Lees. Before another word was spoken, Jones brushed the Sergeant aside and lunged at Lees with a knife. The wound was three inches deep into Lees' left side. He collapsed immediately, bleeding profusely. He never recovered, and died at 11 am the following day.

Jones' guilt was never in doubt, and at the Northamptonshire Assizes was found guilty before the Lord Chief Justice of England himself. He was hanged on Northampton Racecourse on Monday 9 March 1812.

### Husband and Wife — I

1814 *Victim*: Rachael Morris
Wednesday 6 April 1814
Aston-le-Walls
*Offender*: Thomas Morris

The body of Rachael Morris was found with truly horrific injuries, inflicted by her husband Thomas. The murder weapon was a spade, which had been left sticking in her skull. One ear had been chopped off, one eye had been gouged out and her skull had been shattered into pieces by repeated blows with the spade.

No motive was reported for this, and we are left wondering at the emotions and sentiments which lay behind such a ferocious assault. The *Northampton Mercury* reported that Thomas 'solemnly declared that he had murdered his wife from a premeditated resolution; having deliberately gone down stairs to fetch up the spade with which he committed the horrid act'.

Thomas Morris was hanged on Northampton Racecourse on Saturday 23 July 1814, saying that 'Sabbath breaking with drunkenness had brought him to his downfall'.

**The offence that only women can commit.**

Prior to 1828, to prove 'murder' in the case of a new born baby found dead in suspicious circumstances, and to negate the defence of 'being stillborn', the prosecution would have had to show that the child had a completely separate existence from its mother. In other words, that the child had been capable of living a separate life (no matter how brief) physically separated from its mother, indicating, therefore, the cutting of the umbilical cord.

As probably all illegitimate births were in private and unwitnessed anyway, then this 'separate existence' rule was virtually impossible to prove. Some women were therefore going unpunished for criminal homicide upon their children.

To counter this, the 1828 Offences against the Person Act created the new offence of 'Concealment of Birth'. This was where the mother of a child found dead in suspicious circumstances, and who had attempted to conceal the birth from public and official record, could be convicted before a court of an offence without having to prove 'separate existence'. Appropriate legal, medical and social action could then be taken by the authorities.

The first woman to be charged with Concealment of Birth in Northamptonshire was 36 year old Elizabeth Johnson, who was however found not guilty at the 1834 Lent Assizes.

The social disgrace of having an illegitimate child during Victorian and Edwardian times was too much for some young girls to bear. They sought to rid themselves of their problem by killing their child and hiding the body, and the conspicuous number of offences of Concealment of Birth in Northamptonshire in the couple of generations before the first World War bears testament to this. In the period between 1882 and 1919, there were 33 cases, all of them servant girls in the age range 18 to 25.

In 1922, The Infanticide Act gave new definitions to the killing of babies by their mothers, and as social conditions and customs changed, so the incidence of this type of offence declined.

**The last woman to be hanged in Northamptonshire**

1852 *Victim*: Elizabeth Pinckard (52)
Friday 3 October 1851
Thrupp, near Daventry
*Offender*: Elizabeth Pinckard (51) (Housewife) (Daughter-in-law)

Elizabeth and Richard Pinckard were wealthy farmers in the hamlet of Thrupp. Their son, John, however, and his wife, confusingly also called Elizabeth, were in financial difficulties. They could not pay their rent, and were being hard pressed by their landlord, who suggested they borrow money from John's mother.

But Elizabeth senior had constantly refused to lend any money to Elizabeth junior. This animosity between the two women was probably caused by the fact that Elizabeth junior was already twice widowed, and being some 20 years older than her husband, was only one year younger than her mother-in-law.

Early on the morning of Friday 3 October 1851, John and Richard Pinckard left for Daventry Fair. Wanting an opportunity to talk to her mother-in-law about a loan again, Elizabeth left the house at 10 am to walk to her mother-in-law's on the outskirts of the hamlet. The fact that she took no pains to conceal herself, and was in fact seen going into, and leaving, her mother-in-law's by six people, one of them the local village policeman, makes her later indictment for murder rather puzzling.

It was not until 5.30 pm that evening that the body of Elizabeth senior was discovered, and was by then quite cold. She was sitting on the floor in the corner of the room, and around her neck was wound some apron tape which was tied to a hook in the cupboard door above her head. When Elizabeth was told a few minutes later of the death, she apparently 'went as cold and white as death', and slumped shocked into a chair.

A doctor was called and at the scene gave his opinion of death as suicide by strangulation by the apron tape. But a later post-mortem revealed something more sinister. Mrs Pinckard had died of strangulation right enough, but only after she had been knocked senseless by a massive blow to the head.

Mrs Pinckard's body had not lost any blood, but smears were found on Elizabeth's torn dress, which she had attempted to wash, and also on the hook holding the tape. Identical tape was found in a drawer in Elizabeth's room. A small bloodstain was also found on a mallet used to close dairy churns and which was said to be the thing used by Elizabeth to hit Mrs Pinckard on the head. Because Mrs Pinckard's body had not lost any blood, the fact that Elizabeth had a gashed finger pointed to her connection with the mallet and the hook.

Elizabeth Pinckard was indicted for murder and was found guilty. But there was immense sympathy for her, and agitation for a reprieve by a large faction who contended that her crime was manslaughter and not murder and that she should not hang. The fact that Elizabeth had killed her mother-in-law was not disputed. But it was voiced that Mrs Pinckard had been struck during a quarrel over money, and that Elizabeth had no intention to kill, which was also borne out by the number of persons seeing her that morning. This idea received a lot of support from a lot of people, but overlooked the fact that tape had been wound around the neck, presumably to make it look like suicide. There was also the strong motive of financial gain for Elizabeth upon her mother-in-law's death.

Because the execution of Elizabeth Pinckard is 'important' as the last to be held in public in the county, an eye witness account of the scene is reprinted from the *Northampton Mercury* of Saturday 20 March 1852.

'On the fatal morning [Tuesday 16 March] she attended prayers in the chapel and when the hymn was sung her voice was heard above the rest, and firmer than any. The last verse she repeated of her own accord. In the pinioning room she offered up an extempore prayer, with great fervour and distinctness. At her own request the cap was drawn over her eyes before she went up to the drop; but her remarkable firmness and self-possession continued to the last, and she ascended the steps, happening to tread on her dress, she raised it well as she could with her pinioned hands, and went on without further assistance. She stood quietly and firmly on the fatal spot in which she was placed by Calcraft the executioner, and the bolt was struck immediately after. The fall was considerable, and death ensued in a few seconds. A shriek was heard in many parts of the crowd at the fatal moment and an impression is abroad that it came from the unhappy prisoner. Nothing of the kind however escaped her lips.'

**Follow the footprints**

1855 *Victim*: Benjamin Cheney (81)
Thursday 6 July 1855
Rothwell
*Offender*: Isaac Pinnock (19) unemployed

Isaac Pinnock was a 19 year old crippled youth who was regarded in his home town of Rothwell as a nuisance. He was looked upon as unemployable, so his only past-time was to hang about the town, his boredom leading to petty crime and vandalism. It was inevitable that he would graduate onto something more dramatic.

At 12.45 pm on Thursday 6 July 1855, Sarah Driver and her mother, Rhoda Tye, were walking the public footpath from Kettering going towards Rothwell. What they saw upon reaching the stile into the field called Slates Piece, in Rothwell parish, froze them with horror.

Lying on his back in a large pool of his own blood was a man they both knew well as Benjamin Cheney, an 81 year old farmer from Rothwell. His brains had been spattered over the footpath from a single ferocious wound 4 ins long and 2 ins deep, into his head behind the left ear. Death must have been instantaneous and had obviously only occurred a few brief minutes earlier.

The culprit was never in doubt. Isaac Pinnock had been seen hanging around the stile for an hour before the discovery of the body; and Samuel Taylor, the tenant of Slates Piece, had seen Isaac Pinnock scurrying along the footpath in the direction of Rothwell at 12.42 pm precisely, as though in a great hurry.

And not only that, a clear trail of footprints could be followed away from the body, and these were no ordinary footprints. The left foot was normal, but where the right footprint should have been, there were marks of a walking stick and a series of semi-circular marks where the toe of the right shoe had dragged on the ground. And there was only one person who could have walked like that. The marks were followed into Rothwell before they petered out, at which point the axe belonging to Isaac Pinnock's father was found, still wet with blood.

The Jury only took a few minutes to find Isaac Pinnock guilty of murder. The motive had been robbery, as 14s 6d had been taken from the body. Isaac Pinnock was sentenced to hang, but later had his sentence commuted to life imprisonment.

**Husband and Wife — II**

1871 *Victim*: Mary Addington
Whit Tuesday 30 May 1871, 10.25 am
Holcot
*Offender*: Richard Addington (38) Shoemaker

Elizabeth Warren was visiting her sister at Holcot, who lived next door to Richard and Mary Addington. Elizabeth Warren knew the Addingtons well and on that morning was surprised to see the couple quarrelling in their own backyard. She saw Richard push his wife bodily into the house and slam the door behind him. Suddenly, a few seconds later, terrifying screams were heard, the door burst open and Mary rushed out, with blood spurting from a deep gash in her throat.

'Oh Mrs Warren, he's cut my throat, come and look, I'm a dying woman'. Mary staggered into the house where Elizabeth Warren was standing. Richard immediately followed his wife into the yard, but was confronted by another neighbour, Elizabeth Harris, who had been attracted by the screams.

'Betsy I have cut her throat, you can go and look at her if you like'. But Betsy Harris did not want to look, because on seeing Richard's blood stained hands, she turned tail and ran.

Richard in a daze staggered into the house next door, and in front of the horrified Elizabeth Warren fell on his knees and pleaded before his wife 'Would you forgive me?'

'I have forgiven you, my dear husband'.

Lydia Driver of Rothwell received five years hard labour for starving to death her four year old step-daughter, Hannah, in January 1866. She had had no solid food for three days, and her bones showed through her skin. Her stomach and bowels were completely empty except for a tablespoon of cinders. (NP)

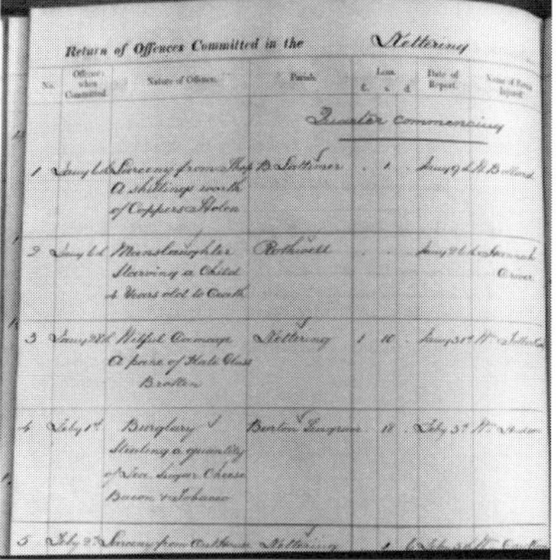

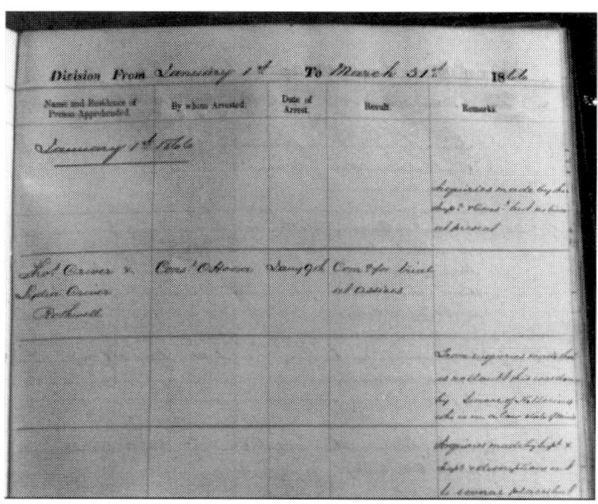

Kettering Divisional Crime Register recording the manslaughter of Hannah Driver. (NP)

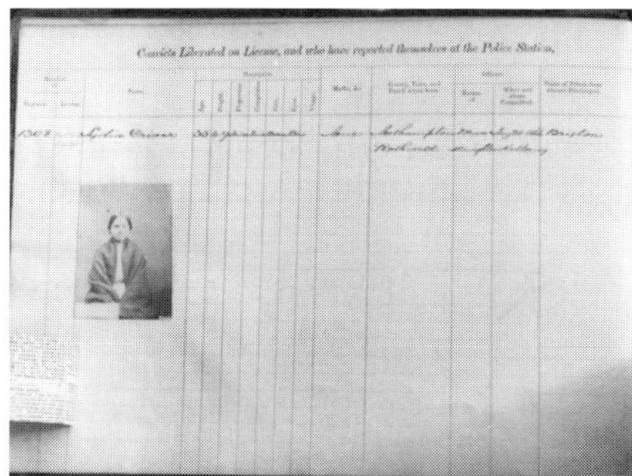

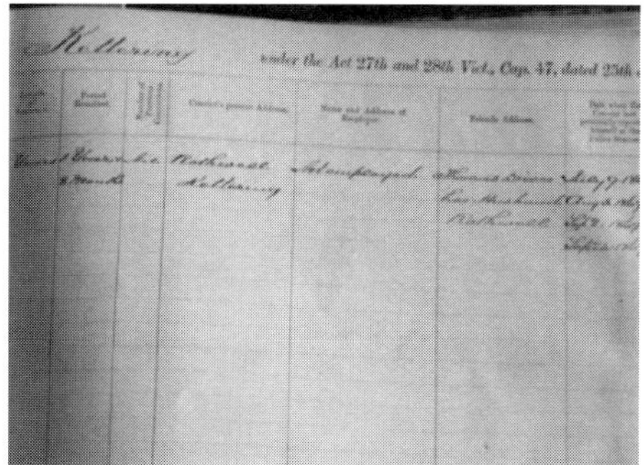

Kettering Divisional Convicts' Reporting Register. Lydia Driver had to report monthly after release. She first reported in July 1869, but died in the following October. (NP)

'I know you won't be long before you die, I shan't be long before I die. You won't be many minutes'. And indeed she was not.

Dr Francis Marshall would find at his post mortem that Mary Addington had received three stab wounds in the neck, chest and stomach. Any one of these could have proved fatal.

At the trial, the defence barrister, Charles Merewether, tried to get a verdict of insanity for his client. But despite calling several witnesses who all said that Richard had been acting strangely, he failed to convince the jury. The verdict was guilty of wilful murder.

But there seems to be a strange lack of motive for this crime. We can speculate, however, upon a phrase used in the *Northampton Mercury*, describing Richard Addington as an 'inoffensive little man'. So do we have here a henpecked husband quietly suffering his wife's tongue for years before suddenly exploding? Walmersley Tarry of Holcot, at the trial, said he witnessed an argument between the couple just one week before the murder. Was this just one more of the many tongue lashings that Richard had endured over the years? Was the argument witnessed by Elizabeth Warren the breaking point? The last straw?

Richard Addington was the first person to be hanged away from public gaze in the newly constructed gallows inside Northampton County Gaol on Monday 31 July 1871, and was buried next to Elizabeth Pinckard inside the Gaol perimeter.

**Simply to see what it felt like.**

1873 *Victim*: John Cox Newitt (72) Farmer
Sunday 30 November 1873
Wood Burcote, near Towcester
*Offender*: Thomas Chamberlain (40) Toll Gate Keeper

Betsy Wright, for the manslaughter of her illegitimate unnamed son, at her parents' house in Peterborough, received eight months hard labour at the 1871 Lent Assizes. The baby was found under a pile of ashes with a fractured skull. (NP)

# Full & True Particulars

Of the

# TRIAL

AND

# EXECUTION

OF

## THOMAS CHAMBERLAIN,

***Who was Hanged at Northampton,***

On **MONDAY MORNING, MARCH 30, 1874,**

For the

# Horrible Murder

OF

## Mr. J. C. NEWITT, AT BURCOTE,

Near Towcester.

THE wretched man, Thomas Chamberlain, has at last met his doom for the cruel murder of Mr. John Cox Newitt, an aged man of 72, and a respectable farmer of Wood Burcote, near Towcester. The fearful crime, which was committed so long ago as the 30th day of last November, on a Sunday evening, created the greatest excitement and consternation at Towcester and the villages around. But justice was soon on the track of the murderer, and within an hour and a-half after the awful crime, Thomas Chamberlain, a shoemaker, and the keeper of the Lord's Field Toll-gate, a mile and a-half from Wood Burcote, was in custody on the charge. On that quiet Sunday evening the old man and a servant girl named Harriett Stevens, were together alone in the house, a lone farm house, half a mile from the nearest cottages. Mr. Newitt had himself been to church at Towcester that morning and partaken of the Holy Communion. His wife and their son John Newitt had gone to church in the evening. At half past seven the girl went into the parlour to take some wood to put on the fire, and her old master was then sitting up to the table reading his Bible, at about 10 minutes before eight o'clock the girl heard the front door open and some body come up the passage. Thinking it was her mistress and her young master, she got up from the table, where she had been writing, to get the supper, as she used to do when they came home from church. She had no sooner got up than Thomas Chamberlain opened the door and came in. She knew it was Chamberlain directly, for she had known him well for fifteen months. He had up to the last October (1873) kept the Wood Burcote Tollgate, only a quarter of a mile from Mr. Newitt's house, until that toll-gate was pulled down. He often brought parcels up to the house, which had been left at the gate by carriers as they passed along the road. She had, too, on Sundays walked with him towards Burcote as she came from church and therefore knew him perfectly well. When he entered the kitchen he had across his right shoulder some long weapon, about a foot and a half or two feet long. Without saying a word he caught hold of her right shoulder with his left hand and dealt her a blow on the left shoulder with this weapon. She struggled with him and he hit her several times on the head, but her chignon saved her head. Her hair and chignon were cut in two and she had a scalp wound under where her hair had been cut. She of course screamed, and this brought in her old master from his Bible to see what was the matter.

The villain then set upon the old man, and a fearful struggle took place. At first Mr. Newitt threw his murderer on to a coal-hod, but Chamberlain was soon up again and dealt him such a savage blow as to knock him to the ground. The poor girl ran out screaming "Murder," and to get help. She fetched Richard Darby and his three sons, who were labourers on her master's farm, and them she told that Chamberlain was murdering her master. Darby and his sons went to the house but found the murderer gone, and their master lying dead in the kitchen. He had some frightful wounds on the head and neck, and must have bled to death in a minute or two. The ceiling and walls were be-spattered with blood, and the kitchen where the terrible struggle took place looked like a slaughter-house. The police of Towcester were soon on the spot and on the alert to discover the perpetrator of his frightful crime. The girl Stevens told them it was Chamberlain who had done the deed, and Superintendent Osborn went to the Lord's Field toll-house, kept by the prisoner and there found he had changed his shirt, trousers, and waistcoat. The trousers were smothered with blood, and the coat, waistcoat, and shirt, which the prisoner had been wearing when he killed Mr. Newitt also had many stains of blood upon them. He also had a cut across the back of his left hand, which it was thought he had made himself when holding the victim down by it, whilst he struck him with the sword. Chamberlain said he had cut his hand when he was cutting some pork for supper; and denied the charge of having murdered Mr. Newitt. He was taken to the police station at Towcester and when the inquest was held the next day, the crowd was so enraged with the man, who they were sure had murdered the good old man, they would have torn him in pieces if they could have got to him. Traces of blood were found the morning after the murder for about 250 yards from Mr. Newitt's house in the direction of the prisoners toll-gate. And traces of blood were also found about the prisoner's premises and also on the road from his house to a little gate, about sixty or seventy yards distant. That little gate leads into a field where there is a pond in which the sword with which Mr. Newitt was murdered and his servant attacked, was found. Chamberlain had bought this very sword of a Daventry man when he kept the Badby toll-gate; and it was seen hanging up in his house at the time he kept the Wood Burcote toll-gate, near the residence of his victim.

## THE TRIAL

of Chamberlain took place at Northampton on Tuesday, March 10th, before my Lord Judge Brett. The murderer was as cool as possible, and declared he was innocent, although everything pointed to his guilt. A jury of his fellow-countrymen found the wretched man guilty of WILFUL MURDER. The Judge put on the black cap, and then passed upon the miserable man

## SENTENCE OF DEATH.

Since his condemnation Chamberlain continued as hardened and indifferent as ever. He said nothing about his crime, nor did he show any signs of contrition. The Chaplain of the Gaol (the Rev. John Dreaper) was in daily attendance upon the condemned man, and earnestly exhorted him to occupy his few remaining hours in repentance and in seeking for pardon; but the rev. gentleman's efforts did not appear to have the slightest effect. He listened patiently to all that was said, though taking no notice of it. The condition of his mind is shown by the fact that, in a box of his, were found a number of cuttings from newspapers, containing accounts of murders, suicides, burglaries, and other similar crimes, which he had preserved. In the prison he talked with his gaolers upon various subjects, but studiously avoided any reference either to the murder he had committed or to his approaching fate. Chamberlain did not seem to care about religion. He ate and slept well, and seemed altogether careless of the terrible fate which awaited him.

## The Convict's Last Farewell to his Wife and Children.

On Friday afternoon (March 27th) the convicts wife and two children, a boy of fifteen and a girl of eight, together with his brother, called to say a last farewell to him. The interview, which lasted about twenty minutes, was by no means of a character which might have been expected on such a solemn occasion, and part of the conversation was of a very unusual description. Some remarks were made with reference to the trial, and the opinion expressed by the prisoner and his family was that the servant girl and the police had told innumerable falsehoods. The condemned man was then told of the subscription being made for the servant, and the wife immediately remarked that it would have been a more sensible plan had the money been given for her benefit. Alluding to his removal from an upstairs cell to his present one, the prisoner asked his brother if he had found among his property a cutting from a newspaper with reference to Victor Townley, who, about five years ago, committed suicide at Pentonville by throwing himself down the steps. The brother replied in the affirmative, and the prisoner then observed that he believed his gaolers were afraid that he would follow that example, and, in order to prevent him, removed him to another cell. Some allusion was also made to the statement at the trial, that the murdered man had always been very kind to the prisoner's children. This the prisoner denied, but, upon being questioned by the wife, the boy admitted that, on one occasion, Mr. Newitt had given him a shilling. The remainder of the conversation was of a similar frivolous character, no allusion whatever being made to the fearful fate awaiting him, and the subject of religion was ignored, with the exception of one remark which fell from the unhappy man, to the effect that, even at the eleventh hour, "it would take a great many parsons to change him," meaning that any entreaty to him to repent would be fruitless. Shortly afterwards the interview terminated. The only manifestation of feeling on the part of the convict was shown at the moment when his family left him.

## THE EXECUTION.

The unhappy man was hanged this (Monday) morning, March 30th, at eight o'clock, within the walls of the County Gaol at Northampton. The workmen began to erect the scaffold at four o'clock in the morning. It was placed in the Gaol-yard, near the same spot where Richard Addington was hung nearly three years ago. The executioner was a man named Marwood, from the neighbourhood of Lincoln. Chamberlain having been pinioned, was led out to the place of execution, the Chaplain, the Rev. J. Dreaper, reading the prayers usual on these occasions. Only the Under-Sheriff and the gaol officials were present, with a number of reporters. The proceedings were quite private. The criminal ascended the scaffold, his head was covered with a cap, and the rope was put round his neck. Then the bolt was drawn, and all was speedily over. When the deed was done, a black flag was put out in front of the gaol, as a sign of the fact to the public, and at nine o'clock a formal inquest was held before the County Coroner. The man's body was buried in a corner of the gaol premises.

Reprinted for Northamptonshire Libraries 1976 at the Alden Press Oxford

The contemporary view of the Wood Burcote murder, told far better. (NRO)

Thomas Chamberlain was to all intents and purposes a happily married man with two children. Although a shoemaker by trade, in November 1873 he was keeping the Lord's Field Toll Gate, two miles outside Wood Burcote. But there was a darker, deeply pathological side to his nature. He was fascinated by murder, crime, and the murkier habits of his fellow human beings. He considered himself an authority on criminal history and had accumulated a substantial collection of newspaper cuttings dealing with murders, suicides, burglaries and other serious crimes.

Indeed, the very lack of any motive for his horrible crime led observers to say that the study of these records had affected his mind so much that he must have committed murder simply to see what it felt like, because there certainly was no obvious motive. And Thomas Chamberlain himself never expressed neither regret nor remorse, nor stated any motive, for his callous murder of a poor defenceless old man of 72. Even on the scaffold, Chamberlain remained so totally blasé of the whole affair, that Marwood the Executioner said later that he had never known a prisoner 'meet death in so careless and unconcerned a manner. The man must have been a monster'.

Because of the local revulsion that this murder provoked, several printers cashed in on the fashion of the times for lurid broadsheets, and several were published. Three of them are reproduced here, and the actual mechanics of the crime is best left to them.

**When soldiers fall out — II**

1878 *Victim*: Samuel Griffiths, Militia Paymaster Sergeant
John Brooks (70) Militia Quartermaster Sergeant
*Offender*: Patrick John Byrne (37) Militia Sergeant

Patrick John Byrne had previously been in the regular army and had an exemplary record as a Colour Sergeant in the Northamptonshire Regiment. He was transferred to the Militia Regiment with the rank of Colour Sergeant, where he was placed in charge of the Sergeants' Mess, with ex-officio living accommodation in the Militia Headquarters (called the Militia Stores) in Great Russell Street, Northampton.

Patrick Byrne was therefore highly thought of to be given the responsibility. But when placed in charge of the Sergeants' Mess, things began to go wrong for him. Easy access to the stocks of drink kept in the Mess would eventually turn him into a near alcoholic.

Not surprisingly, things began to slip, and the accounts of the Mess ended up in such a chaotic state that the officers of the Militia had no choice but to relieve him of the position. He was demoted to Sergeant and ordered to leave his Quarters in the Stores.

On the morning that he was due to leave, Monday 2 September 1878, Byrne had already drunk two glasses of brandy and three pints of beer on an empty

# EXECUTION OF THOMAS CHAMBERLAIN,

## For the MURDER of Mr. JOHN C. NEWITT,

## At Wood Burcote, near Towcester.

The Scene at

the Execution.

The True History of the awful deed for which Thomas Chamberlain was Hung at the County Gaol, Northampton, on the morning of Monday, March 30th, 1874; to which is appended the Lamentation and many important particulars never before made public.

The most cruel crime committed in the county of Northampton during the present century is undoubtedly the murder of John Cox Newitt, farmer, of Wood Burcote, near Towcester, who was horribly butchered by a toll-bar keeper named Thomas Chamberlain, on Sunday, November the 30th, 1873. A brave servant girl, named Harriett Stevens, escaped, after several severe wounds had been inflicted on her by the deadly weapon which Thomas Chamberlain carried with him. This weapon was an old cutlass, which the prisoner bought at Daventry, and which he ground sharp so as to enable him to accomplish the foul deed. When Richard Darby (who had been alarmed by the servant girl) ran to the farm to save his master, he found his mangled corpse lying on the kitchen floor, while all around were patches and pools of blood. The old man's ear had been cut off in the struggle, and after a search the piece was picked up by the surgeon, and placed near the body. The police, on being informed by the servant, at once proceeded to Thomas Chamberlain's house, and found him trying to wash the stains from his bloody garments; his trousers and waistcoat were deep-dyed with the gory marks of the encounter; he was at once handcuffed, and amid the screams of his children and the sobbing of his wife, he was borne away to Towcester Police Station. His own hand had been cut by the cutlass in the struggle. A long search took place for this instrument of destruction, which was afterwards discovered in a pond near the murderer's dwelling. The police also discovered splashes of blood which had dripped from the murderer's own hand as he ran from the farm after committing the deed to his own house. Thus the chain of evidence was complete. But beyond this, there was the evidence of the servant girl, who recognised the man who struck at her savagely with a weapon as Thomas Chamberlain, keeper of Lord's Field Turnpike Gate, on the Buckingham road. The prisoner, when placed in the dock, before Justice Brett, at Northampton Assizes, on March 10, had a most defiant appearance; and the jury without hesitation found him guilty of this horrible crime, thus stamping him as a blood-thirsty criminal. After he had been sentenced to be hung by the neck until quite dead, he coolly said, "Thank you, my Lord," and, laughing, walked from the dock in the custody of the gaoler.

On Monday morning, March 30th, this hardened criminal was hung in the court yard of the Northampton County Gaol—dying as he had lived, a thorough wretch. When the black flag was hoisted, a sigh of relief went up from the crowd assembled outside the walls, as they knew that a brutal murderer had been sent to his last account; and may the Lord have mercy on his soul.

HARRIETT STEVENS, The brave Servant Girl.

The servant girl, Harriett Stevens, was complimented by the Judge for the way in which she gave her evidence, and her bravery under such terrifying circumstances; and to the fact of her acting so wisely she owes her life, and thus lived to identify the murderer.

## The Lamentation of Thomas Chamberlain.

Thomas Chamberlain is my name,<br>
At Lord's Field Gate I did reside,<br>
With a good wife for my partner,<br>
And dear children by my side.

Kind friends, listen to my story,<br>
While to you the truth I tell;<br>
By my shameful end take warning—<br>
Think of the fate that me befel.

In the County Gaol I now am lying,<br>
Doomed on the gallows' tree to die:<br>
None to cheer me, no one near me<br>
Save the turnkey—he's ever nigh.

Farewell, dear wife; farewell, my children;<br>
Farewell, my friends and kindred all;<br>
While your daily work you follow,<br>
Think of my sad and wretched fall.

To get your living, work and labour,<br>
God will give you strength and health;<br>
Seek not to rob your peaceful neighbour<br>
Of his honest, hard-won wealth.

No more I'll hear the light lark singing,<br>
Nor the cuckoo's cheerful song;<br>
No more I'll hear the church bells ringing,<br>
As through the fields I walk along.

I fancy at night, when all are sleeping,<br>
I hear the funeral's solemn toll,<br>
And the Parson's earnest pleading<br>
To God for mercy on my soul.

Now once more, my wife and children,<br>
I bid a long and sad adieu;<br>
My last appeal shall be to Heaven<br>
That peace and joy abound with you.

Northampton,<br>
March, 1874.

And with more illustration. (NRO)

NORTHAMPTONSHIRE LENT ASSIZES, 1874.

# FULL, TRUE, AND PARTICULAR ACCOUNT

OF THE

# Horible Murder

*Of Mr. J. C. NEWITT, at Burcote, near Towcester, with*

# Trial and Sentence of the Murderer.

THE SUNDAY NIGHT, the 30th of last November, the whole neighbourhood of Towcester was thrown into a state of consternation by the report that Mr. John Cox Newitt, an aged man of 72, and a respectable farmer of Wood Burcote, a hamlet of Towcester, had been most foully murdered. But he had been murdered under such circumstances that in an hour and a half after the commission of the crime, the supposed murderer, Thomas Chamberlain, a shoemaker and the keeper of the Lord's Field Tollgate, a mile and a half

or two miles from Wood Burcote, was in custody. On that quiet Sunday evening the old man and a servant girl named Harriet Stevens, were together alone in the house, a lone farm house, half a mile from the nearest [illegible], Mr. Newitt had been himself to church at Towcester that morning and partaken of the Holy Communion. His wife and [illegible] John Newitt had gone to church in the evening. At half past seven the girl went into the parlour to take some wood to put on the fire and her old master was then sitting up to the table reading his Bible, at about 10 minutes before eight o'clock the girl heard the front door open, and somebody come up the passage. Thinking it was her mistress and her young master, she got up from the table, where she had been writing, to get the supper, as she used to do when they came home from church. She had no sooner got up than Thomas Chamberlain opened the door and came in. She knew it was Chamberlain directly, for she had known him well for fifteen months. He had up to the last October (1873) kept the Wood Burcote Tollgate, only a quarter of a mile from Mr. Newitt's house, until that tollgate was pulled down. He often brought parcels up to the house, which had been left at the gate by carriers as they passed along the road. She had, too, on Sundays walked with him towards Burcote as she came from church and therefore knew him perfectly well. When he entered the kitchen he had across his right shoulder some long weapon, about a foot and a half or two feet long. Without saying a word he caught hold of her right shoulder with his left hand and dealt her a blow on the left shoulder with this weapon. She struggled with him and he hit her several times on the head, but her chignon saved her head. Her hair and chignon were cut in two and she had a scalp wound under where her hair had been cut. She of course screamed and this brought in her old master from his Bible to see what was the matter.

The villain then set upon the old man, and a fearful struggle took place. At first Mr. Newitt threw his murderer on to a coal-bed but Chamberlain was soon up again and dealt him such a savage blow as to knock him to the ground. The poor girl ran out screaming "Murder," and to get help She fetched Richard Darby and his three sons who were labourers on her master's farm and them she told that Chamberlain was murdering her master. Darby and his sons went to the house but found the murderer gone and their master lying dead in the kitchen. He had some frightful wounds on the head and neck and must have bled to death in a minute or two. The ceiling and walls were bespattered with blood, and the kitchen where the terrible struggle took place looked like a slaughter house. The police of Towcester were soon on the spot and on the alert to discover the perpetrator of this frightful crime. The girl Stevens told them it was Chamberlain who had done the deed and Superintendent Osborn went to the Lord's Field toll-house, kept by the prisoner and there found he had changed his shirt, trousers, and waistcoat. The trousers were smothered with blood, and the coat, waistcoat, and shirt, which the prisoner had been wearing when he killed Mr. Newitt also had many stains of blood upon them. He also had a cut across the back of his left hand which it was thought he had made himself, when holding the victim down by it, whilst he struck him with the sword. Chamberlain said he had cut his hand when he was cutting some pork for supper; and denied the charge of having murdered Mr. Newitt. He was taken to the pol[illegible] at Towcester and when the inquest was held the next day the crowd was so enraged with the man, who they were sure had murdered the good old man they would have torn him in pieces if they could have got to him. Traces of blood were found the morning after the murder for about 250 yards from Mr. Newitt's house in the direction of the prisoners toll-gate. And traces of blood were also found about the prisoner's premises and also on the road from his house to [illegible] gate, about sixty or seventy yards distant. That [illegible] a field where there is a pond in which the sword with which Mr. Newitt was murdered and his servant attacked, was found. Chamberlain had bought this very sword of a Daventry man when he kept the Badby toll-gate; and it was seen hanging up in his house at the time he kept the Wood Burcote toll-gate, near the residence of his victim. Everything points to the guilt of the wretched man, Chamberlain,

and on Tuesday (March 10th) he was tried before Mr. Justice Brett for the foul crime he had committed and found guilty of

"WILFUL MURDER"

By a Jury of his fellow-countrymen. The Judge then put on the Black Cap, and passed upon the miserable man

## Sentence of Death ! ! ! !

Chamberlain will be Hanged within the walls of the County Gaol.

The fact that there were three separate broadsheets published, points to the local abhorrence felt over this murder. (NRO)

# EXECUTION

OF

## Sergeant Patrick John Byrne

**For the Murder of Quarter-master Sergt. Brooks and Paymaster-Sergeant Griffiths, at the Militia Stores, Northampton, on September 2nd.**

Tried at Bedford Assizes, for the Double Murder on Saturday, October 26th, 1878.

Executed at the Upper Prison, Northampton, on Tuesday, November 12th, 1878.

Yet mourn ye not as they
Whose spirit's life is quenched! For him the past
Is sealed: he may not fall, he may not cast
His birthright's hope away!
All is not here of the beloved and blessed;
Leave ye the sleeper with his God at rest.

Byrne was tried at the late Bedford Assizes and found guilty of murder. When sentenced to death, he said, "I am very sorry for it, Sir. I had been drinking from July to August, and part of September. I have a wife and five children. I must ask for the mercy of the Court."

The criminal had served 20 years in the Army in different parts of the world; he had been Color Sergeant in the Militia, but was lately reduced and had to give up his quarters at the Stores. The murders were most cool and deliberate, there being no cause for disagreement between the murderer and his victims.

The above unhappy murderer was executed on the morning of the 12th November, at the Borough Gaol, Northampton, the black flag giving notice to the assembled people that Byrne was that minute launched into eternity. Who can picture to themselves the remorse of the unfortunate man for the deed he had committed; who can describe the feelings of the man who, after shedding the blood of his comrades-in-arms, sees the tearful faces of the widows and children of his victims gazing with compassion upon him. It must have been heart-breaking to Byrne to have had interviews with his former comrades, and, worse than all, with the women whom he, by his bloodthirstiness, had left husbandless and their children fatherless. It must have been heart-breaking to listen to the ministrations of the good Priest (Byrne was a Catholic), and it must also have been more heart-breaking to know that he had offended the God who made both him and his victims, and who, in his Holy Law says "A life for a life."

This is the first execution that has taken place at the Borough Gaol, now called Her Majesty's Upper Prison, and we hope it will be the last. Byrne seemed previous to his death resigned to his fate, and admitted his sentence was just. He attributes his rash act to drink, and says if he had only paid more attention to his religious duties, and the advice of his wife, he would not have had to answer for the fearful charge of murder. The Poet says of the Soldier:—

He had left his home in his spirit's pride,
With his father's sword and blessing;
He stood with the valiant side by side,
His country's wrong redressing.

He came again, but an altered man,
The path of the grave was before him,
And the smile that he wore was cold and wan,
For the shadow of death hung o'er him.

There were tears that fell from manly eyes,
There was woman's gentle weeping,
And the wailing of age and infant cries
O'er the grave where he lies sleeping.

Dr. Scott (the Romish Priest), attended the unhappy man to the scaffold, trying to cheer his last moments with the thoughts of a better world, and the culprit seemed to listen with marked attention.

Comrades and friends farewell;
Take warning by my fate;
Your temper guard, the drink eschew,
Before it is too late.

Like me you may be mad
With that vile compound Drink;
Like me may kill a friend—
Think comrades! only think!

I leave behind a loving wife,
Also five children dear;
I hope the Saints their lives will guard,
And then I have no fear.

I served my country true,
In lands beyond the sea
And could have died, with Soldier pride,
For the land of the brave and free.

My prospects in life were fair,
And my heart was filled with hope;
But now, instead of by sword,
I die by the hangman's rope.

Oh, Mary, Mother of God;
Hear my sad parting cry;
And when my Spirit my body leaves
Waft it to Christ on high.

†

REQUIESCAT IN PACE.

The Militia Stores Murder of 1878. Note the printer's use of the same stock woodcut as in the Chamberlain broadsheet. (NRO)

stomach, when he was seen in the Reading Room by QMS John Brooks, who had the task of escorting Byrne out of his Quarters.

The Militia Stores, from a turn of the century post card. The double murder was in the front court yard.

'Now Byrne, have you got those Quarters ready? For if they are not ready, I must report you', said Brooks, and followed it up by making some remarks about the dirty state that the Quarters were in. This must really have jarred on Byrne's nerves, and it was these very remarks by Brooks that were shown later to have lit the fuse of Byrne's drunken temper.

'Aye well then' said Byrne 'I'll go and see about it' and he burst out of the Reading Room, now blindly driven by an uncontrolled temper. Fetching a loaded rifle straight away, he returned to the square in front of the Stores. So blinded by fury was he that he intended to shoot anybody that came along. The unfortunate John Brooks happened to be the first to appear, and Byrne duly shot him dead with one bullet straight through the heart.

Hearing the crack of a rifle, Paymaster Sergeant Samuel Griffiths rushed out into the yard and promptly had his brains blown out by a single shot from twelve yards range.

Just at that very moment, into the yard from Great Russell Street, came the son of QMS Hill on his way to his father's house inside the grounds of the Militia Stores. Byrne turned round and blindly shot at the boy, but missed.

The rifle was now empty and Byrne was immediately disarmed by men who all pounced on him before he could reload and do any more mischief. All Byrne could say was 'they've turned me out of my Quarters'. The whole incident had lasted no more than a few minutes.

Because of the tremendous local abhorrence of the crime, Byrne was not tried at Northampton, but at the Bedfordshire Assizes the following month. His guilt was never in doubt, and he was hanged in Northampton Borough Gaol on the Mounts on Tuesday 12 November 1878. He expressed extreme contrition for his crime, blaming everything on 'the demon drink'.

**Jealousy and unrequited love**

1885 *Victim*: Mary Ann Tite (25)
Tuesday 3 March 1885, 10 pm
Stoke Bruerne
*Offender*: Thomas Brookes (44) Labourer

When Thomas Brookes looked through the window of the village school on one late winter evening in 1885, what he saw made his mind snap. Inside the hall he had seen his 'fiance', Mary Tite, talking with another man. This was just too much for him to bear, and he just had to do something about it.

Thomas Brookes had been a railway guard, and up until then, was considered normal and sober. But in 1883, he had left the railway and had gone to live with his father at Stoke Bruerne. It was at this stage that he began acting strangely, and on several occasions had been seen walking about the village in his slippers.

Thomas, still unmarried at 44, took a liking to 25 year old Mary Ann Tite who lived in Stoke. It is doubtful whether Mary wanted a relationship with a man old enough to be her father, but there seemed to be a certain fondness between the two. Thomas, though, obviously read into it more than there actually was, and started trailing Mary about the village. So when on following Mary to a meeting in the school hall, he looked through the window and saw her talking to another man, his temper just exploded.

Mary returned home at 10 pm on the night of Tuesday 3 March 1885, and Thomas went to call upon her. He found her talking to her father, Ham Tite. Ham went upstairs to bed, leaving the couple alone downstairs.

Thomas accused Mary of looking at another man. He told her that he had seen them together at the meeting earlier that night. Mary did not have time to reply, as by then Thomas was completely raving. He pulled out a revolver and fired one shot at point blank range at Mary's right ear. She collapsed, mortally wounded. How or when Thomas had acquired a gun has never been explained, but on hearing the shot, Ham Tite came rushing downstairs to find his daughter in a pool of blood, and the cottage door open. Of Thomas there was no sign.

Completely now without sanity or reason, Thomas made his way to his house just a few minutes walk away and went in. The first person he saw was Mrs Webb, his father's 50 year old housekeeper. Without saying a word he pointed the gun at the woman, who showing great courage, or perhaps just terrified reaction, knocked the gun aside.

But this caused the gun to fire, and the bullet grazed her cheek leaving severe powder burns on her face. Thomas' 75 year old father, attracted by the commotion, entered the room, saw what was happening, and started grappling with his son, even though Thomas then pointed the gun straight at him.

The gun went off again, and Brookes senior was shot in the left hand. He staggered back, expecting the worst.

But Thomas immediately put the gun to his own head, and pulled the trigger. The gun exploded, and Thomas collapsed in a pool of blood.

Too shocked to do anything more, Mrs Webb and Thomas' father left the cottage, leaving Thomas unconscious on the floor. They went to fetch help, as they obviously thought that Thomas was dead.

Ten minutes later they returned with neighbours, only to find that Thomas was missing. As was the gun.

Search parties of policemen were out all through that night, combing woods and fields surrounding the village. All to no avail, Thomas had seemingly disappeared.

PC Wren's allotted area was Stoke Park Wood. At 8 am the next morning, he was walking through the wood, when suddenly he heard a shot. He dived to the floor expecting other shots to follow. But there was silence. Eventually, he picked himself up.

PC Wren found the body of Thomas Brookes just a few yards from where he had sought cover. Thomas was lying face down in a pool of his own blood; blood from his earlier wound and blood from the newly inflicted one. Miraculously he was still alive.

Thomas Brookes appeared at the Assizes of July 1885, was certified insane, and was ordered to be detained at a hospital for the criminally insane.

**The youngest ever**

1897 *Victim*: Sarah Ann Pittam (5 weeks)
Friday 26 February 1897
Syresham
*Offender*: Arthur Pittam (7 years of age)

Certainly the youngest person in the county to appear before Judge and Jury, seven year old Arthur Pittam was charged with the manslaughter of his five week old sister, Sarah Ann.

One Friday evening in 1897, Arthur came home to find his mother suckling his young sister. He asked his mother for food, and she pointed to bread and butter on the table, telling the boy to help himself. Arthur apparently was hotly impetuous in temper and the fact that his mother did not attend to his wishes straightaway seemed to make him angry. He picked up a butter knife and threw it at his mother, but missed her and hit the baby on a tender spot on the top of her skull. As a result, Sarah Ann died two days later.

For a seven year old child to appear before a court was unusual even in those days, and the Judge had to acquaint the court with the legal position. 'The prisoner being only seven years of age' said Mr Justice Pollock, 'the inference of the law was that he could not suppose to be guilty of a crime because he was wanting in that wicked mind which alone could constitute a crime. But ... there may be cases with defendants as young as this, there might be express malice which showed that he might be treated as another person should be. It would be a matter for the jury as to what the real act of this child was'.

In throwing out the charge against Arthur Pittam, the jury, through the prosecuting barrister, Mr Ryland Adkins, said that they did not wish for any punishment and would be very thankful if the boy could be looked after in some home. Mr Adkins obviously got very close to the essence of this affair when he added at the end of his speech that 'the mental health of this family is terrible.'

**The most horrible of murders**

1897 *Victim*: Albert Smith (13) Schoolboy
Saturday 10 July 1897
Stuchbury, near Sulgrave
*Offender*: James Shaw (25) Labourer

What prompts a man to kill in the most horrible way imaginable? James Shaw had been in the Scots Guards, but had served his time and had been discharged on pension. He was 25 years old, unmarried and living with one of his sisters in Banbury.

On the morning of 10 July 1897, a beautifully hot summer Saturday, James went to Stuchbury to visit his brother-in-law, Frank Smith, the widower of another of his sisters. Finding only his little nephew Albert, aged 13, and his niece Alice, aged nine, at home, James took them both out for a walk in the sunshine. They all walked for a mile out of the village and finally came to a field called Stone Pits. It was in this field that James, to use a euphemism of the times, committed an 'outrage' on little Alice, which presumably would be some kind of sexual assault.

James then sent Alice away back home leaving him alone with Albert. Albert, who was the only witness of the assault was never to be seen alive again.

Witnesses at the trial would determine the times of the events of that day. Emma Smith, sister of Alice and Albert, who was 'in service' in the village, saw her brother and sister walking out of the village with their uncle at 2 pm. Joseph Franklin would see all three together in Stone Pits; as would Martha Wootton at 2 pm, and then little Alice walking home alone at 4 pm. And finally, Walter Kent would see James Shaw walking away from Stuchbury alone just before 4 pm. The landlord of the public house at Helmdon would then serve James with a glass of beer later in the afternoon and would describe him as 'wild and strange looking'. James evidently then returned to Banbury as if nothing had happened.

Because of Albert's disappearance, the following day, a Sunday, another brother, George Shaw, was sent off to Banbury, where James told him he had left Alice and Albert at the village blacksmiths. In the meantime a search was organised by PC Coles, the local policeman, who was to find the horribly mutilated body of Albert in Stone Pits field.

The boy's head had been completely hacked from his body and was found about 20ft away partially hidden by grass. Nearby was found a blood stained open-bladed razor which had been the murder weapon and which James had used to sever the head from the body, including, of course, cutting through the spinal column, for which considerable strength would have had to be needed.

At his trial four months later, James' appearance in the dock caused a stir. He had put on several stones in weight and his clothes were hardly big enough for him. Not only that, but three prison warders stood with him in the dock, and two police officers stood close by, a precaution considered necessary on account of his actions in prison since his committal hearing.

He had been extremely violent in prison, and had attempted suicide on several occasions, behaviour which as the *Northampton Mercury* truistically put it has 'been such as to lead to the most careful investigation as to his sanity'. Indeed, a plea of insanity was all that the defence could hope for, but in summing up, Mr Justice Wills instructed the jury to form their own opinion on that question.

The jury decided that James Shaw was sane when he had murdered Albert Smith, and so he was sentenced to death. However, he was further examined whilst in prison, and the death sentence was quashed. James Shaw was subsequently detained in a secure asylum for the criminally insane at Her Majesty's pleasure.

**What was the motive?**

1899 *Victim*: Mary Elizabeth Meadows (26):
Saturday 11 March 1899, 5.30 am
Kingsthorpe Hollow, Northampton
*Offender*: Joseph Cornelius Parker (24) Striker

Joseph Parker and Mary Meadows had been courting for four years, apparently so happily that during that time they had never had a single quarrel. Just before midnight on Friday 10 March 1899, Joseph and Mary returned from an evening out to her mother's house in Salisbury Street, Semilong, Northampton.

Joseph was 'very drunk' and so Mary's mother, Charlotte, said she would allow him to stop the night on the sofa. Charlotte left Joseph and Mary talking and went to bed. At 5 am the next morning, she was woken by sounds of the couple downstairs making a cup of tea, and then leaving the house.

The next sighting of the couple is by George Jelly who was on his way to work. At 5.30 am he was in Kingsthorpe Hollow, when walking towards him he saw a young couple who stopped to ask him the time before walking on. Later, he was to recall his impression of that meeting as being one of complete serenity, because the couple (for it was Joseph and Mary) seemed 'so very happy together'.

George walked on. But suddenly he heard two gun shots from behind him. Walter Crofts was also walking in Kingsthorpe that morning and on hearing the two shots turned a corner to see Mary Meadows lying on the pavement. She was still alive, but failing fast, and by 5.35 am when PC Herbert Swift arrived, she was quite dead. Of her attacker, there was no sign.

Five minutes later in Royal Terrace, PC Charles Marlow is quietly walking his beat. When a policeman walks onto the streets, he has no idea what his tour of duty will contain for him. Often it is dull routine, with nothing happening of any difference to anything that he has not already dealt with hundreds of times before. However there are times when fate picks him out for something quite extraordinary. As PC Marlow walks along, a man approaches and speaks.

'Do you want a job? I've shot my girl'.

'When and where?'

'On the new road. I put two shots through her head and she is quite dead'. Parker hands the gun to the astonished officer. 'This is what I did it with. Be careful there are two more shots in it'.

'Be careful what you're saying, as this is a serious charge'.

But Parker continues, probably the emerging shock forcing on him the need to talk to someone, remember it is only ten minutes or so after the murder. 'She wanted me to shoot her and then myself. She wanted me to do it in the house saying that no one would hear us. I would not do it in the house and we came outside and stood a few minutes. Then I lifted it up and pulled the trigger and she fell to the ground. As she lay on the ground I put another shot through her head. I could not shoot myself and so I thought I would give myself up'.

Faced with all the evidence, Mr Magee, the defence barrister could not dispute that Joseph had shot Mary, so his main ploy was to throw doubts on his client's sanity and thus mitigate the offence. Delving back into Parker's family, he set out to prove for three generations past, there was evidence of insanity and epilepsy.

Mr Justice Lawrance summed up.

'It was a peculiarity of the case that not a single person had been called from beginning to end, who, having known the prisoner was able to speak to any peculiarity about the prisoner. There was no indication whatever of what was called "uncontrollable impulse", on the contrary, there seemed some little evidence of pre-meditated arming for the crime'.

This last remark of the Judge referred to the witness Hector Harmer, a work mate of Parker's, who said that on Thursday 9 March (two days before the murder) Parker had said to him 'I shall have to do away with my girl'; and at 7 pm on the eve of the murder had also said 'I don't know what to do with my girl'. Evidence also showed that Parker brought the revolver from a local gunsmith's in the few days previous.

The jury took only ten minutes to arrive at the verdict of guilty to murder. Joseph Cornelius Parker was hanged at Northampton Gaol on Tuesday 11 July 1899.

**A ghoulish murder**

1901 *Victim*: Louisa Claydon (43) Housewife
Sunday 7 July 1901, 1 am
Portland Street, Northampton
*Offender*: Alexander Claydon (43) Shoe Finisher

Louisa and Alex had been childhood sweethearts, but had gone their separate ways and had married others. In 1897 however, Louisa being widowed, and Alex already a widower, they married. Alex had no children, but Louisa had a 14 year old daughter Kate.

Louisa was a hard working woman, she had to be, because she had had to support her first husband who was a drunkard. Marriage to Alex did not change her nature. Nor did it need to, because Alex was also of intemperate habits. Finding that his wife was bringing in money by outwork shoe finishing and by taking in washing, coupled with step-daughter Kate bringing in a working wage, Alex turned more and more to drink, and less and less to work.

Things got so bad that in January 1899 a separation order was made and the couple parted. But by Christmas 1900, they were back together again, renting a house in Portland Street, Northampton. Alex, though, did not learn his lesson. At the end of June 1901, Louisa had turned him out of the house, or as Alex put it, 'put the key on him'.

During the week before the murder, Alex drank all his money away and slept rough under hedges. So by Saturday 6 July 1901, he was in desperate need of food, shelter and beer, and not in that order. He knew that his wife delivered washing to the landlady of 'The Globe' public house, so he hung about there on that evening hoping to see Louisa for another chance, and to scrounge some beer money.

Successful scroungers are successful talkers; and Alex was no exception. Louisa gave him money and said that he could go back to her. She left the pub early, and would return to Portland Street by 10.45 pm. Alex was left drinking in 'The Globe', but left at 11 pm, reaching Portland Street by 11.05 pm.

What happened next is first described by Alex himself, in his signed confession taken soon after his arrest at Moulton by PC William Bailey:

'I met my wife at the old Globe public house on the Kettering Road, I asked her whether she was all right. She said "Are you?" I said "Yes". I remained there until 11 pm and then went direct home and up to bed. I had no light. My wife was in bed. She called me a dirty dog, and would sooner have a serpent beside her than me. I did nothing, I said nothing. I then went to sleep and slept until 1 am. I believe I got up and went into the shop and got my file and struck my wife with it on the head. She shouted out "Kate!" I could not say how many times I struck her. I then went and ate two eggs and some bread and butter. After that I went back upstairs and put a light in the daughter Kate's room. I then went back to bed and went to sleep until a quarter to four, when I woke. I put my hand on my wife's body and found it cold. I believe she was dead. I then got up and went for a long walk, and now I wish to give myself up as the murderer of my wife. Alex Claydon'.

In fact, what had really happened was incredible. Waking up at 1 am, Alex went downstairs to his shop (shoe outworkers referred to their workrooms as their 'shop') and fetched a shoemakers' file. It was steel, 16 ins long with a sharp pointed spike at one end which was designed to fit into a wooden handle, although on this one, the handle was missing. He crept back to the bedroom.

How many times Alex smashed the heavy file on Louisa's head is unknown — the pathologist later found it impossible to count the separate wounds — and Alex certainly could not remember. Not content with that, he used the pointed end of the file to stab Louisa in the head and chest repeatedly. Louisa died within seconds, and her blood and brains saturated the bedclothes.

The state of Alex's mind at this point must be marvelled at, because he then went into Kate, who was unaware of what had happened, and asked if there was anything to eat. She said there was and went back to sleep. Downstairs Alex found himself a couple of eggs, and calmly made himself some egg sandwiches.

Then feeling sleepy, Alex returned to the bedroom and lay down beside the mutilated corpse of his wife, which meant laying down in the pools of her blood and brains still wet in the bed. He woke two hours later, by which time his shirt was saturated with Louisa's blood. Poor Louisa by this time was quite cold, and her blood had matted her hair and congealed upon the bedclothes.

Alex Claydon left the house at 4 am still wearing his blood soaked shirt. He would then walk for nearly five hours, during which time, with returning sobriety, the realisation of the dreadful thing that he had done would so affect his mind that he would give himself up voluntarily to PC William Bailey at Moulton police station.

Because the murderer had been found and his guilt was never in doubt, the question of motive never seemed of much importance at the time. Indeed, no satisfactory explanation of why Alex had so callously and horribly murdered his wife was ever given. Even at his trial, the question of motive was of secondary importance as the defence barrister concentrated on trying to get a verdict of insanity for Alex. He failed.

Alexander Claydon was hanged at Northampton Gaol on Friday 13 December 1901.

**Edwardian comic 'nasties'**

1904 *Victim*: Elsie Jane Burrows (11) Scholar
Wednesday 17 February 1904, 8.30 pm
Ivy Road, Northampton
*Offender*: George Scott Burrows (15) Shoe Finisher

The youngest person to be indicted for murder in Northamptonshire (although not the youngest person to be indicted for criminal homicide, see Arthur Pittam in 1897), George Burrows stood trial for the brutal murder of his sister, and the reasons given at his trial bear some remarkable parallels to today's habits.

George Burrows, senior, was a widower living in Ivy Road, Northampton with five of his six children; Beatrice aged 18, Elsie aged 11, Thomas 10, Harry 8, and George, junior, aged 15.

At 8.20 pm on Wednesday 17 February 1904, George senior left his house leaving Beatrice and George junior downstairs, and Elsie, Thomas and Harry all in bed. Beatrice left at 8.30 pm leaving George alone downstairs.

Thomas and Harry heard Beatrice go out, and then heard George coming upstairs. This so scared Thomas that he immediately got up and locked his bedroom door. When asked later why he had done this, he said it was because he thought George would come in and start hitting them, which he had done several times before.

Instead, Thomas heard George go into Elsie's bedroom and quite plainly heard Elsie cry out several times 'Stop it, our George'. Then hearing George hurriedly leaving the house, Thomas knew instinctively that something was wrong, but was too frightened to do anything, and he burst into tears, thankful to hear his father return a few minutes later.

Elsie was found lying on her bed, her head smashed in by heavy blows with a blunt instrument. She was still alive, but despite medical treatment her injuries were too horrific for anything to be done. She died at 10.15 pm without ever regaining consciousness. The murder weapon was an axe, the heavy blunt part of the head, not the blade, being used.

The trial, not surprisingly, revolved around George's sanity. It emerged that he was extremely fond of Elsie, always bringing her little presents, and had actually kissed her good night only minutes before he had murdered her! So why had George killed her?

He was forever reading what was referred to as 'sensational literature' and comics of 'criminal adventure' such as *Buffalo Bill* and *Charlie Peace*. Dr Harding of Northampton Berry Wood Asylum described George as suffering from 'homicidal mania-homicidal insanity'. So when he was asked by defence counsel whether sensational literature would peculiarly affect a boy having homicidal mania, replied 'I believe it would'.

The jury returned a verdict of not guilty by reason of insanity, and George Scott Burrows was ordered to be detained at His Majesty's pleasure.

The Charles Peace referred to was a real life character who was hanged in Armley Gaol, Leeds in 1879. He had been convicted of the murder of Arthur Dyson at Sheffield, the murder of PC Nicholas Cock at Manchester both in 1876, and also the attempted murder of PC Edward Robinson at Blackheath, London in 1878. Because of several escapes from custody, after which he boasted that no prison could hold him, a cult grew up around him, and *Charlie Peace* comics with their lurid sensationalism were the Victorian and Edwardian equivalent of today's 'video nasties'.

**The eternal triangle**

1912 *Victim*: Mary Jane Pursglove
Saturday 27 July 1912 7 pm
Northall Street, Kettering
*Offender*: Isaac Edward Sewell (35) Shoehand

Isaac Sewell had lived with Mary Pursglove for only one month, but their relationship was a stormy one. The couple had frequent quarrels, with Isaac jealously accusing Mary of seeing another man called Bell.

On that Saturday evening, Mary was lying asleep on her bed with Isaac beside her. Leaving Mary asleep Isaac went downstairs and fetched his shoemaking knife, and returned to the bedroom. Lying on her back, Mary presented the ideal target, and Isaac with all his strength, slashed down twice at Mary's unprotected throat. The first cut was straight across her throat, and the second was from the centre of the throat to the left ear. So ferocious was the attack that Mary's head was almost severed from her body.

Isaac Edward Sewell was tried at the Northamptonshire Assizes in October 1912 and was found guilty of murder, but because of insanity, was ordered to be detained at His Majesty's pleasure.

Although there are obviously many more murders which occurred after the two world wars, these will not be listed. Relatives of the victims and offenders can still be alive, and may not welcome any reminder of past tragedies. We must respect the privacy and feelings of others. However, these last two cases are given, as they are directly attributable to the two great world wars of this century, and show that casualties of war are not necessarily those under direct fire of the enemy.

1920 *Victim*: Alice Maud Copperwaite (23) Housewife
Friday 30 January 1920, 8.30 pm
Billing Road, Northampton
*Offender*: Frederick Cecil Copperwaite (27) Shoehand

Frederick Copperwaite served throughout the Great War in the Royal Army Medical Corps and saw much action in France as well as Macedonia and

Salonika. After being demobilised in 1919, he came back to live with his young wife Alice, in Northampton. But there was something wrong.

From being a bright, outgoing, lively young man, he had changed into a sullen, morose and introspective human being, brooding on the horrors that he had seen. And the discovery that Alice had had a baby by another man during his absence, was the final blow.

On the evening of Thursday 29 January 1920, Frederick was involved in a fight with another man, probably the baby's father, and on the very next day Frederick cut Alice's throat as they were walking together in Billing Road. His attempted suicide with the same razor was foiled by passers-by.

Frederick Copperwaite was found not guilty of murder by reason of insanity, and was ordered to be detained at His Majesty's pleasure. One of the few cases where sympathy is equally with the offender as with the victim.

### The GI Murder

1945 *Victim*: Harold William Newton (19) Merchant Seaman
Monday 17 September 1945, 10.30 pm
Silver Street, Brixworth
*Offender*: William Raymond Knight, Private, United States Army

Harold Newton was shot with an American service revolver by one bullet straight through his heart which killed him instantly. William Raymond Knight, an American service man with the American army in England, and whose home was in Segno, Texas, was indicted for the murder.

In the 'Coach and Horses' public house in Brixworth, Knight started talking to two local girls, and the inevitable fight broke out between Knight and three local lads, Newton included. The argument continued in the street outside after closing time, with one lad trying to pick a fight with Knight, who was accompanied by one of the girls.

Whether it was true or not, the youth backed off after Knight allegedly pulled his gun in a threatening manner. The lad ran off to fetch both his mates, who returned to the telephone kiosk at the Spratton turn to see the American and the girl with their arms around each other's necks. This was just too much. In the ensuing fight, Newton was shot dead.

On Thursday 4 October 1945, William Knight appeared at a Court Martial held at the United States Army Headquarters, Grosvenor Square, London, presided over by Lt-Col W. W. Hayes. He was found guilty of manslaughter, given a dishonourable discharge, and imprisoned for four years.

# CHAPTER 3

## 'BURSTING WITH SIN AND SORROW' OTHER CRIME IN NORTHAMPTONSHIRE

"We live together in a world that is bursting with sin and sorrow"
*Miscellanies*: Samuel Johnson (1709-1784)

- **i) Arson and Damage**
- **ii) Assaults, Assaults on Police, and bare knuckle prize fights**
- **iii) Burglary**
- **iv) Drunkenness**
- **v) Heresy**
- **vi) Organised criminal gangs**
- **vii) Poaching**
- **viii) Rape and sexual offences**
- **ix) Riot and public order**
- **x) Robbery**
- **xi) Theft**
- **xii) Treason**
- **xiii) Vagrancy**
- **xiv) Witchcraft**

ONLY these categories of crime will be described, but they will give an indication of the type and level of criminality that Northamptonshire has had to contend with throughout its history. Blackmail, forgery, kidnapping, firearms offences and so on, will not be dealt with, primarily because of lack of space. Neither will traffic offences, as these are of comparatively modern date, and some consider them not crimes at all.

To provide some sort of comparison, statistics will be given for 1852 and 1993, and sometimes for 1202 and 1657 where the information is available. The only way that any sort of comparison can be made is by reducing numbers of crimes into rate per 1,000 population. It must be stressed, however, that statistically, this is a fairly crude and unsophisticated method, and there are a lot of factors which can affect the result. But given the data we have to go on, it is the best we can do, and at least, indicates the trend.

National crime statistics did not start in earnest until 1856, but in any case tended to be London biased. So locally published crime statistics are preferred over the national ones. The year 1852 was chosen because that is the only year that crime statistics both for the borough of Northampton and the county of Northamptonshire were published, thus giving a total for the whole of the county. And because of a change in the Chief Constables' reports, the latest modern figure we have is for 1993.

**i) Arson and Damage**

Four men have been hung for arson in Northamptonshire. The first was John Lavendar, only 17, who was hung in August 1750 for setting fire to the house of John Brooksby at Kettering.

But the other three men were all hung within the 15 year period of 1819 to 1834, which is highly significant. Rick burning, or incendiarism as it was called, was particularly prevalent in the early 19th century, as it was one of the few ways that the labouring classes could draw the authorities' attention to the extremely depressed state of agriculture, when farm labourers' wages fell to 9d per day.

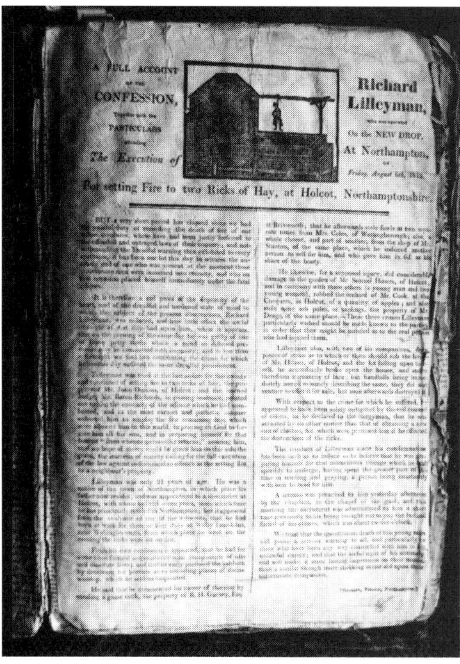

A FULL ACCOUNT OF THE CONFESSION, together with the PARTICULARS attending The Execution of Richard Lilleyman, who was executed On the NEW DROP, At Northampton, on Friday, August 6th, 1819, For setting Fire to two Ricks of Hay, at Holcot, Northamptonshire.

For setting fire to two hay stacks at Holcot, Richard Lilleyman was hanged on Friday 6 August 1819. (NRO)

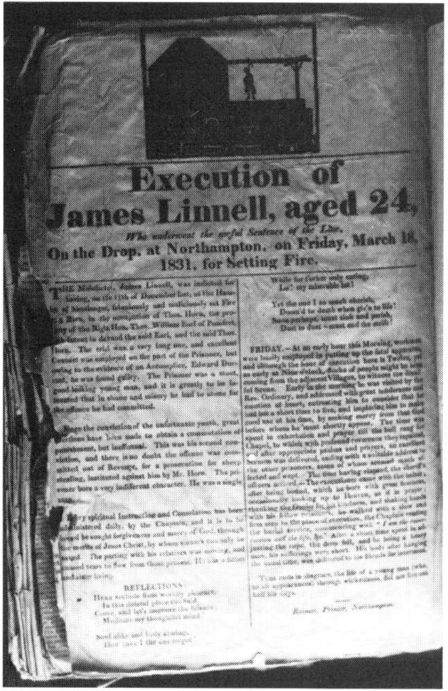

Execution of James Linnell, aged 24, Who underwent the awful Sentence of the Law, On the Drop, at Northampton, on Friday, March 18, 1831, for Setting Fire.

The barn at Shutlanger set alight by James Linnell was so big, it took 100 men to fight the blaze, including Linnell himself before he was discovered as the arsonist. (NRO)

Sir Robert Peel stopped hangings for non-homicide offences after 1837. So on Monday 31 March 1834, for the firing of a wheat stack belonging to Samuel Sharp at Guilsborough the previous December, Thomas Gee became the last man in Northamptonshire to hang for a non-homicide offence.

At the trial, Samuel Sharp, the farmer, described his own actions:

'I was in bed when the fire happened, and was called up at 11 o'clock; I found the stack on fire; we saved some of it; . . . I know the prisoner, he lives near the bottom of the village; I saw him in custody on Sunday after the fire and asked him how he came to do me this spiteful trick, and whether I ever did him any injury? He said "No, never". I said "I cannot think how you could think of it"; he seemed confused, he then burst out crying, and said "I hope Mr Sharp you'll forgive me". I asked how long he had it in his mind to do it; he said he did not

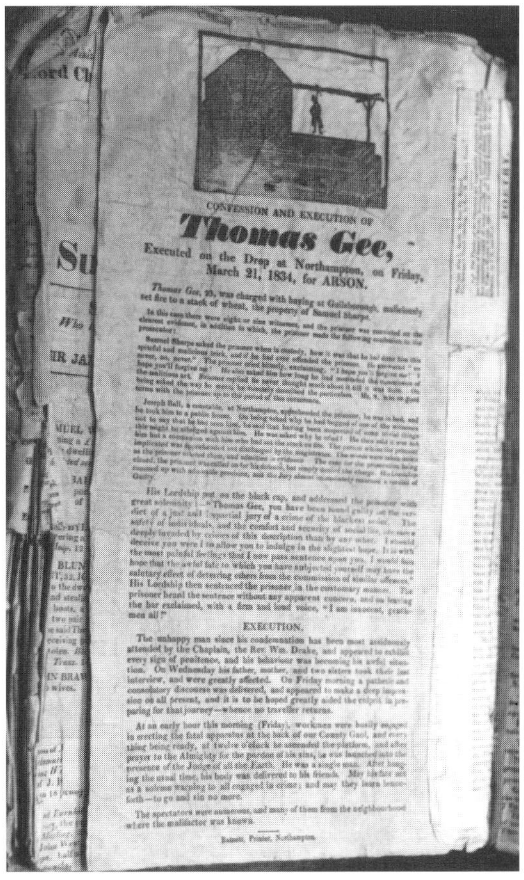

CONFESSION AND EXECUTION OF

**Thomas Gee,**

**Executed on the Drop at Northampton, on Friday, March 21, 1834, for ARSON.**

*Thomas Gee*, 25, was charged with having at Guilsborough, maliciously set fire to a stack of wheat, the property of Samuel Sharpe.

[illegible]

His Lordship put on the black cap, and addressed the prisoner with great solemnity:—"Thomas Gee, you have been found guilty [illegible] of a just and impartial jury of a crime of the blackest order. The safety of individuals, and the comfort and security of social life, [illegible] deeply invaded by crimes of this description than by any other. I should deceive you were I to allow you to indulge in the slightest hope. It is with the most painful feelings that I now pass sentence upon you. I would fain hope that the awful fate to which you have subjected yourself may have the salutary effect of deterring others from the commission of similar offences." His Lordship then sentenced the prisoner in the customary manner. The prisoner heard the sentence without any apparent concern, and on leaving the bar exclaimed, with a firm and loud voice, "I am innocent, gentlemen all!"

EXECUTION.

The unhappy man since his condemnation has been most assiduously attended by the Chaplain, the Rev. Wm. Drake, and appeared to exhibit every sign of penitence, and his behaviour was becoming his awful situation. On Wednesday his father, mother, and two sisters took their last interview, and were greatly affected. On Friday morning a pathetic and consolatory discourse was delivered, and appeared to make a deep impression on all present, and it is to be hoped greatly aided the culprit in preparing for that journey—whence no traveller returns.

At an early hour this morning (Friday), workmen were busily engaged in erecting the fatal apparatus at the back of our County Gaol, and every thing being ready, at twelve o'clock he ascended the platform, and after prayer to the Almighty for the pardon of his sins, he was launched into the presence of the Judge of all the Earth. He was a single man. After hanging the usual time, his body was delivered to his friends. May his fate act as a solemn warning to all engaged in crime; and may they learn henceforth—to go and sin no more.

The spectators were numerous, and many of them from the neighbourhood where the malefactor was known.

[illegible], Printer, Northampton.

The last person to be hung in Northamptonshire for a non-homicide offence. Because of a bungled execution, his neck was not snapped cleanly, and he took 20 minutes to die from asphyxiation. Note again the printer's stock woodcut. (NRO)

think much about it till he did it . . .; there was between 30 and 40 quarters of wheat in the straw.'

Incendiarism continued for many years into the 19th century, but by the 1850s it had ceased to be a form of agricultural protest. So in 1852, only 16 reports of arson occurred in Northamptonshire, for a population of 242,000, giving a rate per 1,000 of .065. But setting fire to things continues to fascinate some people, and in 1993, there were 435 offences for 575,000 population, a rate of .75.

No person has ever been hung in Northamptonshire for causing damage to other peoples' property, other than arson. Nevertheless, the crime of causing damage has always figured largely, and has consistently been near to the top of the lists of the most common crimes. It is one of those 'niggling' offences which is always being committed, but presents more 'nuisance' value than criminality, although the owners of damaged property may not agree. In 1852 there were 283 cases of malicious or wilful damage in the county, a rate per 1,000 population of 1.17 offences. In 1993, 575,000 population produced 9,214 cases, or 16.02 offences per 1,000.

In October 1869, William Harrison (20) together with Henry Mills (28) set fire to two hay ricks at Brixworth. At the 1869 Winter Assizes, Harrison only received nine months hard labour because he was thought to be under the influence of Mills, who received two years. (NP)

Edmund Treadgold had six convictions for damage, including three in a seven month period during 1867, all at Little Bowden. He continually broke down fences to let his animals graze on other peoples' pastures. He received sentences ranging from 14 days to two months in prison. (NP)

**ii) Assaults, Assaults on Police, and bare knuckle prize fights**

Society has always been (and always will be) plagued by people who think they have the right to settle matters by hitting other people. Assaults have always been offences under the Common Law (law not written down in statutes, but which has been around for so long that everybody accepts it) but were subsequently made Statute offences by the two Offences against the Person Acts of 1828 and 1861.

For an assault at Daventry in 1849, 22 years before this picture was taken, John Hillyer received one month hard labour. No details are known. (NP)

Ever since records began, every criminal court in the land has dealt with hundreds of cases year in and year out. For instance, in the 1202 Northamptonshire Assize rolls, Hawis of East Carlton accused Richard the parish priest of East Carlton, Eda his wife, and Hugh, his servant, of wounding her husband, Hugh, the local builder. Hawis was reported to have said that she would persist with her accusation, even if Hugh declined to. In the event, neither of them turned up for court, and so the accusation was dropped. The background to this story makes fascinating conjecture: a hen-pecked husband being led by a fiery tempered nagging wife incensed over a trivial matter? Or the realisation that they could not win against the socially more powerful parish priest?

In the 1202 Assize rolls, there are 12 cases of wounding, involving 28 defendants. Given an estimated population of 20,000 for the county at that time, this gives a rate of .6 offences per 1,000 of population. In 1852, there were 64 assaults in Northampton, and 321 assaults in the county, not including assaults

Mark Prestidge received 21 days in prison for an assault at Brackley in 1851, when he was involved in an argument over a civil debt. (NP)

George Thorpe in company with George Binley attacked William Curtis in a bar room brawl at 'The King's Arms' pub in Desborough in December 1864. Curtis' injuries were so serious that the case went to the 1865 January Quarter Sessions, where Thorpe and Binley each received one month imprisonment. (NP)

on police officers. The population was 242,000, which gives a rate of offence per 1,000 population of 1.59. And in 1993, 2,767 assaults from 575,000 population, is 4.81 assaults per 1,000.

Assaults on police officers have always been given as separate figures. In 1852 there were 40 assaults in the county and 12 in the borough, a total of 52, a rate per thousand of .21. In 1993, 171 assaults is a rate of .3.

However, when the numbers of officers 'available' to be assaulted (in other words, not including those who have desk jobs) is considered, a completely different picture emerges. In 1852, there were 73 'available' officers, and 52 assaults upon them, which indicates that a staggering 71.2 per cent of the force had been assaulted during that year. This may not be strictly true, as we do not know whether some officers were assaulted more than once. In other words there may have been 52 assaults on 52 separate officers (giving the 71.2 per cent) – or 52 assaults on one officer (giving only 1.4 per cent of the force being assaulted) – or any number pro rata in between. But even so, the possibility of 71.2 per cent of the force being assaulted is breathtaking.

In 1993, an estimated 970 'available' officers produced 171 assaults. Using the same method as on the 1852 figures, we arrive at an assault rate of anywhere between .1 per cent and 17.6 per cent of the force being assaulted during the year. Nearly a 25 per cent reduction in 140 years.

Bare knuckle prize fights, which are a form of assault, have always been unlawful. Consequently, prize fights were hushed up, but it is known that at least two of the 'greats' of the old bare knuckle fighters fought matches for the 'English championship' in Northamptonshire – William Caunt and William 'Bendigo' Thompson – in the 1830s. The 'ring' was in Paulerspury parish, in a clearing of Whittlewood forest deliberately chosen because it was right on the borders of Northamptonshire and Buckinghamshire, so that if any constables came snooping round, the participants could just step over the border and be immune to arrest.

Several other prize fights are known to have taken place in Northampton itself, with purely local contestants. In July 1844, for example, Daniel Cumberpatch fought John Fitzhugh in Billing Road, which resulted in the death of Fitzhugh and Cumberpatch receiving three months for manslaughter.

But certainly the most notorious (and probably the last 'organised') prize fight, was on Saturday 10 September 1892 in a field at Duston. The date was chosen deliberately, as that was the day of the committal hearing of Andrew MacRae for the murder of Annie Pritchard and their illegitimate child in a bacon warehouse in Northampton. It was thought that the majority of the Northampton Borough Police would be pre-occupied with the crowds outside the court.

After clashing in a pub brawl, it was decided that Stephen Memory, a 23 year old shoe worker, and William Langley, also 23, should settle their differences in an old style bare knuckle fight. The McRae committal gave the perfect opportunity, and an estimated 25 to 30 men turned up at Duston Hill to witness the spectacle.

For 40 gruelling rounds the two men slugged it out. Langley, although physically bigger, was continually on the receiving end, being knocked down 30 times. But each time he got up, egged on by his seconds and onlookers, only to be felled again by the bare knuckle fists of Memory. He was nearly blind, half insensible and badly beaten and bruised about the head. After one and a half hours of punishment he collapsed unconscious, and would die later that night from massive blood clots on the brain.

When the death of Langley became public knowledge, police enquiries began. Although *attendance* at a prize fight was not in itself illegal, nevertheless because of the circumstances, those who had been there were extremely tight lipped. Consequently, only Memory and six others were indicted, including

James Jeyes, a 51 year old shoe factory owner, and thus a man of some social standing in Northampton.

The fact of the fight was never disputed, so Memory as the principal was to be found guilty of manslaughter. The others were charged with aiding and abetting.

Mr Justice Kennedy summed up the legal position. A man at a prize fight was not necessarily an aider and abetter, but only so if he encouraged the fight, and if death ensued, then he was equally guilty with the principal. However, there must be sufficient evidence to show this. The only evidence available was from a group of young boys who were playing cricket in a nearby field. Under cross examination, they became (or were made to be) completely confused, and so the case against five of the accused collapsed.

But on the evidence against Jeyes, the boys could not be shaken. Jeyes they said, had arranged for a taxi to take Langley away. By this and other actions, he was therefore clearly involved in the management of the fight, and the jury found him guilty of aiding and abetting. He received seven months hard labour, whilst Memory received 12 months hard labour.

### iii) Burglary

The act of entering premises or buildings, by force, when the owner of the property would rather you did not, has been called several things over the centuries. It was called Forcible Entry by statutes of Richard II in 1381, Henry VI in 1429, and James I in 1623; Breaking and Entering or Housebreaking, depending on the time of day, by the Larceny Acts of 1827, 1861 and 1916; and finally, Burglary by the Theft Act of 1968, although this Act removed the ingredient of entering by force. The concept however is the same: entering a building which you are not legally entitled to, to commit some form of crime. Burglaries, therefore, are different from robberies, you cannot rob a building, only people.

The old medieval records however, are vague on this point. In the 1202 Assize roll, there is no mention of burglary (or Forcible Entry), but it can be safely assumed that some of the crimes recorded as robberies were in fact burglaries. And the same for the 1630 and 1657/1658 Quarter Sessions, no specific mention of burglary is made, though there were plenty of non specified offences, some of which must have been burglaries.

The first person to be hung in the county where the crime specifically states it was burglary, was John Woodroff in 1731, followed by Samuel Bayley a year later. However, the most 'distinguished' burglars to have been hung in the county, were the five who were the first to be hung at the same time on the newly erected 'New Drop', at the county gaol, Angel Lane, Northampton, on Friday 19 March 1819.

William Minards (27) a miller from Wootton and William George (21) from Renhold in Bedfordshire, were both awaiting trial for burglary in Northampton county gaol. On Friday 24 July 1818, however, they escaped through a window,

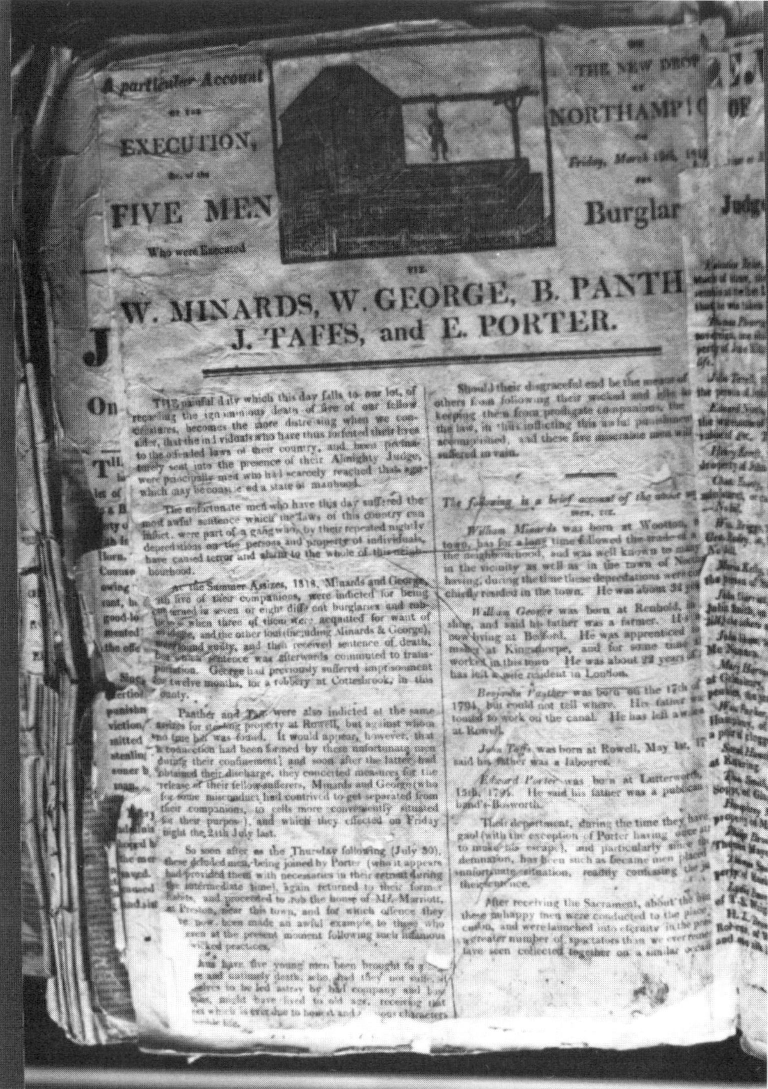

A particular Account of the EXECUTION, of the FIVE MEN Who were Executed on THE NEW DROP at NORTHAMP[illegible] on Friday, March [illegible] for Burglar[illegible]

viz.

W. MINARDS, W. GEORGE, B. PANTH[illegible]
J. TAFFS, and E. PORTER.

THE painful duty which this day falls to our lot, of recording the ignominious death of five of our fellow creatures, becomes the more distressing when we consider, that the individuals who have thus forfeited their lives to the offended laws of their country, and been prematurely sent into the presence of their Almighty Judge, were principally men who had scarcely reached that age which may be considered a state of manhood.

The unfortunate men who have this day suffered the most awful sentence which the laws of this country can inflict, were part of a gang which, by their repeated nightly depredations on the persons and property of individuals, have caused terror and alarm to the whole of this neighbourhood.

At the Summer Assizes, 1818, Minards and George, with five of their companions, were indicted for being concerned in seven or eight different burglaries and robberies, when three of them were acquitted for want of evidence, and the other four (including Minards & George), were found guilty, and then received sentence of death, but which sentence was afterwards commuted to transportation. George had previously suffered imprisonment for twelve months, for a robbery at Cottesbrook, in this county.

Panther and Taffs were also indicted at the same Assizes for stealing property at Rowell, but against whom no true bill was found. It would appear, however, that a connection had been formed by these unfortunate men during their confinement; and soon after the latter had obtained their discharge, they concerted measures for the release of their fellow-sufferers, Minards and George (who for some misconduct had contrived to get separated from their companions, to cells more conveniently situated for their purpose), and which they effected on Friday night the 24th July last.

So soon after as the Thursday following (July 30), these deluded men, being joined by Porter (who it appears had provided them with necessaries in their retreat during the intermediate time), again returned to their former habits, and proceeded to rob the house of Mr. Marriott, at Preston, near this town, and for which offence they have now been made an awful example to those who even at the present moment following such infamous wicked practices.

[illegible] have five young men been brought to [illegible] and untimely death, who, had they not suffered [illegible] to be led astray by bad company and [illegible], might have lived to old age, receiving that [illegible] which is ever due to honest and [illegible] characters [illegible] life.

Should their disgraceful end be the means of [illegible] others from following their wicked and idle [illegible] keeping them from profligate companions, the [illegible] the law, in thus inflicting this awful punishment [illegible] accomplished, and these five miserable men will [not have] suffered in vain.

*The following is a brief account of the above* [illegible] *men, viz.*

*William Minards* was born at Wootton, [illegible] town, has for a long time followed the trade of [illegible] the neighbourhood, and was well known to many in the vicinity as well as in the town of No[illegible] having, during the time these depredations were [illegible] chiefly resided in the town. He was about 24 [illegible]

*William George* was born at Renhold, [illegible] shire, and said his father was a farmer. H[illegible] now living at Bedford. He was apprenticed [illegible] maker at Kingsthorpe, and for some time [illegible] worked in this town. He was about 22 years [illegible] has left a wife resident in London.

*Benjamin Panther* was born on the 17th of [illegible] 1794, but could not tell where. His father [illegible] found to work on the canal. He has left a w[illegible] at Rowell.

*John Taffs* was born at Rowell, May 1st, 17[illegible] said his father was a labourer.

*Edward Porter* was born at Lutterworth, [illegible] 15th, 1793. He said his father was a publican [illegible] bard's-Bosworth.

Their deportment, during the time they have [been in] gaol (with the exception of Porter having [illegible] to make his escape), and particularly since [their con]demnation, has been such as became men placed [in their] unfortunate situation, readily confessing the ju[stice of] their sentence.

After receiving the Sacrament, about the [illegible] these unhappy men were conducted to the place [of exe]cution, and were launched into eternity in the p[resence of a] greater number of spectators than we ever re[member to] have seen collected together on a similar occa[sion].

The first outing of the 'New Drop', when Minards, George, Panther, Taffs and Porter were all hung for a burglary at Preston Deanery in 1818. (NRO)

opened on the outside, by their colleagues Benjamin Panther (25) and John Taffs (19) from Rothwell, and Edward Porter (25) from Lutterworth.

On their flight away from town, they burgled the home of Mr William Marriott at Preston Deanery, just outside Northampton. But they were soon captured, and this time there was no escape, and they were all hung together.

# 20 POUNDS
## REWARD.

WHEREAS last Night, the 9th, or early this Morning, the 10th of April, Instant, the Dwelling House of the Hon. and Rev. JAMES DOUGLAS, of Broughton, was feloniously broken into, and the whole of his valuable PLATE, together with CASH to the amount of above £40 stolen therefrom.

*On each piece of Plate is engraved a Salamander, supported by a Coronet.*

Whoever will give information which will lead to the apprehension and conviction of the Offender or Offenders will receive the above Reward.

**Broughton Rectory, April 10, 1836.**

DASH, PRINTER, KETTERING.

The Reward Notice issued for the Broughton Rectory burglary in 1836. Note the speed of printing and publishing, as this notice was obviously printed before the burglars' capture, which occurred at 2 pm that same day. (NRO)

## Northamptonshire.

# A CALENDAR OF THE SEVERAL PRISONERS

*Now confined in His Majesty's Gaol and House of Correction for the said County, as well as those who remain in Custody under former Sentences, and Justices' Orders as those*

WHO ARE TO TAKE THEIR TRIALS BEFORE

THE HONOURABLE SIR JAMES ALLAN, PARK KNIGHT,

One of the Justices of our Lord the King of his Court of Common Pleas; and

THE HONOURABLE SIR WILLIAM BOLLAND, KNIGHT,

One of the Barons of our said Lord the King of his Court of Exchequer of Pleas,

## AT THE SUMMER ASSIZES,

COMMENCING JULY 11TH, 1836.

## WILLIAM HARRIS, ESQUIRE, SHERIFF.

PRISONERS ON ORDERS IN THE GAOL AND HOUSE OF CORRECTION:—

Richard Page, Thomas Blinkhorne, James Cox, William Ward, Thomas Coleman, Ambrose Woods, William Robins, Edward Liddington, Henry Maudesley, Richard Ellat alias Elliott, Elijah Groves, Francis Clarke, Robert Slater, Samuel Wills, Charles Finedon, John Blunt, William Gardner William Flintfarrow, Samuel Bonham, Samuel Frisby, Samuel Hollowell, James Henson, William Massey, John Stanton, John Cunnington, John Fisher, William Ash, Charles Tee, John Archer, Richard Nichols, James Hoskins, Thomas Willis, William Willis, James Elmore, George Enfield, Edward Miller, Thomas Robinson, John Meakins, Patrick M'Guire, Sarah Collins, Caroline Wilson, Joyce Coe, Mary Nutt, Sarah Lilley.

ALPHABETICAL LIST.

| NO. | NAME. | AGE. |
|---|---|---|
| 5 | Anstice John | 22 |
| 7 | Andrew Robert | 30 |
| 16 | Brown Thomas | 26 |
| 15 | Coles Thomas | 26 |
| 22 | Chattel John | 20 |
| 24 | Collins Daniel | 19 |
| 10 | Dent Josiah | 19 |
| 8 | French Thomas | 26 |
| 3 | Gore Benjamin | 21 |
| 14 | George James | 20 |
| 12 | Howe Thomas | 39 |
| 17 | Harris John | 18 |

| NO. | NAME. | AGE. |
|---|---|---|
| 4 | Jones William | 21 |
| 23 | Jinks George | 36 |
| 20 | King William | 32 |
| 19 | Morby John | 40 |
| 2 | Powell Thomas | 23 |
| 6 | Powell Thomas | 19 |
| 13 | Paviour Esther | 48 |
| 18 | Page James | 33 |
| 25 | Panter Samuel | 22 |
| 11 | Rogers John | 18 |
| 9 | Southam William | 18 |
| 21 | Suitor James | 16 |
| 1 | Waples William | 25 |

NOTE.—Those marked, N, can neither read nor write; those R, read only; those IMP., read and write imperfectly; those WELL, read and write well; those SUP., superior education.

The Calendar for the 1836 Summer Assizes, where the Broughton burglars, Gore, Jones and Anstice are listed overleaf. They were found guilty and had their Death Sentences commuted to life imprisonment. (NRO)

## PRISONERS FOR TRIAL.

N. 1. WILLIAM WAPLES, aged 25,—Committed 17th March, 1836, by Edward Bouverie, Esquire, and Edwd. Robt. Butcher, D.C.L. charged on the oaths of George West and others, on suspicion of having, on the night of the 3d of March last, burglariously broken open the dwelling-house of William Cole, at the parish of Upper Heyford, and feloniously stolen, taken, and carried away therefrom, three yards and half of velveteen, six yards of cotton print, two pair of black worsted stockings, and other articles of the value of £10, the property of the said George West.

The same WILLIAM WAPLES, aged 25, } Committed the same day, by the same
N. 2. THOMAS POWELL, aged 23, } Magistrates, charged on the oaths of William Marriott and others, of having, on the night of the 27th, or early in the morning of the 28th of February last, feloniously and burglariously broken open the dwelling-house of the said William Marriott, at the parish of Duston, and stolen, taken, and carried away therefrom, eight knives and forks, a black-silk handkerchief, and divers other articles of the value of £10, his property.

Well. 3. BENJAMIN GORE, aged 21, } Committed 10th April, 1836, by Thomas Philip Maunsel,
R. 4. WILLIAM JONES, aged 21, } Esquire, charged on the oath of the Honorable and Rev.
Well. 5. JOHN ANSTICE, aged 22, } James Douglas and others, of having feloniously broken into the dwelling-house of the said Honorable and Rev. J. Douglas, at the Parish of Broughton, and stolen therefrom, divers articles of plate, gold and silver trinkets, and bank notes.

Imp. 6. THOMAS POWELL, aged 19,—Committed 11th April, 1836, by the Rev. James Hogg, Clerk, charged on the oaths of William Rayson and William Pridmore, with unlawfully entering into an inclosed Park, in the parish of Rushton, in the night of the 31st of December last, with two other persons, with a gun and bludgeons for the purpose of destroying game.

Imp. 7. ROBERT ANDREW, aged 30,—Committed 20th April, 1836, by John Yorke, Esquire, charged on the oath of George Smith, of Sudborough, with having, on the night of Wednesday the Thirteenth of April last, between the hours of half-past Ten and half-past Eleven o'clock, on the King's highway, in the parish of Oundle, feloniously assaulted the said George Smith, with intent to rob him.

Imp. 8. THOMAS FRENCH, aged 26, } Committed 30th April, 1836, by William Willes,
N. 9. WILLIAM SOUTHAM, aged 18, } Esquire, charged on the oath of William Chesley, with having, on the night of the 7th day of March, 1835, at Grimsbury, in the parish of Warkworth, feloniously and burglariously entered the dwelling-house of Elizabeth Rymill, and stolen and taken away therefrom, one coat, three pair of breeches, and other property of the goods and chattels of the said William Chesley.

N. 10. JOSIAH DENT, aged 19, } Committed 5th May, 1836, by the Rev. John Rose, Clerk,
R. 11. JOHN ROGERS, aged 18, } charged on the oath of Benjamin Bull, with having, on the 4th day of November last, feloniously stopped the said Benjamin Bull, on the King's highway, in the parish of Floore, and robbed him of a silver watch of the value of 15s. a purse of the value of threepence, and a shilling, the property of the said Benjamin Bull.

Imp. 12. THOMAS HOWE, aged 39,—Committed 18th May, 1836, by George Mallaber, Esquire, Mayor of the Borough of Daventry, charged on the oaths of John Hyde, John Holland, and others, with having, on the 11th day of May last at the Borough of Daventry aforesaid, feloniously, knowingly, and willingly, and without lawful excuse, had in his possession a certain forged and counterfeited Bank Note for the payment of £5, and one piece of counterfeit money to resemble the lawful current coin of this realm, called a sovereign, he the said Thomas Howe well knowing the same to be forged, false, and counterfeited.

R. 13. ESTHER PAVIOUR, wife of William Paviour, aged 48,—Committed 6th June, 1836, by the Rev. Francis Clerke, Clerk, charged on the oath of George Bliss, with having, on the 23d day of May last, feloniously stolen and taken away a pair of shoes, two sheets, a gown, and other articles of the goods and chattels of the said George Bliss, from his dwelling-house, at the parish of Aston-le-Walls.

N. 14. JAMES GEORGE, aged 20, } Committed on the 9th June, 1836, by Chas. Hill, Esquire,
N. 15. THOMAS COLES, aged 26, } charged with having, in the night of the 6th of April last, broken and entered the dwelling-house of Wm. Houghton, at Wellingborough, and stolen therefrom 9lbs. of beef, a loaf, about 2lbs. of butter, a box, containing eight knives and eight forks, and several other articles, the property of the said William Houghton.

The same THOMAS COLES, } Committed on the 7th June, 1836, by Chas. Hill, Esquire,
Imp. 16. THOMAS BROWN, aged 26, } charged on the oath of William Harper, of Lowick,
Imp. 17. JOHN HARRIS, aged 18, } tailor, with having in the night of the 21st of May last, feloniously broken into and entered the shop, being part of the dwelling-house of his father, and stealing therefrom about three yards of cotton cord or corduroy, about five yards of fustian, eight yards of jean or nankeen, two Valentia waistcoat pieces, several remnant pieces of cotton cord, a remnant of light kerseymere, and a pair of breeches linings.

3

The same THOMAS BROWN also stands charged with having in the month of April, 1835, feloniously stolen a gun from the coach-house of James Everard, at Wellingborough, the property of the said James Everard.

The same THOMAS COLES also stands charged with having in the night of the 14th May last, feloniously stolen a bag of pollard or shorts, and an axe, from a barn in the yard of Wm. Sears, at Wellingborough.

The same THOMAS COLES also stands charged with having in the night of the 24th of May last, feloniously stolen from the same barn a sack containing a quantity of pollard, and another sack containing a quantity of barley flour, the property of the said William Sears.

The same THOMAS COLES also stands charged with having late on Saturday night the 4th, or early on Sunday morning the 5th of June last, feloniously stolen from the workshop of William Valentine, at Wellingborough, three hand-saws, two axes, two drawing knives, two smoothing planes, several chisels, several gimlets, a gouge, a large augur, two gages, a wood rasp, a large basket, and other articles, the property of the said William Valentine.

The same THOMAS COLES also stands charged with having stolen from a barn at Wellingborough, in the night of the 4th of June last, six fowls, the property of John Collins Scott.

The same THOMAS COLES also stands charged with stealing from a certain close in Wellingborough, a shovel, the property of William Rixon.

The same THOMAS COLES also stands charged with having in the night of the 2d of June last, feloniously stolen from a garden at Wellingborough, a hen and eleven chickens, the property of William Hardwick.

The same THOMAS COLES also stands charged on the oath of George Walter, of Great Harrowden, with having in the night of the 8th of April last, feloniously broken open his workshop at Great Harrowden aforesaid, and stealing therefrom a single-barrelled gun, and other articles, the property of the said Geo Walter.

18. JAMES PAGE, aged 33, 19. JOHN MORBY, aged 40, 20. WILLIAM KING, aged 22, Committed 5th July, 1836, by William Willes, Esquire, charged on the oath of William Franklin, of Newbottle, in this county, with having in the month of March, 1831, entered a barn in the occupation of the said William Franklin, in the parish of Newbottle aforesaid, and feloniously stealing therefrom 20 bushels of wheat of the goods and chattels of the said William Franklin.

21. JAMES SUITOR, aged 16,—Committed 7th July, 1836, by Geo. Mallaber, Esquire, Mayor of the Borough of Daventry, charged on the oath of John Lench and others, with having on the 5th day of July instant, obtained from the said John Lench, the sum of one shilling and sixpence, under a false ticket, pretending that it was written by James Powell, the foreman of the said John Lench, as due to one Ashby, whereby the said James Suitor defrauded the said John Lench of one shilling and sixpence.

22. JOHN CHATTEL, aged 20, 23. GEORGE JINKS, aged 30, Committed July 9th, 1836, by William Willes, Esquire, charged on the oath of John Horwood, with having in the month of April last, feloniously stolen and taken away four bushels of barley, of the goods and chattels of the said John Horwood, at the parish of Stean, in this county.

24. DANIEL COLLINS, aged 19, 25. SAMUEL PANTER, aged 22, Committed 11th July, 1836, by the Rev. James Hogg, Clerk, charged on the oaths of Joseph Wingell and others, with stealing a pair of stockings, and various articles of wearing apparel, from the dwelling-house of Joseph Brooks, at the parish of Kettering, in this county, the property of the said Joseph Brooks.

Another crime that was definitely a burglary, occurred at Broughton Rectory during the early hours of Sunday 10 April 1836. John Anstice (22), William Jones (21) and Benjamin Gore (21) got away with all the Reverend and Honourable James Douglas' family crested silverware (he was to become the 4th Baron Douglas of Douglas in 1849) and goods and cash worth another £40.

Unfortunately their combined brain power was evidently not of the highest, and they were caught at 2pm that very same afternoon as they were sleeping under a haystack just three miles away, between Pytchley and Burton Latimer. All the silverware was found buried nearby. Anstice, Jones and Gore appeared at the 1836 Summer Assizes, were found guilty, and had their death sentences commuted to life imprisonment.

In 1852 there were 35 reported burglaries in Northamptonshire, from a population of 242,000, giving .14 burglaries per 1,000 population. In 1993, a population of 575,000 produced 16,816 burglaries, a rate of 29.25 per 1,000.

Henry Abbott (22) burgled the house of Edward Haynes at Woodford in January 1870. He climbed up a tree and into an open window, stealing a watch, a pair of boots and £2. 5s. He was wearing the boots when he was arrested. At the 1870 Lent Assizes he received eight months hard labour. (NP)

### iv) Drunkenness

Drunkenness in itself has never been considered a serious 'crime', more anti-social than criminal. However, the role of drink in the cause of crime has always been well known from earliest times through to our 'lager louts' of today. And so, from earliest times the alehouse has always been strictly controlled and regulated.

We thus discover the dilemma that has faced the authorities from the beginning. Alehouses can, of course, provide genuine refreshment and entertainment for honest patrons. But sometimes these patrons were far from honest, and history is peppered with many Acts of Parliament that tried to stop landlords from harbouring criminals who looked upon the local pub as the hatchery of criminality.

Worries about the link between crime and alcohol, and the places where alcohol could be obtained, were consistently being voiced. For instance, the *Northampton Mercury* of Saturday 9 July 1836 called village alehouses 'parochial nurseries . . . for the encouragement of criminals and the growth of crime'. And in a letter to the same paper in September 1859, 'A Ratepayer' said that village pubs were 'sources of vice, crime and social debasement'.

And the court records are full of evidence of this anxiety. At the Michaelmas Quarter Sessions of 1630, the whole of the parish of Staverton petitioned the Quarter Sessions to stop Richard Williams frequenting the Staverton alehouse, saying that he 'has for these three or four years last past much haunted the alehouse in our town . . . and it has been very offensive to many not only for his living from his family where it is fittest for him to be but also because he is generally supposed and suspected to be so much there for no good end . . .'

But more direct evidence of drink and the cause of crime is given in the Michaelmas Quarter Sessions of 1657, when the Reverend Joseph Newell, vicar of Paulerspury complained, in the form of an Information, about the behaviour of a certain Robert Clarke of Potterspury. Robert Clarke, said the Information, 'doth for the most part in the week abuse himself of the blessings of God by continual excessive drinking, and is for the most part every day in the week overcome with beer'.

Robert's crimes are catalogued in the Information, including the time that he 'took away the keys of the church door (it being the Lord's Day) from the [Parish] Clerk and locked up the doors and kept the whole parish out of the church'. Also, that 'the said Robert Clarke, being drunk did . . . go into his house and bring out a gun and offer to shoot the said Mr Newell . . .'

This Robert Clarke was described as 'gentleman', so he must have been of some social standing, and when he was bound over to keep the peace against the Vicar of Paulerspury, his surety was £20, a fairly tidy sum for those days. But notice the importance that the complainant put on alcohol in these crimes.

But it was not until the 19th century that Cesare Lombroso, the first of the great criminologists, actually produced statistics to 'prove' the link between drink and crime. In 1880 he reckoned that there were 4,938 public houses in London which were exclusively for the resort of criminals and prostitutes. In Northampton, in the area known as the 'Boroughs', there were over 90 public houses in less than one square mile. Whilst not every one of them can be considered a 'criminal pub', of course, nevertheless there must have been a lot that were.

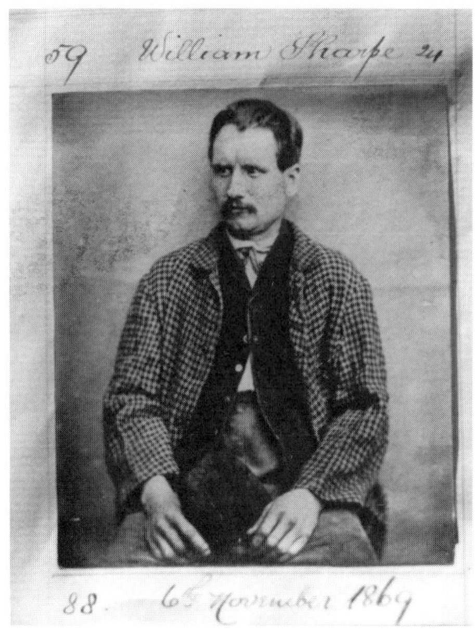


William Sharpe (24) spent five and a half months doing hard labour in a 14 month period, as a result of four convictions for drunkenness: March 1868 at Thrapston; June 1868 at Oundle; May 1869 at Northampton; and May 1869 at Oundle. (NP)

However, from the earliest times, simply being drunk in a public place, was also regarded as a criminal offence, and arrests purely for drunkenness, with no other crime attached, were being made all the time. In 1852, 180 cases of drunkenness were reported, and a population of 242,000 gives a rate per 1,000 of .74. In 1993 however, different police procedures apply, and so a strict comparison based purely on numbers cannot be valid. But what it is worth, only 44 cases of drunkenness got to the courts during 1993, a rate per 1,000 population of .08.

**v) Heresy**

Heresy was both an ecclesiastical offence and a criminal one. In 1678, however, the criminal part of the offence was dropped, and it is now punishable only by the church authorities.

Although the murder of the Reverend William Losse took place in Lois Weedon church on Sunday 2 July 1643, this was more for political, rather than theological reasons, and as such, was not a true martyrdom. The only real martyrdom in Northamptonshire, was in the reign of Mary Tudor, the aptly named 'Bloody Mary'. During her five years reign (1553-1558), hundreds of Protestants were put to death for their religious beliefs, as she tried to reverse her father's split with Roman Catholicism.

John Kurde was a shoemaker from Syresham who had been arrested for refusing to attend Holy Communion in his parish church, and for denying the doctrine of Transubstantiation. He was imprisoned in Northampton Castle and stood trial at All Saints Church in 1557. He was found guilty and sentenced to be burnt at the stake, the usual treatment for 'heretics'.

In September 1557, Kurde was led out of the town by the north gate (Barrack Road) to Kingsthorpe Hollow. In front of thousands of people, whilst the bundles of sticks were still being piled about him, the Vicar of St. Giles, John Roote told him that he would be pardoned if he recanted. John Kurde's answer was simple. 'I have had my pardon by Jesus Christ'. His martyrdom is included in Foxe's *Book of Martyrs*.

**vi) Organised criminal gangs**

Over the years there have been several notorious gangs in Northamptonshire, from medieval times right the way through until perhaps the most famous of them all, the Culworth gang. When there is no police force to stop them, gangs of criminals can roam the countryside marauding just as they please.

Travelling bands of criminals were the scourge of England, and indeed, so much were these gangs part and parcel of English social life, that the greatest folk hero that England has ever produced was just one such gang leader. Every county had its gangs, Nottinghamshire had Robin Hood, and Northamptonshire had Thomas the Baker.

Thomas the Baker was finally captured and appeared at the Northamptonshire Assizes in September 1202. But instead of appearing as a noble Robin Hood figure trying to right wrongs of an unjust society, Thomas turned 'approver', and poured out a long list of crimes and accomplices in an effort to save his own skin. An 'approver' was the medieval equivalent of 'turning Queen's Evidence'; in other words, giving evidence against fellow criminals in return for a pardon.

He named 18 members of his gang, including Reginald of Wellingborough, Roger Gulger, Scot of Higham Ferrers and Hudde the forger, and also 14 others who had given them shelter and protection from the authorities. The gang's crimes included burglaries, thefts and robberies, where all manner of plunder was taken, from foodstuffs and wheat, through to clothing, bedding and money. All in all, Thomas confessed to about 20 crimes, and you can bet there were probably many, many more.

The area covered by the gang was amazing. Northamptonshire was obviously their main stamping ground, but they roamed as far south as Bury St Edmunds, and as far north at Nottingham. And by visiting Nottingham in the 1190s, they obviously knew of, and perhaps even met, their Nottingham equivalents, perhaps even Maid Marion.

Perhaps Thomas could compare Robin Hood's Maid Marion to his own 'Maid Marion', a certain Emma Brunfustian, who must have been quite a 'gal'. Thomas said that Emma went daily to Daventry or Northampton markets, and 'was of the worst repute, so that she has killed men and leads robbers to rob houses'. And Adam Falc, who keeps her, 'is likewise of the worst repute'.

Luck was not with Thomas however. Although he had turned 'approver', he was still hanged. But what happened to Emma and all the rest of the gang is unknown, the Assize rolls are silent.

When William Bacaunt was found murdered in Saint Andrew's churchyard, Northampton, on Christmas Eve 1305, it was found to be just one consequence of a gang war that rocked medieval Northampton.

William Bacaunt, William Tubbe, John of Ireland, Henry of Peatling (Leicestershire), Walter of Oxford and William le vileyn had all been members of a criminal gang that had numerous robberies in the county to their credit. However, all six had been captured somehow and had been imprisoned in Northampton castle.

Whilst in prison, Bacaunt, Tubbe, William of Peatling and William le vileyn all became 'approvers', against a rival gang of criminals who were still at large. On Christmas Eve 1305, all the six broke out of Northampton castle gaol, and fled for sanctuary to Saint Andrew's Priory church, Northampton. It was there, on that same day, that the other gang led by John, son of John de Aston, came to Saint Andrews, looking for the 'narks who had grassed them up'.

John's luck was in when they saw William Bacaunt outside the church, and he was promptly murdered. But being unable to get to the main gang inside the church in sanctuary, John and his men had to slink away, and history can tell us nothing more about them.

The remaining members of the band stopped in sanctuary until Saturday 18 March 1306, which was the eve of Palm Sunday. Why they were allowed to stop in sanctuary for over 80 days, double the official sanctuary time, is not made known.

On that Saturday night, all four remaining members of the gang broke out of the priory church, and in order to do so, had to assault two of the Prior's household. So severely did they beat them up, that their lives were despaired of. William Tubbe, William le vileyn and Henry of Peatting all escaped and were never heard of again.

Walter of Oxford, however, sought sanctuary again, this time in the Church of the Friars Preachers in Northampton, but chose to go to gaol instead of abjuring the realm. But he broke out yet again, and yet again sought sanctuary, this time in the Church of the Friars Minor also in Northampton. And yet again, Walter surrendered himself to the prison instead of exile abroad. But this time, he died in prison.

This was quite an extraordinary saga, which if it had happened today, would have been spread all over the tabloids for months.

## *Guilty M'Lud!*

The 'Culworth Gang' has gone down in the folk history of Northamptonshire. For nearly ten years the 'Culworth Gang' committed robberies and burglaries throughout south Northamptonshire and north Oxfordshire, and although some of its exploits must have been common knowledge, fear of reprisals kept anyone from giving evidence against it. In its heyday, in the early 1780's, the Gang was about 15 strong. This number fluctuated over the years as members joined and left, but the original founders remained at its core, and came from the villages centred around Culworth.

The most prominent members were: John Smith, senior, his two sons John, junior and William, William Bowers, William Pettipher, William Tervill, Thomas Malsbury and Richard Jack, all labourers from Culworth; Richard Law, a carpenter from Culworth; and one William Abbott. William Abbott was the Parish Clerk of Sulgrave and was reputed to carry a brace of pistols everywhere he went, even when performing his parish duties in church.

Starting off by simple poaching, the gang graduated to more serious stuff. The exact number of crimes committed by individual members of the Gang is unknown, but by their own confessions after their capture, owned up to 47 robberies, and doubtless there were a good many more, including the highway robbery of William Adams in 1785 for which James Tarry had already been executed.

In 1837, a certain James Beesley published his account of the gang in the manuscript magazine of the Banbury Mechanics' Institute. The list of crimes given by him was only a small number of the total, but as he drily adds 'it is sufficient to show that they were wholesale plunderers, not your mere petty larceny men.'

In all Beesley describes 21 robberies with violence on 17 different occasions, ranging from poor travellers right up to lawyers and clergymen in broad daylight. In one description of a violent burglary and robbery at Sulgrave, Beesley was actually able to speak with the victim, although by then (1837) an old lady of over 80.

All in all, over a period of nearly ten years, the Culworth Gang amassed a large amount of cash and property, and gained a reputation for violence which stopped anyone thinking of giving evidence against it. The Gang built a crime empire equivalent to the London East End gangs of the 1960s.

However the end of the Gang came in the early months of 1787. Law and Pettipher returning from a burglary at Blakesley, stopped overnight at an Inn in Towcester. The landlord was suspicious and searched their bag whilst they were asleep, and found two smocks and two masks. He called the Parish Constable, but they decided to do nothing. It was not until they heard the news of the Blakesley burglary some two days later, that they decided to report their find. Law and Pettipher were captured, taken before a Magistrate and committed for trial.

12

*Copy of a Letter from JOHN SMITH, (a Prisoner in Northampton Gaol, under Sentence of Death) to his Wife,*

July 21th, 1787.

*My dear and loving Wife,*

THESE come with my kind Love to you and all my dear children, begging you will come to see me before I depart this wicked world, and beg of God to forgive me all my sins, and I will endeavour to make my Peace, with God before I die. My Dear, I desire my Son William will make my Coffin, and let me have it here before I die; and I desire you will have my Body taken home to my own house, that you may see me buried. And beg of my children to take warning by my unhappy end, that they may turn to the path of virtue, and beg of them to beware of bad company and Sabbath breaking, which is the wish of their dying Faither. My Dear, I hope you will come to see me; and let my Daughter Molly know, that she my meet you here, for I cannot die in Peace without I do see her, so I beg you will desire her to come,

So no more, from your dying Husband.

JOHN SMITH.

P. S. My. Dear, desire my Son John to marry Elizabeth Beard, and beg of him to be good to her and the Child, and take warning by me that they may live in Comfort.—I desire you will take care of these lines, and cause them to be read to all my Children every Sabbath-Day; and I hope that God will give them Grace to take warning—it is the Prayer of a dying Father.

JOHN SMITH.

13

*Copy of a Letter from DAVID COE, (a Prisoner under Sentence of Death in Northampton Gaol) to his Parents.*

July 28th, 1787.

*Honoured Father and Mother,*

THESE come with my Duty to you both, with my kind Love to my dear, and loving wife, and all my dear Children, I beg that you will not grieve for me, but for yourselves. For I am only going a little before you; and I pray God grant us to meet in Heaven, where we shall never part no more. I hope my untimely Death will be a Warning to all that know me, that they may beware of bad Company, and Sabbath-breaking, I must leave this wicked World on Friday next, and I pray God to receive my departing Soul, through Jesus Christ my Lord and Saviour. *Amen. Amen.*

I desire you would let me see my Coffin before I die, and I beg you will be hear on Thursday Night, and all my Friends that desire to take their Leave of me before I die, so the Lord be with you all.

So no more, from your dying Child.

DAVID COE.

A contemporary printing of the Culworth Gang's leader, John Smith's letter to his wife. It is printed alongside a letter from David Coe, who together with his accomplice John hulbert, were hanged for theft of foodstuff on the same day as the Culworth Gang. (NRO)

And once it was shown that someone had the courage to stand up against the Gang, the beginning of the end was in sight. Whilst in gaol, Law and Pettipher implicated and named all the surviving members of the Gang, who were all rounded up within days, except for Richard Jack who fled the country and was never heard of again.

Nine members of the Gang appeared at the Northamptonshire Spring Assizes of 1787; the Smith trio, Law, Pettipher, Bowers, Abbott and Tervill, all on charges of robbery. Tervill and the two younger Smiths were acquitted, Abbott was transported for life, but the rest were sentenced to death.

John Smith, senior, whilst under sentence of death, wrote a letter to his wife. This shows that he was not an illiterate farm labourer, but a reasonably educated man, at least educated enough to have known the full implications of the life he was leading.

John Smith's exhortations to his son fell on stony ground. Within two years, John, junior would be hung for highway robbery in Warwickshire, leaving the devoted Elizabeth Beard to bring his body, strapped to the back of a donkey, all the way from Warwick back to Culworth for burial, travelling throughout the night so as not to attract attention.

William Smith fared better. Giving up his criminal life, he settled to be an industrious and hard working man. Thomas Malsbury, although part of the Gang, never stood trial, and would seem to have escaped justice. But some years later, at Culworth, he was accidentally run over by a heavy horse and cart, and was killed instantly.

John Smith, senior, William Bowers, Richard Law and William Pettipher, the 'Culworth Gang', were all hanged together on Northampton Racecourse on Wednesday 3 August 1787, before one of the largest crowds ever.

George Catherall came from a highly respectable family from Bolton in Lancashire. His early life is obscure, but it seems he had been dishonourably discharged from the army, as his back and shoulders were scarred with 'cat o' nine tails' marks. He spurned the respectable life of his family and turned to crime, earning the disapproval of his mother who told him that 'he would die with his shoes on'.

Taking the nickname of 'Captain Slash', in imitation of an old highwayman, Catherall gathered around him a gang of violent thieves and pickpockets. Their main targets were the county fairs where large numbers of people gathered, which made thieving, pickpocketing and robbery easy. In such activities the gang toured around England visiting each fair in turn.

The 1826 Midsummer fair at Boughton Green, Northampton attracted the attention of 'Captain Slash', and he descended on the fair with 100 of his gang.

# EXECUTION OF
# George Catherall,
## ON THE NEW DROP, NORTHAMPTON, ON FRIDAY, JULY 21, 1826,
*For Highway Robbery, at Boughton Green Fair.*

GEORGE CATHERALL, aged 29, and HUGH ROBBINSON, aged 18, stood charged with stealing from James Henley, 11 half crowns, one crown, one waistcoat, a neckerchief, a corkscrew, and some halfpence, at Boughton Green Fair. Catherall, who is known by the name of "CAPTAIN SLASH," appeared in a shabby dress, having his head bound up in a silk handkerchief, in consequence of the fracture of the skull. In taking him his left hand also was broken, and two of his ribs; the prisoners are strangers in this neighbourhood, and are supposed to belong to a party of thieves and pickpockets who frequent the different fairs of the kingdom.—Jas. Henley, the prosecutor, is a shoemaker residing in this town, and was employed as a waiter at one of the booths during the fair. Between one and two o'clock on the morning of the 28th of June, as witness was walking across the Green, he saw Catherall a few yards distant from him, who came up, and without saying a word, struck him a violent blow across the face with a large stick, which felled him to the ground. A number of other persons immediately surrounded him, and the other prisoner Robinson, beat him violently while lying on the ground. Witness perceiving that they were rifling his pockets, put up his knees, on which Catherall said, "d— your eyes why don't you put your legs down." —Witness then cried out "murder," and the prisoner Catherall, setting his foot on his throat, said, d— you, there shall be murder too." The prisoner Robinson lay on him while he was down. Whilst witness was on the ground his right-hand breeches pocket was cut off, as also a bundle which he held in his hand, containing various articles, was taken from him. George Warwick swore that the former witness was knocked down in the manner before described, and during the affray, which lasted a considerable time, he, in company with another person, went up and struck Catherall, with a view to get him away. He also followed the prisoner Robinson, and took him into custody. Geo. Ealum, corroborated the evidence of the former witness, and added that he saw the prisoner Robinson take something like a pocket from the person on the ground, which Robinson threw to some of his companions, who ran away with it. The Judge, in summing up, observed that the knocking a person down and robbing him in any open place, constituted highway robbery. Verdict—Guilty. *Robinson, Transported for Life.*

CATHERALL also stood charged with robbing Jas. Hannell, at Boughton Green Fair, on the above night. James Hannell, is a Confectioner, and regularly attends the above fair. About twelve o'clock in the night of the 27th of June, as he was walking up the Green, he received a violent blow on the right side of his head from a stick, but upon turning round he could not see any one near him. A number of persons immediately came up, and one of them again struck him on the left side of the head, which brought him to the ground. Five or six men immediately fell upon him, and rifled his pockets of silver to the amount of £1. The prisoner Catherall then said "d — you, you have got some notes somewhere," to which witness replied "No I have not." Catherall, having raised him up from the ground by his collar, threw him down again with great violence, at the same time saying "D— it, go it boys, blood or money."—Witness then became insensible.—Elizabeth Palmer, who kept a stall corroborated the above statement, and added she heard Hannell say "I have nothing but silver, take that, but pray spare my life." When they had left him they went to a booth where beer was sold. She there heard Catherall say, "Now then, Madam, give us half a crown's worth of beer." She also heard him say, "What a spree we have had," to which the other replied, "Ay, two bobs a piece." When they had drank the ale, Catherall said to his companions "Now my lads, one and all, and d— the man who flinches." They then went into the fair. Thos. Dickins, a waiter, corroborated the evidence of the former witness, and said he heard Catherall say, "Come, my lads, form into a line, soldier-like." Richard Dines saw Hannell knocked down by Catherall, who at the same time said, "D— and b— your eyes, blood or money." Catherall cross-examined the several witness with some degree of skill. In his defence he merely said that he knew nothing of the transaction, and that all the witnesses said was false. Verdict—Guilty. On the following morning the prisoners were brought up to receive sentence of death.—His Lordship entreated Catherall not to be deluded into any false hopes of pardon, as, from the aggravated nature of his crime, no mercy could be extended to him in this world. The Judge informed Robinson his life would be spared.

It is gratifying to observe that the Conduct of this unfortunate Culprit has been becoming his awful situation; every kind of consolatory Instruction has been daily administered by the Chaplain, the Rev. Mr. Drake. The Sunday after his Condemnation, the unfortunate Man appeared deeply affected while the Rev. Gentleman prayed for him, and nearly fainted, his mind since appeared more tranquil.

At an early hour on Friday morning he was again visited by the Rev. Chaplain, and at nine o'clock a pathetic and impressive sermon was delivered on the occasion. The Sacrament was then administered, and at Twelve o'cock he ascended the fatal platform, and in a few minutes he was launched into eternity.

During his confinement, the unfortunate Culprit has stated that he was the Lancashire Youth who fought the battle at Warwick, with Shelton, about 12 months since. He was a single man, and a native of Bolton.

*(Ratnett, Printer, Bridge-street, Northampton).*

A contemporary broadsheet of the execution of 'Captain Slash' in 1826. (NRO)

CORRECT ACCOUNT OF THE EXECUTION OF

# George Catherall,

ALIAS

# CAPTAIN SLASH,

## On the New Drop, Northampton,

## ON FRIDAY, JULY 21, 1826,

### For Highway Robbery, at Boughton Green Fair.

GEORGE CATHERALL, aged 29, and HUGH ROBINSON, aged 18, stood charged with stealing from James Henley, 11 half-crowns, one crown, one waistcoat, a neckerchief, a cork-screw, and some half-pence, at Boughton Green Fair. Catherall, who is known by the name of CAPTAIN SLASH, appeared in a shabby dress, having his head bound up in a silk handkerchief, in consequence of the fracture of his skull. In taking him his left hand also was broken, and two of his ribs. The prisoners were strangers in this neighbourhood, and are supposed to belong to a party of thieves and pickpockets who frequent the different fairs of the kingdom.—James Henley, the prosecutor, is a shoe-maker residing at Northampton, and was employed as a waiter at one of the booths during the fair. Between 1 and 2 o'clock on the morning of the 28th of June, as witness was walking across the Green, he saw Catherall a few yards distant from him, who came up, and without saying a word, struck him a violent blow across the face with a large stick, which felled him to the ground. A number of other persons immediately surrounded him, and the other prisoner, Robinson, beat him violently while lying on the ground. Witness perceiving that they were rifling his pockets, put up his knees, on which Catherall said, "D— your eyes, why don't you put your legs down." Witness cried out "Murder," and the prisoner Catherall, setting his foot on his throat, said "D— you, there shall be murder too." The prisoner Robinson lay on him while he was down. Whilst witness was on the ground his right hand breeches pocket was cut off, and a bundle which he held in his hand, containing various articles, was taken from him.—George Warwick swore that the former witness was knocked down in the manner before described, and during the affray, which lasted a considerable time, he, in company with another person, went up and struck Catherall, with a view to get him away. He also followed the prisoner Robinson, and took him into custody. George Ealum corroborated the evidence of the former witness, and added that he saw the prisoner Robinson take something like a pocket from the person on the ground, which Robinson threw to some of his companions, who ran away with it. The Judge, in summing up, observed that the knocking a person down and robbing him in any open place constituted highway robbery. Verdict—GUILTY. ROBINSON TRANSPORTED FOR LIFE.

CATHERALL also stood charged with robbing Jas. Hannell at Boughton Green Fair on the above night.—James Hannell is a confectioner, and regularly attends the above fair. About twelve o'clock in the night of the 27th of June, as he was walking up the Green, he received a violent blow on the right side of his head from a stick, but upon turning round he could not see any one near him. A number of persons immediately came up, and one of them again struck him on the left side of the head, which brought him to the ground. Five or six men immediately fell upon him, and rifled his pockets of silver to the amount of £1. The prisoner Catherall then said, "d— you, you have got some notes somewhere," to which witness replied, "No I have not." Catherall having raised him up from the ground by his collar, threw him down again with great violence, at the same time saying, "D—it, go it boys, blood or money." Witness then became insensible. Elizabeth Palmon, who kept a stall, corroborated the above statement, and added she heard Hannell say, "I have nothing but silver, take that, but pray spare my life." When they had left him they went to a booth where beer was sold. She there heard Catherall say, "Now then, Madam, give us half-a-crown's worth of beer." She also heard him say, "What a spree we have had,' to which the other replied, "Ay, two bobs a-piece." When they had drank the ale, Catherall said to his companions, "Now my lads, one and all, and d— the man who flinches.." They then went into the fair. Thos. Dickins, a waiter, corroborated the evidence of the former witness, and said he heard Catherall say, "Come, my lads, form into a line soldier-like." Richard Dines saw Hannell knocked down by Catherall, who at the same time said, "D—and b—your eyes, blood or money." Catherall cross-examined the several witnesses with some degree of skill. In his defence he merely said that he knew nothing of the transactions, and what all the witnesses had said was false. Verdict—Guilty. On the following morning, the prisoners were brought up to receive sentence of death.—His Lordship entreated Catherall not to be deluded into any false hopes of pardon, as, from the aggravated nature of his crime, no mercy could be extended to him in this world. The Judge informed Robinson his life would be spared.

It is gratifying to observe that the conduct of this unfortunate culprit has been becoming his awful situation; every kind of consolatory instruction has been daily administered by the chaplain, the Rev. Mr. Drake. The Sunday after his condemnation, the unfortunate man appeared deeply affected, while the Rev. gentleman prayed for him, and nearly fainted, his mind since appeared more tranquil.

At an early hour on Friday morning he was again visited by the Rev. chaplain, and at nine o'clock a pathetic and impressive sermon was delivered on the occasion. The sacrament was then administered, and at twelve o'clock he ascended the fatal platform, and in a few minutes he was launched into eternity.

During his confinement, the unfortunate culprit stated that he was the Lancashire youth who fought a battle at Warwick, with Shelton, about twelve months previous. He was a single man, and a native of Bolton.



[Arlidge, Printer, Northampton.

Judging by the typography, a much later reprint, by a different printer, of the contemporary 'Captain Slash' broadsheet. The text is exactly the same. (NRO)

On the last night of the fair, the gang moved into action and they started attacking the booths and stallholders, committing brutal robberies and damage. But the proprietors of the stalls, and the law abiding local men, had armed themselves with swords and muskets.

A tremendous fight took place, which eventually resulted in the banishment of the gang. 'Captain Slash' and six of his gang were captured, to stand trial for robbery. One of his subordinates was transported for life, and the others received substantial gaol sentences.

George 'Captain Slash' Catherall was hanged at the 'new drop' on Friday 21 July 1826 before a large crowd. Just before the executioner pulled the bolt, Catherall kicked off his shoes into the crowd. He died knowing that he had proved his mother wrong.

**vii) Poaching**

Poaching, or the illegal taking of game and fish, is one of the criminal offences that has diminished drastically. This is because our modern society does not provide the stimulus for poaching that it did in times gone by.

The classic ingredients for poaching are two fold: to compensate the (lower class peasant) poacher for the large number of abeyances or unpaid services he was forced to render to the (upper class lord of the manor) the land owner; and to obtain food for his family at no cost. Modern society does not require bond-service anymore, and food is readily available.

In 1993 there were 50 offences under the Game laws, from a population of 575,000, a rate per 1,000 population of .08. In 1852, 242,000 population produced 244 cases of poaching, a rate per 1,000 of 1.01.

Because the land owning classes also made the laws, acts against poaching have run well into double figures over the years. During the 19th century for example, over 20 acts of parliament were passed concerning the illegal taking of game or fish. And because of this, the punishments upon conviction were severe as well.

Poaching was usually tried at Petty Sessions, but the more serious cases went to the Quarter Sessions. The 1630 Northamptonshire Michaelmas Quarter Sessions recorded five cases of poaching of deer from Grafton Regis Park and Higham (Ferrers) Park, and fish from a lake at Boughton.

These same sessions also include a case of what sometimes went hand-in-hand with poaching, the assault upon the gamekeeper. Normally assaults on gamekeepers were just sufficient enough to enable the poachers to escape, as was the case on Tuesday 16 July 1630, when Henry Thompson assaulted the gamekeeper of Sir Simon Bennett, Bart at Grafton Regis. But sometimes things got serious, and in Northamptonshire we have an example of a gamekeeper being murdered: see Chapter 8.

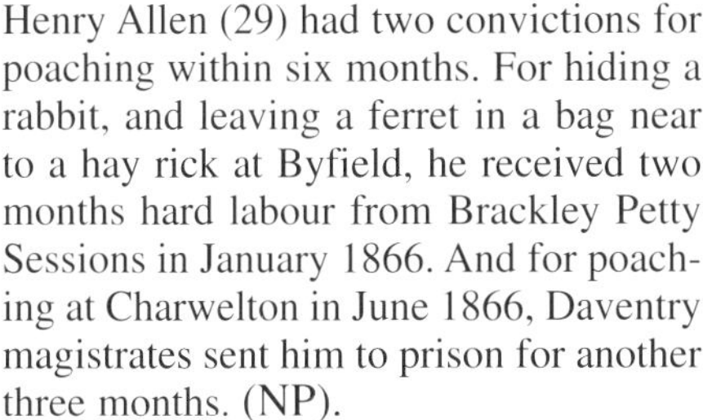

Henry Allen (29) had two convictions for poaching within six months. For hiding a rabbit, and leaving a ferret in a bag near to a hay rick at Byfield, he received two months hard labour from Brackley Petty Sessions in January 1866. And for poaching at Charwelton in June 1866, Daventry magistrates sent him to prison for another three months. (NP).

Another committed poacher. Richard Egan had three convictions for poaching in the Brackley area in the 1860s, with sentences of three months, two months and three months. (NP)

The authentic voice of the peasant poacher is very hard to come by, but Northamptonshire is lucky in having a Victorian poacher of such intellect that he has left his memoirs. James Hawker was born in Daventry in 1836, of very poor parents. He does not hide his contempt for the land and property owning classes, and after his parents were ejected from their house when he was 14, the two classic ingredients were present, and he turned to poaching. His memoirs are steeped in his own brand of philosophy justifying his numerous poaching expeditions, and he also gleefully describes the times when he escaped from 'dim witted' village policemen.

The social history of poaching, and the effect it has had on the fabric of rural society, is such a vast subject in itself, that there is not space available here to do it the justice it deserves.

**viii) Rape and sexual offences**

The sexual drive of other people is so fascinating to all of us, that probably this section of the book will be the first one that the reader will turn to.

The sexual offences of rape, bestiality, incest, indecent assault, pornography, unlawful abortion, unlawful sexual intercourse (or USI, mainly concerning girls under the age of 16) and, of course, prostitution, have all appeared in the county's courts in various numbers throughout the years. But at the infamous Summer Assizes of 1910, the county really 'hit the jackpot' when the time allowed had to be increased in order to cope with an excessive number of cases of a serious sexual nature. No other court, before or since, has had that number to deal with, and which led to the disapproving comment of Mr Justice Lawrence that 'morality does not seem to prevail in abounding force in this county'.

At the 1202 Northamptonshire Assizes, there were three rape cases. Helewisa accused Geoffrey, son of Walter of raping her, but Geoffrey never turned up, and so the process of outlawing him was started. However, the process could work in reverse. Rohesia of Addington, who had accused Richard, son of William of raping her, also failed to turn up, and because of this, she was deemed to be at fault, and her arrest was ordered.

Collet, however, did turn up, to defend himself after he was accused by Christina, daughter of William, son of Norman, of dragging her 'from the way and taking from her her virginity'. The result of this, unfortunately, is not recorded.

The three rapes reported for 20,000 population of the county in 1202, is .15 offences per 1,000 population. In 1993, 575,000 population produced 58 rapes, a rate of .1 per 1,000. Four rapes in 1852 from 242,000 is .017 per 1,000 population.

Five men have been hung in Northamptonshire for rape, and strangely enough, these all occur within the ten years between 1821 and 1830. This seems strange, given the harshness of the 'Bloody Code', that nobody was hung for rape before 1821. We know rapes occurred before then, so did our ancestors think the death penalty inappropriate before 1821?

But rape was punished, as we see from the case of a 16 year old servant girl, Fanny Bott, on Tuesday 14 March 1865 at Nether Heyford. To make matters worse, the accused was a police Inspector, John Jackson. He had returned to the house at 7pm after he had visited in the morning asking questions about a village incident. Jackson, who had joined the force in 1862, received ten years imprisonment, making him the only police officer of the county force to be imprisoned for rape.

In rural areas, bestiality may be commonplace, who is to know? The only time we do know is when a case appears in the court lists: see the Assize Calendar for 1856 and the Quarter Sessions Calendars for 1857 and 1881.

The offences of incest, indecent assault and USI are not mentioned in the local

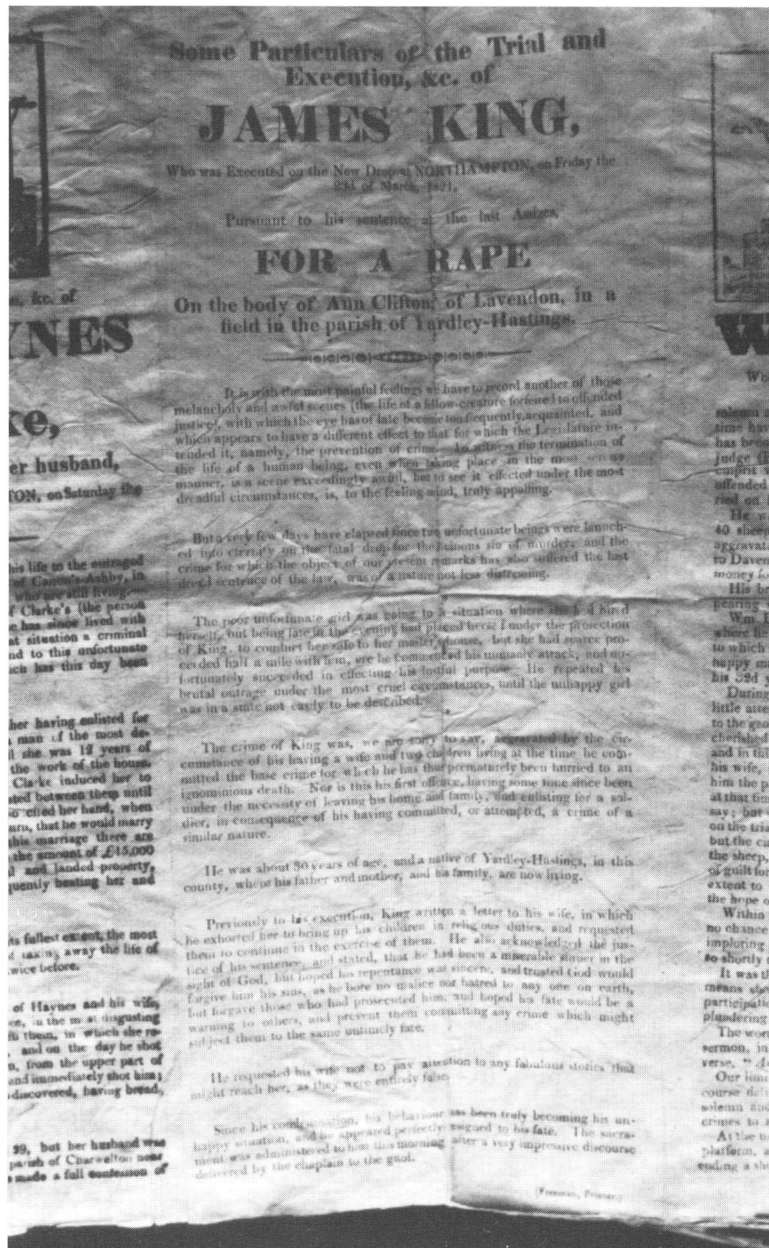

Some Particulars of the Trial and Execution, &c. of

JAMES KING,

Who was Executed on the New Drop at NORTHAMPTON, on Friday the 23d of March, 1821,

Pursuant to his sentence at the last Assizes,

FOR A RAPE

On the body of Ann Clifton, of Lavendon, in a field in the parish of Yardley-Hastings.

It is with the most painful feelings we have to record another of those melancholy and awful scenes (the life of a fellow-creature forfeited to offended justice), with which the eye has of late become too frequently acquainted, and which appears to have a different effect to that for which the Legislature intended it, namely, the prevention of crime. [illegible] the termination of the life of a human being, even when taking place in the most [illegible] manner, is a scene exceedingly awful, but to see it effected under the most dreadful circumstances, is, to the feeling mind, truly appalling.

But a very few days have elapsed since two unfortunate beings were launched into eternity on the fatal drop for the heinous sin of murder; and the crime for which the object of our present remarks has also suffered the last dread sentence of the law, was of a nature not less distressing.

The poor unfortunate girl was going to a situation where she had hired herself, but being late in the evening had placed herself under the protection of King, to conduct her safe to her master's house, but she had scarce proceeded half a mile with him, ere he commenced his unmanly attack, and unfortunately succeeded in effecting his brutal purpose. He repeated his brutal outrage under the most cruel circumstances, until the unhappy girl was in a state not easily to be described.

The crime of King was, we are sorry to say, aggravated by the circumstance of his having a wife and two children living at the time he committed the base crime for which he has thus prematurely been hurried to an ignominious death. Nor is this his first offence, having some time since been under the necessity of leaving his home and family, and enlisting for a soldier, in consequence of his having committed, or attempted, a crime of a similar nature.

He was about 30 years of age, and a native of Yardley-Hastings, in this county, where his father and mother, and his family, are now living.

Previously to his execution, King written a letter to his wife, in which he exhorted her to bring up his children in religious duties, and requested them to continue in the exercise of them. He also acknowledged the justice of his sentence, and stated, that he had been a miserable sinner in the sight of God, but hoped his repentance was sincere, and trusted God would forgive him his sins, as he bore no malice nor hatred to any one on earth, but forgave those who had prosecuted him, and hoped his fate would be a warning to others, and prevent them committing any crime which might subject them to the same untimely fate.

He requested his wife not to pay attention to any fabulous stories that might reach her, as they were entirely false.

Since his condemnation, his behaviour has been truly becoming his unhappy situation, and he appeared perfectly resigned to his fate. The sacrament was administered to him this morning after a very impressive discourse delivered by the chaplain to the gaol.

(Freeman, Printer.)

James King raped Ann Clifton in a field at Yardley Hastings in October 1820. He was hanged on Friday 23 March 1821, expressing great sorrow, and continually acknowledging the justice of his sentence. (NRO)

crime statistics of 1852. The only category that comes anywhere near is 'Unnatural offence', of which, in 1852, there were two. As this is so vague, no conclusion can be drawn. However, in the national statistics after 1856, these offences were mentioned. The 1866 figures are held at the Northamptonshire Record Office, and for that year, three indecent assaults were reported for the whole of the county.

Unlawful abortion and pornography have not figured highly in the county's court lists. By their very nature, they are difficult to unearth, as the 'victim' in both crimes actively seeks to keep quiet and not to publicise any complaint. There was a case of 'unlawfully procuring a miscarriage' at the 1910 Summer Assizes (see below); and in 1917, John Mitchell was tried, but found not guilty, of inducing an abortion on his girl friend, at Thrapston.

Photography was tailor-made for pornography, and after its invention and worldwide mushrooming of photographers' studios in the 1850s, it can easily be appreciated that pornographic pictures were probably turned out in their hundreds. What is believed to be the first case of pornography in Northamptonshire came before the Spring Assizes of 1865.

William Cox, aged 45, had a studio in Bridge Street, Northampton. From a tip-off, he was arrested and in his possession had an obscene slide. Fifteen more obscene slides were found when his studio was searched. He said that his assistant had taken them, but he had since dismissed him. Mr Justice Smith found Cox not guilty, saying that mere possession was no offence, only producing them with intent to sell, and there was no evidence of that against Cox, only against his assistant, who had subsequently disappeared. No description was made in the local press of why the slides were considered to be obscene.

The 1866 crime statistics record that in Northamptonshire there were 84 known prostitutes, three of whom were under 16. And of that 84, only 17 were ever taken to court during that year. Although prostitution was regarded as a social evil, it seems to have been tolerated fairly well. Apart from these national figures, there are no other series of figures for prostitution in Northamptonshire, as the subject never seems to have been studied closely.

Further back in time, figures for prostitution are even harder to obtain. The 1657 Quarter Sessions contain references to an act of parliament 'for suppressing of the abominable crying sins of incest, adultery and fornication', and seven women were convicted. It is not specified exactly which of the three categories of offence each conviction was for, but more likely than not, it was for prostitution.

All the above activities have always been regarded as criminal. In the past, however, having children outside wedlock was also regarded as criminal, although, it has to be admitted, not on morality grounds, but on financial ones, as the parish in which the illegitimate birth took place had to pay for the upkeep. Bastardy orders to putative fathers to pay money were therefore pursued rigor-

An Account of the Life, Behaviour, and Execution of

**William Meadows, William Gent, & Redmond Middleton,**

Who were executed at Northampton,

On Friday, August 2, 1822,

For committing a Rape upon *ANN NEWMAN*, and robbing her on the King's Highway, of her Wearing Apparel, &c.

WITH the most painful feelings we have to record another of those awful and melancholy scenes which the eye has of late been too much accustomed to witness in this part of the kingdom, and which appears to have a different effect to what was intended by the Legislature, viz. *the Prevention of Crimes.*—To witness the termination of the life of a human being, even when it takes place in the common course of nature, and in the most calm and serene manner, is exceedingly awful; but to see three of our fellow creatures, all young men, as soon as they had entered into life, doomed to forfeit their lives to the law of the land, is, under such dreadful circumstances, to the feeling mind, truly appalling.

---

*William Meadows*, aged 27, *William Gent*, 22, and *Redmond Middleton*, 20, who have this day forfeited their lives, were committed to prison on the 1st of June last, charged with having, in company with six others, committed a Rape upon Ann Newman, of Bozeat, in this county, on her return from Wellingborough fair, and robbed her of various articles of wearing apparel.—They were tried and convicted at our last assizes, before Mr. Baron Graham; together with *Charles James*, aged 18, and *Thomas Bales*, aged 17; but the two latter have, in consequence of their youth, been since reprieved.——The three unfortunate sufferers were natives of Wellingborough, and Meadows was by trade a tailor, and Gent and Middleton were shoemakers; and what renders it still more distressing, they were all married men, and have left several children, as well as aged parents, to lament their untimely end.

Since their condemnation they conducted themselves in a manner becoming their awful situation, but did not shew that contrition and repentance for the dreadful crime they had been guilty of, and for which they were to forfeit their lives, as could have been wished.—They repeatedly stated that their untimely end was to be attributed to drunkenness, sabbath-breaking, and bad company.

They were attended by the Chaplain of the prison, and some other Clergymen, and Gent, at his own request, as well as of his parents, was visited by a Dissenting Minister, whose united endeavours were strenuously exerted in endeavoring to prepare them to seek forgiveness from their offended Maker.

On Thursday they were visited by their wives and relations, to take their last farewell of them in this world.—The scene was truly affecting, particularly with Gent and his wife, who is in a very advanced state of pregnancy.

Having received the sacrament, they ascended the fatal platform, and after spending a short time in prayer, were launched into eternity, in the presence of the greatest number of spectators ever assembled here on such an occasion: and may the untimely end of these unfortunate young men, prove a warning to those who are still pursuing the paths of vice and wickedness, and convince them of the dreadful precipice on which they stand.

Cordeux, Printer, Northampton.

Contemporary broadsheet of the rape of Ann Newman. The three men, all from Wellingborough, never showed any contrition, and their behaviour after sentence did not 'generally evince a due sense of the turpitude of the crime ... or the awfulness of their situation'. (NRO)

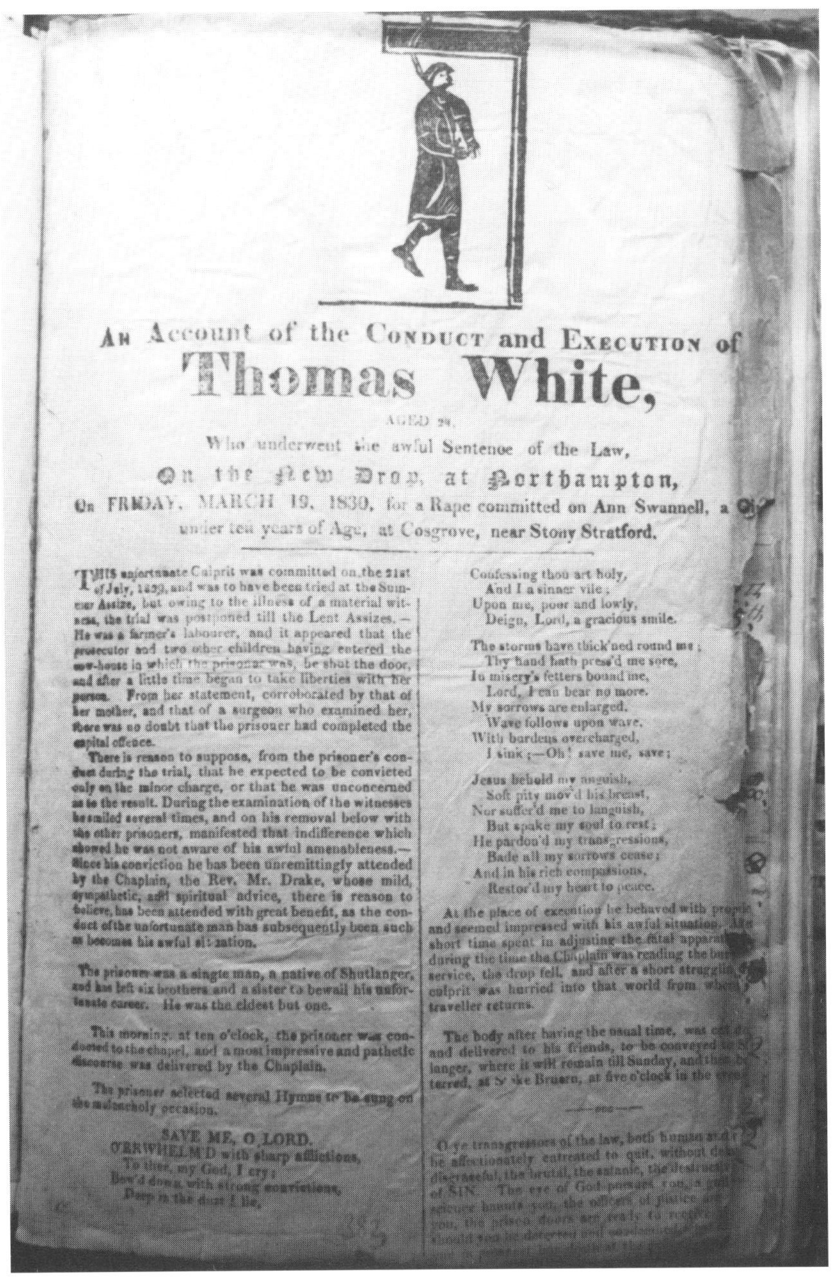

AN ACCOUNT of the CONDUCT and EXECUTION of

# Thomas White,

AGED 28,

Who underwent the awful Sentence of the Law,

On the New Drop, at Northampton,

On FRIDAY, MARCH 19, 1830, for a Rape committed on Ann Swannell, a Gi[illegible] under ten years of Age, at Cosgrove, near Stony Stratford.

THIS unfortunate Culprit was committed on the 21st of July, 1829, and was to have been tried at the Summer Assize, but owing to the illness of a material witness, the trial was postponed till the Lent Assizes.—He was a farmer's labourer, and it appeared that the prosecutor and two other children having entered the cow-house in which the prisoner was, he shut the door, and after a little time began to take liberties with her person. From her statement, corroborated by that of her mother, and that of a surgeon who examined her, there was no doubt that the prisoner had completed the capital offence.

There is reason to suppose, from the prisoner's conduct during the trial, that he expected to be convicted only on the minor charge, or that he was unconcerned as to the result. During the examination of the witnesses he smiled several times, and on his removal below with the other prisoners, manifested that indifference which showed he was not aware of his awful amenableness.—Since his conviction he has been unremittingly attended by the Chaplain, the Rev. Mr. Drake, whose mild, sympathetic, and spiritual advice, there is reason to believe, has been attended with great benefit, as the conduct of the unfortunate man has subsequently been such as becomes his awful situation.

The prisoner was a single man, a native of Shutlanger, and has left six brothers and a sister to bewail his unfortunate career. He was the eldest but one.

This morning, at ten o'clock, the prisoner was conducted to the chapel, and a most impressive and pathetic discourse was delivered by the Chaplain.

The prisoner selected several Hymns to be sung on the melancholy occasion.

SAVE ME, O LORD.

O'ERWHELM'D with sharp afflictions,
To thee, my God, I cry;
Bow'd down, with strong convictions,
Deep in the dust I lie,
Confessing thou art holy,
And I a sinner vile;
Upon me, poor and lowly,
Deign, Lord, a gracious smile.

The storms have thick'ned round me;
Thy hand hath press'd me sore,
In misery's fetters bound me,
Lord, I can bear no more.
My sorrows are enlarged,
Wave follows upon wave,
With burdens overcharged,
I sink;—Oh! save me, save;

Jesus beheld my anguish,
Soft pity mov'd his breast,
Nor suffer'd me to languish,
But spake my soul to rest;
He pardon'd my transgressions,
Bade all my sorrows cease;
And in his rich compassions,
Restor'd my heart to peace.

At the place of execution he behaved with prop[illegible] and seemed impressed with his awful situation. A[illegible] short time spent in adjusting the fatal appara[illegible] during the time the Chaplain was reading the bu[illegible] service, the drop fell, and after a short struggl[illegible] culprit was hurried into that world from whe[illegible] traveller returns.

The body after having the usual time, was cut d[illegible] and delivered to his friends, to be conveyed to S[illegible]langer, where it will remain till Sunday, and then b[illegible]terred, at Stoke Bruern, at five o'clock in the even[illegible]

O ye transgressors of the law, both human and [illegible] be affectionately entreated to quit, without d[illegible] disgraceful, the brutal, the satanic, the destructi[illegible] of SIN. The eye of God pursues you, a [illegible] [illegible]

In contrast to the Wellingborough trio, Thomas White expressed extreme penitence for his rape of Ann Swannell, who was not yet ten years old. (NRO)

ously when cash from the fathers was not forthcoming. In 1852, for example, there were 107 claims for non-payment of Bastardy orders.

At the Epiphany Quarter Sessions in 1658, William Morris of Duddington was summoned for Bastardy by Anne Key, who had been one of his servants. Her statement to the court said that the first time William 'had the carnal knowledge of her body, was about a month before Easter last past, in the servants chamber, about seven or eight of ye clock in ye morning; and [then] about May Day last past in the same chamber, and about ten of ye clock in ye morning . . .; and the last time . . . was about the beginning of June last past in ye chamber aforesaid about five or six of ye clock in ye morning'. Thomas Lambert, another servant, said that at the beginning of June, he 'went into [William's] chamber, between five and six of ye clock in ye morning, he did see his master . . . upon his mayd, the said Anne Key, with his breeches half downe, between her leggs, and . . . [he] . . . said Here is good doeings, her cloathes being up . . .'.

During the year 1657/1658 there were 14 examinations for bastardy. From a population of 110,000, this is .13 per 1,000, which even beats theft for the same period, at .07.

George James (27) received 18 months hard labour at the 1869 January Quarter Sessions for the attempted rape/indecent assault of 11 year old Charlotte Coleman as she had gathered acorns at Glendon in October 1868. She had cried when being assaulted, and had been told by James not to tell her mother, which she did not until three days later when she fell ill. (NP)

**Cases at the infamous 1910 Summer Assizes**.

Henry Cook (60) received six months imprisonment for an indecent assault on an 11 year old girl at Irthlingborough. He had a similar conviction ten years previously.

Charles Flinders (24) received nine months for an indecent assault on a 12 year old girl at Benefield. The fact he had pleaded guilty 'was the only act of merit' the judge could find.

Harry Lovell was found guilty of making a false declaration so that he could marry his niece at Towcester. There was more to this, however, as he was only bound over for £25. From the newspaper report, it can be surmised that he may have married his niece who was pregnant, in order to save her name.

Frank Wright (25) was found guilty of USI with a 15 year old girl, and an attempted USI with 'another little girl', both at Towcester. This was his fourth conviction for this, and so he was sent to prison for five years.

John Graham (19) was found guilty of USI with a 14 year old girl, and Charles Trix (34) was found guilty of USI with a 15 year old girl. The two men had picked up the two girls, plied them with drink in numerous Northampton town centre public houses, and then hired two rooms for the night at the 'Woolpack

The Grand Jury found 'No true Bill' (see Chapter 5) against Thomas Farrer when he was accused of raping Eliza Carpenter at Middleton Cheney in May 1865. Eliza said she only made the complaint after badgering by the police. (NP)

John Berry Langley (36) was convicted at Brackley Petty Sessions in August 1869, for Bastardy Order arrears. He received three months hard labour. (NP)

Inn'. Graham was only bound over for £25 as there were mitigating circumstances, but Trix received four months imprisonment.

Emily Holmes (31) was found guilty of 'unlawfully procuring a miscarriage' at Kettering, which resulted in the death of the illegitimate baby of Ella Johnson. Inspector Tebby told the court that the police believed that 'this was not an isolated incident'.

Clara Beasley (25) was found guilty of the concealment of birth of her illegitimate baby at Lamport, but discharged on her own recognizances; and Charlotte Loasby (44), because of medical evidence, was found not guilty of the concealment of birth of her illegitimate baby at Kettering.

**ix) Riot and public order**

There are two sorts of riots, the ideological and the spontaneous. It has been said that English society ran smoothly – until the people had a legitimate grievance – which then provoked such an almighty riot as to bring the authority's attention to it. The grievance was rectified, and society continued on its merry way again, until the next time. This was the ideological riot, and was thus looked upon as an essential part of English social administration.

But the other sort of riot the spontaneous, was different. No ideological aim was attempted, just a big free-for-all punch-up, triggered by one (probably totally unconnected) incident.

By the Riot Act of 1714, a riot was defined as 'twelve or more persons being unlawfully, riotously and tumultuously assembled together to the disturbance of the public peace'. And where it appeared to any two magistrates, that a rowdy meeting was going to turn into a riot, they had powers to swear in special constables purely for the controlling, or dispersing, the riot. Remember, there was no organised police force in those days, so special constables were the only way of dealing with it, until the army arrived. In the meantime, the crowd would be read the Riot Act, which had to be done by a magistrate or the mayor, who had to stand in front of the mob and shout it out at them, which in some instances, took a lot of courage.

The Riot Act Proclamation was: 'Our Sovereign Lord the King chargeth and commandeth all persons, being assembled, immediately to disperse themselves, and peaceably to depart to their habitations, or to their lawful business, upon the Pains contained in the Act made in the first year of King George the First for preventing tumults and riotous assemblies. God Save the King'. The rioters were then given one hour to disperse, and any remaining thereafter committed a felony for which they could be arrested.

This was a wonderful piece of prevarication, in that it gave the authorities one hour before they need do anything, in the hope that by then the problem would have gone away, or they had sworn in sufficient special constables, or the army had arrived.

Northamptonshire has had lots of both sorts of riots.

**The ideological Riots:**

1) 1607 Enclosure Riots

Enclosures were bad news for the peasants, as they stood to lose land and livelihood to the landlords of the newly enclosed fields, so they rioted. On May Day Eve 1607, riots began in Northamptonshire and eventually spread to all the midland counties. In Northamptonshire, there were riots at Thrapston, Rushton and Pytchley, but on Friday 8 June 1607, the revolt was finally crushed at Newton, near Geddington, and some of the ringleaders were hanged.

2) 1693-1695 Food Riots

About ten separate riots occurred in Northamptonshire protesting about moving grain out of the county to other parts of the country to counteract bad harvests.

3) 1757 Militia Riots

An unknown number of riots occurred in Northamptonshire in protest at the Militia Act of that year, which in effect, introduced conscription into the Militia for all men between 18 and 50.

4) 1760-1800 Enclosure riots

About 19 separate riots in various Northamptonshire villages.

5) 1796 Militia Riots

Three separate riots in Northamptonshire.

6) 1830 'Captain Swing' Riots

The 'last of the labourers' revolts' swept the southern counties of England in 1830, mainly taking the form of smashing and destroying threshing machines. It was the agricultural equivalent of the 'Luddite Riots', as threatening letters signed by 'Captain Swing' were sent to farmers who were seen to be using new technology instead of traditional hand methods, thus putting farm labourers out of work. There were several 'Captain Swing' riots in Northamptonshire, including one at Finedon on Wednesday 1 December 1830.

Ten Finedon men appeared at the 1831 Lent Assizes for this riot: Philip Desborough (68) for inciting the riot the previous day, by going round Finedon shouting that no labourer should go to work the next day for less than 2s 3d per day; John Warren and Joseph Munns for stealing parts of a threshing machine belonging to William Page; and John Blundell (37), Joseph Clapham (25), John Desborough (31) Ambrose Freeman (31), John Mould (23), Michael Munns (20) and Robert Munns (30) for actually smashing William Page's threshing machine.

Joseph Clapham received two months hard labour for his part in the Finedon 'Captain Swing' Riot of December 1830, 41 years earlier than this picture. (NP)

All received varying amounts of imprisonment. Joseph Clapham received two months hard labour. This photograph was taken when he had just been convicted of theft in 1871 when he was 66, a far cry from the committed young social protestor of 40 years before.

7) 1842-1846 Corn Law riots

The introduction of a fixed price for corn sparked off opposition. In Northamptonshire, there were several Anti-Corn Law riots, the biggest being in Northampton in February 1842, and in Wellingborough in October 1842 where there were 29 arrests for assaults on police. The Corn Laws were abolished in 1846.

8) 1839-1848 Chartist 'Riots'

Chartism was a movement for working-class electoral and social reform. Serious rioting took place in various parts of the country, but in Northamptonshire, very little occurred. There were never any riots as such, only lots of noisy meetings which never made much threat to the county's public order. The Corn Law riots were much more trouble.

9) 1887 Shoe Dispute Riots, Northampton

Essentially an inter-branch dispute within the National Union of Boot and Shoe Operatives. However, lock outs and strikes between June and December 1887 led to several riots in Northampton. The dispute was settled in January 1888.

**The spontaneous riots:**

1) 1277 Good Friday Jewish Massacre, Northampton

By their money lending habits, The Northampton Jews had gained ownership of virtually all property within the Borough, and other townspeople were placed in the classic debtors' dilemma. They could only pay the interest on what they already owed by borrowing more. At this time, during the reign of Edward I, anti-Semitism was being actively encouraged, and taking advantage of this, the Northampton townspeople saw a way of ridding themselves of the Jews and their debts to them.

On Good Friday 26 March 1277, a rumour was circulated in the town that the Jews had stolen a Christian boy from his parents, and killed him in their Passover rites by nailing him hand and foot to a wooden cross. This was completely untrue, but so incensed did the Northampton townspeople become that they dragged out 50 leaders of the Jewish community, beat them up, and put them 'on trial'. All 50 were sentenced to death, and the rest of the Jews were banished from the town immediately, not being allowed to take anything with them.

The 50 Jews were tied to the tails of great heavy cart horses, some by their hands, some by their heads, and others by their feet and waists. The terrified horses were then whipped to such a pitch that they were stampeded up and down the road that is now called York Road, dragging the screaming Jews behind them. Several times the horses were driven, getting more and more panic stricken as they trampled over screaming bodies which were becoming increasingly mangled by their great iron shod hooves.

Eventually the flushed and elated townspeople were satiated. Then all the bodies, living and dead, were strung up on a row of trees where they were allowed to rot for months.

So, by the 'Good Friday Massacre', Northampton purged itself of its Jewish community within just one day. All their property was then shared between the executioners, which was, of course, the reason for the whole episode. No person was ever tried for these murders, as the anti-Semitism of the times made such behaviour excusable. It was just 13 years later, that king Edward I ousted the whole of the Jewish community from England, transferring his money lending requirements instead, to the newly arriving Lombardy merchants.

2) 1727 Timber stealing riots, Whittlebury Forest

During June 1727, when residents of the forest villages centred around Towcester excercised their right to cut timber from the royal forest in celebration of the forthcoming coronation of George II, other people took advantage. Soon, whole gangs of people were cutting timber wholesale (nearly 200 trees were felled), which needed the military to restore order. Eventually 147 people (including the Reverend John Welch, curate of Abthorpe) from 44 villages in south Northamptonshire and north Buckinghamshire appeared at the Northamptonshire Assizes, charged with riot and theft.

3) 1852 Election riot, Wellingborough
A General Election took place on Monday 19 July 1852, and polling in those days was a fairly rumbustious affair. So much so, that a large body of men assembled at Wellingborough Town Hall in the hopes of being sworn in as Special Constables for the day ( plus of course, the 3s 6d that went with it). When eventually they were all dismissed without their services being required, they promptly rioted. The mob tore down the actual polling booth itself, then ripped up the cobble stones and started throwing them about. The Chief Constable of the county, Henry Bayly, and Superintendent Luke Knight of the Wellingborough Division, were both attacked with stones, receiving injuries to the head. Knight was actually knocked out, so seriously that at one point it was considered to be nearly fatal. Although he recovered, he never returned to work, and was medically pensioned seven months later.

4) 1854, The First Militia Riot, Northampton
Monday-Wednesday 14-16 August 1854. Three days of rioting followed an incident in the 'Rose and Punch Bowl' in Marefair, when drunken soldiers took exception to one of their number being arrested on suspicion of theft.

5) 1874, The Bradlaugh Riot, Northampton
Tuesday 6 October 1874. rioting after the General Election by supporters of Charles Bradlaugh when he failed to get elected to parliament.

6) 1878, The Second Militia Riot, Northampton
Sunday-Wednesday 2-5 June 1878. Four days of rioting by the local Militia stationed in the town, were sparked off when a rumour (completely erroneous) was circulated that one of their number had been killed by the Northampton Borough Police.

Just one more thing. By the Riot Damages Act of 1886 (which is still in force), the police are liable for financial compensation for any damage caused by a riot. The theory is, that the police should have prevented the riot and/or damage in the first place, so if the police allow damage to occur, they must pay for it.

The other aspect of public order is the 'breach of the peace'. As explained in Chapter 4, our ancestors went to great lengths to preserve 'the peace', and any abnormal or rowdy behaviour was looked upon as a breach of the peace, and was not tolerated. This still happens today, as every weekend numerous young men (and sometimes women) are arrested for breach of the peace.

The method of dealing with it, is not a prison sentence, or anything like that, but by the 'bind over to be of good behaviour', where they give their own surety that they will behave themselves in future. The bind over has been used by the courts ever since a Statute of 1361, and court records are full of them, all down the ages.

The Northamptonshire Quarter Sessions records of 1657 give 76 bind overs, for an estimated population of 110,000, a rate of .7 offences per 1,000. There were 142 bind overs in 1852 for 242,000 population, or .6 per 1,000. And in 1993, for 575,000 population there were 436 bind overs, a rate of .75 per 1,000. Thus for well over 300 years, the level of breach of the peace in Northamptonshire appears to have hardly changed.

**x) Robbery**

By and large, robbery is theft from a person either by using violence or threats of violence. This has always been the case, but in olden times, the term robbery has been used in a cavalier fashion, and sometimes was used to describe offences which were not robberies at all, but burglaries or thefts.

However, the robberies in the 1202 Assize Rolls are the real thing, and there were seven of them, not counting the robberies confessed to by the Northamptonshire Robin Hood's gang. With an estimated population of 20,000, this gives a rate per 1,000 of .35. In 1993, there were 304 robberies in the county, with 575,000 population, a rate of .53 per 1,000. The 20 robberies in the county in 1852, population 242,000, gives .08 per 1,000.

The 1202 robbery cases are really unremarkable: John David accuses Ralph of Elstow and Hugh his servant of robbing him of ten marks; Thomas Southam accuses Henry of Tenerchebrai (the original Dr Finlay?) and Peter his brother, of robbing him of a sword, a cloth cap and corn worth £2; and so on, and so on. No results or sentences are recorded.

But what really springs to mind when talking of robbery, is the robbery committed on the road, by that romantic figure known as the Highwayman. The 'golden age' of the Highwayman was during the eighteenth century, and many famous names became folk heroes and legends, fuelled by popular works such as 'The Beggar's Opera', which has the Highwayman Macheath as its hero.

One of the folk tales from Whittlebury forest in the south of the county concerns the 'Green Man' public house at Syresham. It was said that Dick Turpin the famous Highwayman used to ply his trade on the road between Oxford and Peterborough (the present day A43), and that one night near to the pub, the Bow Street Runners, who frequently stayed at the 'Green Man', almost captured Turpin nearby, who had to flee into Whittlebury Forest leaving his horse (presumably Black Bess) behind with the saddle still warm.

Complete nonsense of course, folk tales nearly always are, as it overlooks the fact that the Bow Street Runners started in 1749 and that Turpin was hanged in 1739, ten years before. But that is the romance of the highwayman. The reality was totally, and brutally, different. Consider this from the *Northampton Mercury* of Monday 18 September 1769.

'Between the hours of nine and ten on Wednesday night last as Mr William Walker the Younger of Kingsthorpe . . . Farmer, was going from this town to Kingsthorpe . . . he was stopped at a place called Wallbank, in a little three cornered close in the Footway, by a Footpad, who on a sudden came up to him, and without speaking to him, immediately fired a large Horse Regimental Pistol at him, but missing him.

Mr Walker immediately struck the fellow with his Fist upon the Head or Face, and knocked him down, and siezed him, but the Fellow, imagining himself overpowered, immediately cried out for help, when one, if not two, other Fellows, who were lurking just by, instantly came up to his Assistance, and beat Mr Walker about the Head and Face with their pistols, and other weapons in a very inhuman Manner, and after robbing him of a yellow canvas Purse and about Three or Four Shillings in Money, they made off leaving Mr Walker insensible upon the Ground Wallowing in his blood; who after some little time so far recovered himself as to be able with very great difficulty to get to the Cock Inn at Kingsthorpe, where a surgeon was immediately sent for, who dressed his wounds. He now lies dangerously ill, but there are hopes for his recovery'.

Anthony Harwood, 26 years old from Durham, and William Craddock, 21, a weaver from Wellingborough, were both hanged for this robbery on Tuesday 14 August 1770. It was Craddock who had confessed to the initial firing of the pistol at the unfortunate Mr Walker.

Twenty five men have been hanged for robbery in Northamptonshire, or as near as can be guessed, given the confusion over the term robbery. After 1837, of course, only imprisonment could be given. Consider these two robberies taken from the 1870 Northamptonshire Summer Assizes.

Frederick Abel (20) and Charles Stanton alias George Clark (24) appeared charged with robbing John Goodman at Daventry on Wednesday 16 February 1870. When walking towards Badby at 11pm, John Goodman was accosted by a man, who turned out to be Frederick Abel, who asked for money to buy some beer. He was given 1½d, but wanted more. Abel then knocked Goodman down and took his purse containing five £5 notes. Charles Stanton alias George Clarke was nearby, and because he had instigated the robbery, and received his share of the £25, he received eight months hard labour, whilst Abel received six months.

Thomas Streeton (18) appeared at the 1870 Summer Assizes, together with John Goss (47), for the robbery of £3 3s from Joseph Cole at Finedon on Monday 4 April 1870. Cole had met Streeton and Goss at the 'Stone Cross' public house at Finedon, and had bought them beer. Whilst all three were walking towards Wellingborough, Goss grabbed Cole around the throat so tightly that his

Frederick Abel (20), left, and Charles Stanton, right, alias George Clark (24) appeared together at the 1870 Summer Assizes charged with robbery at Daventry in February 1870. Stanton received eight months hard labour, whilst Abel received six months. (NP)

This sullen young man, Thomas Streeton (18) was convicted at the 1870 Summer Assizes for his part in a highway robbery at Finedon. (NP)

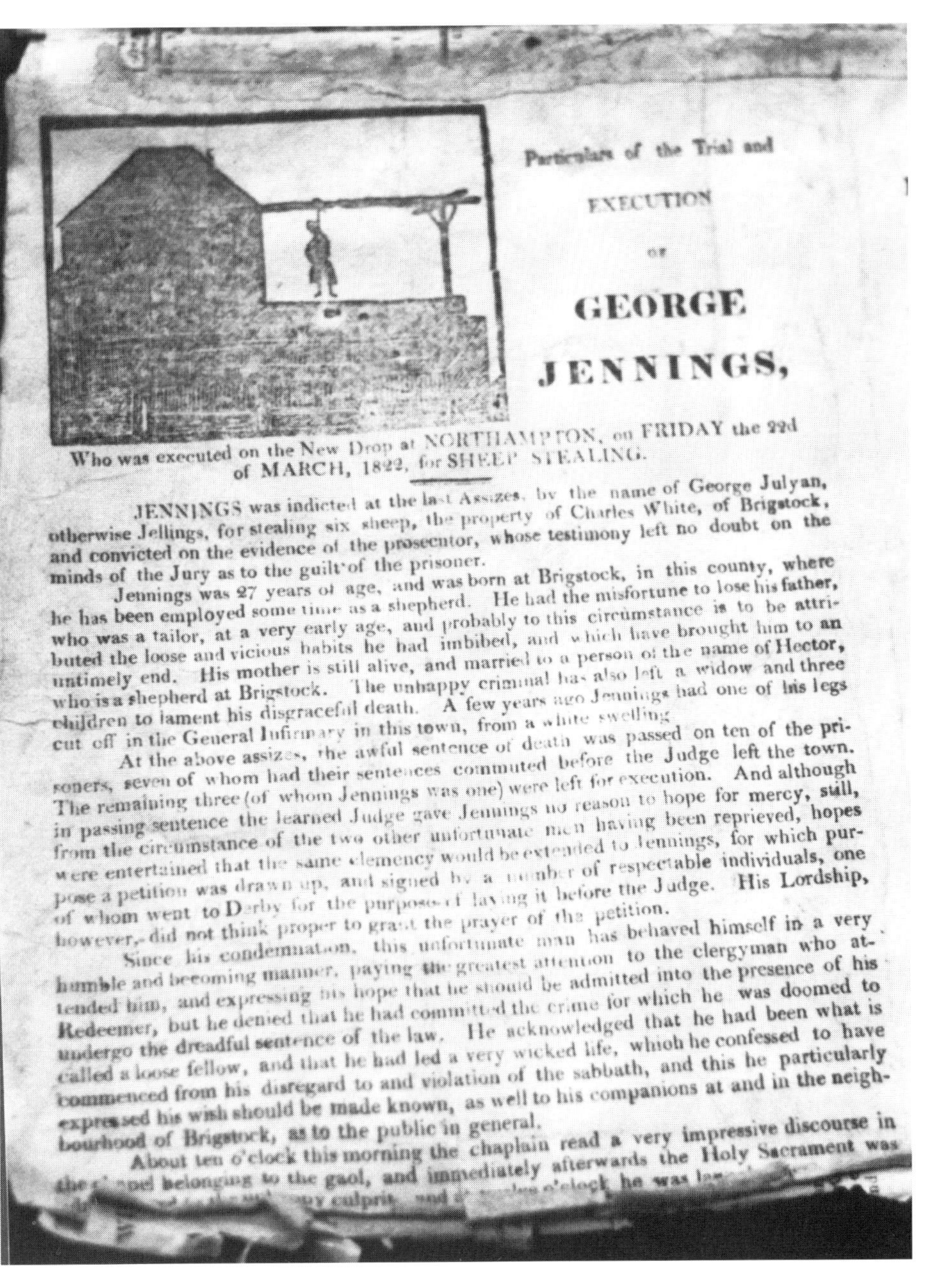

Particulars of the Trial and

EXECUTION

OF

GEORGE

JENNINGS,

Who was executed on the New Drop at NORTHAMPTON, on FRIDAY the 22d of MARCH, 1822, for SHEEP STEALING.

JENNINGS was indicted at the last Assizes, by the name of George Julyan, otherwise Jellings, for stealing six sheep, the property of Charles White, of Brigstock, and convicted on the evidence of the prosecutor, whose testimony left no doubt on the minds of the Jury as to the guilt of the prisoner.

Jennings was 27 years of age, and was born at Brigstock, in this county, where he has been employed some time as a shepherd. He had the misfortune to lose his father, who was a tailor, at a very early age, and probably to this circumstance is to be attributed the loose and vicious habits he had imbibed, and which have brought him to an untimely end. His mother is still alive, and married to a person of the name of Hector, who is a shepherd at Brigstock. The unhappy criminal has also left a widow and three children to lament his disgraceful death. A few years ago Jennings had one of his legs cut off in the General Infirmary in this town, from a white swelling.

At the above assizes, the awful sentence of death was passed on ten of the prisoners, seven of whom had their sentences commuted before the Judge left the town. The remaining three (of whom Jennings was one) were left for execution. And although in passing sentence the learned Judge gave Jennings no reason to hope for mercy, still, from the circumstance of the two other unfortunate men having been reprieved, hopes were entertained that the same clemency would be extended to Jennings, for which purpose a petition was drawn up, and signed by a number of respectable individuals, one of whom went to Derby for the purpose of laying it before the Judge. His Lordship, however, did not think proper to grant the prayer of the petition.

Since his condemnation, this unfortunate man has behaved himself in a very humble and becoming manner, paying the greatest attention to the clergyman who attended him, and expressing his hope that he should be admitted into the presence of his Redeemer, but he denied that he had committed the crime for which he was doomed to undergo the dreadful sentence of the law. He acknowledged that he had been what is called a loose fellow, and that he had led a very wicked life, which he confessed to have commenced from his disregard to and violation of the sabbath, and this he particularly expressed his wish should be made known, as well to his companions at and in the neighbourhood of Brigstock, as to the public in general.

About ten o'clock this morning the chaplain read a very impressive discourse in the [illegible] belonging to the gaol, and immediately afterwards the Holy Sacrament was [illegible] o'clock he was [illegible] culprit [illegible]

George Jennings alias Julyan, upon his conviction for sheep theft, turned over a new leaf and became extremely pious, and 'paid great attention to the prayers offered for him at the place of execution'. (NRO)

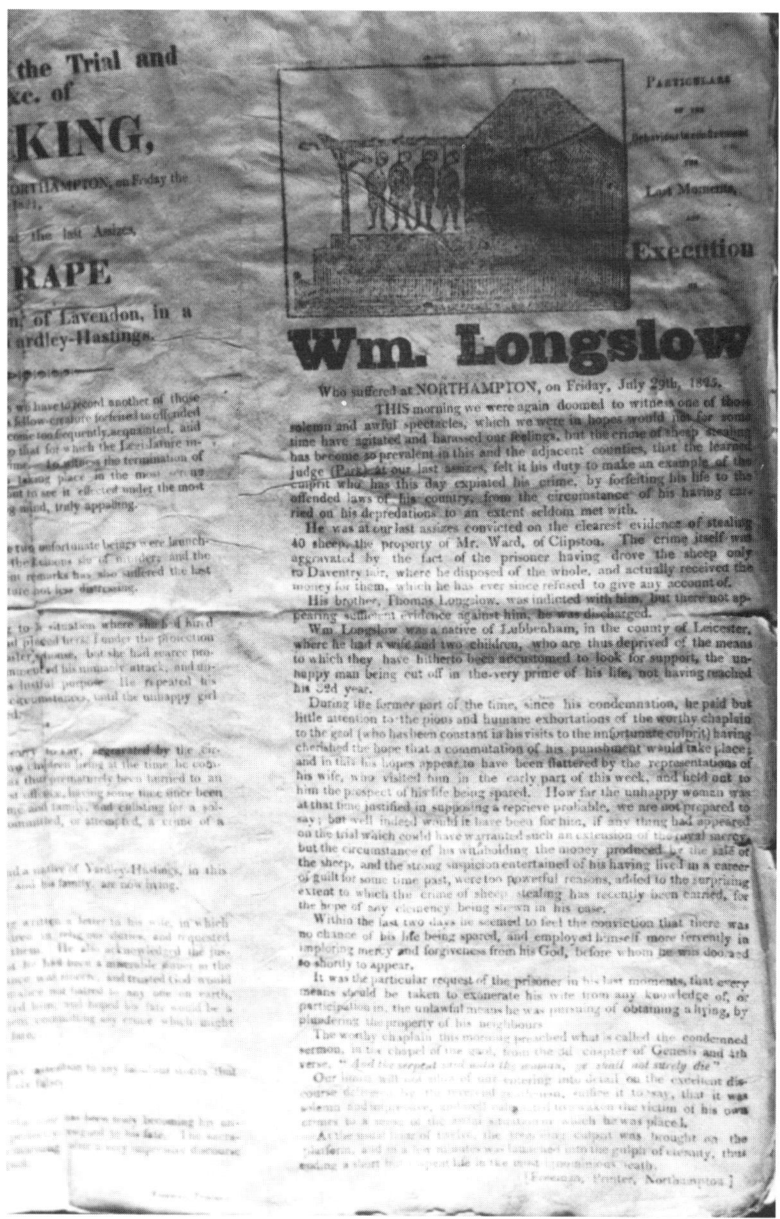

...the Trial and ...c. of ...KING, ...RTHAMPTON, on Friday the ... the last Assizes, ...RAPE ...of Lavendon, in a ...ardley-Hastings.

PARTICULARS of the [illegible] Last Moments, and Execution of

# Wm. Longslow

Who suffered at NORTHAMPTON, on Friday, July 29th, 1825.

THIS morning we were again doomed to witness one of those solemn and awful spectacles, which we were in hopes would [illegible] for some time have agitated and harassed our feelings, but the crime of sheep stealing has become so prevalent in this and the adjacent counties, that the learned judge (Park) at our last assizes, felt it his duty to make an example of the culprit who has this day expiated his crime, by forfeiting his life to the offended laws of his country, from the circumstance of his having carried on his depredations to an extent seldom met with.

He was at our last assizes convicted on the clearest evidence of stealing 40 sheep, the property of Mr. Ward, of Clipston. The crime itself was aggravated by the fact of the prisoner having drove the sheep only to Daventry fair, where he disposed of the whole, and actually received the money for them, which he has ever since refused to give any account of.

His brother, Thomas Longslow, was indicted with him, but there not appearing sufficient evidence against him, he was discharged.

Wm Longslow was a native of Lubbenham, in the county of Leicester, where he had a wife and two children, who are thus deprived of the means to which they have hitherto been accustomed to look for support, the unhappy man being cut off in the very prime of his life, not having reached his 32d year.

During the former part of the time, since his condemnation, he paid but little attention to the pious and humane exhortations of the worthy chaplain to the gaol (who has been constant in his visits to the unfortunate culprit) having cherished the hope that a commutation of his punishment would take place; and in this his hopes appear to have been flattered by the representations of his wife, who visited him in the early part of this week, and held out to him the prospect of his life being spared. How far the unhappy woman was at that time justified in supposing a reprieve probable, we are not prepared to say; but well indeed would it have been for him, if any thing had appeared on the trial which could have warranted such an extension of the royal mercy, but the circumstance of his withholding the money produced by the sale of the sheep, and the strong suspicion entertained of his having lived in a career of guilt for some time past, were too powerful reasons, added to the surprising extent to which the crime of sheep stealing has recently been carried, for the hope of any clemency being shewn in his case.

Within the last two days he seemed to feel the conviction that there was no chance of his life being spared, and employed himself more fervently in imploring mercy and forgiveness from his God, before whom he was doomed so shortly to appear.

It was the particular request of the prisoner in his last moments, that every means should be taken to exonerate his wife from any knowledge of, or participation in, the unlawful means he was pursuing of obtaining a living, by plundering the property of his neighbours.

The worthy chaplain this morning preached what is called the condemned sermon, in the chapel of the gaol, from the 3d chapter of Genesis and 4th verse, "*And the serpent said unto the woman, ye shall not surely die*"

Our limits will not allow of our entering into detail on the excellent discourse [illegible] by the reverend gentleman, suffice it to say, that it was solemn and impressive, and well calculated to awaken the victim of his own crimes to a sense of the awful situation in which he was placed.

At the usual hour of twelve, the [illegible] culprit was brought on the platform, and in a few minutes was launched into the gulph of eternity, thus ending a short [illegible] spent life in the most ignominious death.

[Freeman, Printer, Northampton.]

William Longslow, the last man to be hanged for sheep stealing in Northamptonshire, was a complete contrast to George Jennings, when on the gallows. He ‘paid but little attention to the ... pious ... exhortations of the chaplain’ when he was hung on Friday 29 July 1825. (NRO)

nails drew blood. Cole was wrestled to the ground, and Streeton rifled his pockets. Not content with that, Goss kicked Cole twice in the head, cutting his eye open, and was left unconscious and bleeding in the road. Goss received 10 years hard labour, but Streeton, because he was thought to have been led by Goss, received one year hard labour.

**xi) Theft, or larceny**

Because it is so easy to do, theft is the most common crime of all time, continually at the top of the lists, ever since the lists were started. In 1852, there were 607 thefts of all kinds reported (property and livestock), with a population of 242,000, a rate per 1,000 of 2.51. In 1993, 29,929 thefts (all property, including cars) were reported with a population of 575,000, a rate per 1,000 of 52.1.

Generally speaking, theft is the taking away of someone else's property without their permission, and over the years has been governed by lots of statutes. The most recent are the Larceny Acts of 1827, 1861 and 1916, and the present day Theft Act 1968.

John Cooper (20) had his own butchery shop in Raunds, but fell into financial difficulties. He tried to solve these by getting his stock for nothing. He received six months hard labour at the 1870 Lent Assizes for stealing five sheep at Raunds in February 1870. (NP)

George Tewson (26) received 12 months hard labour for horse theft. In June 1870 at Broughton Fair, he had taken a pony which was tied at the back of the beer tent run by Benjamin Cox. He was caught by Cox's brother whilst he was riding away towards Moulton. (NP)

Joseph Atkins (19). Three convictions for theft by the age of 19. He received one week hard labour at the 1865 Lent Assizes for stealing cheese; three months at Northampton Borough Petty Sessions for stealing nuts in 1869; and 12 months followed by seven years police supervision at the 1870 April Quarter Sessions for stealing a duck. (NP)

What can we learn from this young man's body language? John Brown alias Daniel Bryan received nine months hard labour at the 1870 Michaelmas Quarter Sessions for pickpocketing a purse containing 8s 6d. (NP)

All kinds of things have been stolen over the years, with each age putting its own emphasis on what it regards as materialistically valuable, which probably reflects more about the social outlook and values of those times than anything else could. The confessions of the gang of Thomas the Baker in the 1202 Assize Rolls, for instance, include a greater number of thefts of clothing and textiles, than any other commodity, including foodstuffs.

The Northamptonshire Quarter Sessions of Michaelmas 1630 record ten theft cases, all of which, apart from three unspecified, are for the foodstuffs of hay, corn and fish. But by the 1657 Quarter Sessions, we detect a change, for we have thefts of ropes and fences, clothing, corn, live hens, and a pistol and knife. The 1852 criminal records do not specify the item stolen.

But in agricultural areas such as Northamptonshire, theft of livestock, (a farmer's livelihood) was always thought of as particularly despicable, and enormous energy was spent on getting the animal back. For example, between 1835 and 1840, out of 70 reward notices placed in the *Northampton Mercury* by all the private prosecution associations in the county, 57 were for stealing livestock (43 for sheep, nine for horses, four for pigs and one for cattle).

Five men have been executed in the county for sheep theft, the last being William Longslow in 1825; and seven for horse theft, the last being William Walters in 1801. Today's equivalent of the horse theft, taking a conveyance without consent of the owner (or 'TWOC', pronounced 'twock', as all fans of *The Bill* would know) and theft of pedal cycles, totalled 9,706 in 1993, out of a grand total of all theft of 29,929 offences, or 32.4 per cent.

Thefts were normally tried only at Quarter Sessions or Petty Sessions, and these court records are full of them. All of them are pretty much the same, but occasionally, one turns up which lifts it above the boring run-of-the-mill. One

Angelic little mite, or calculating criminal? Twelve years old Hannah Martin got three months hard labour at the 1870 Michaelmas Quarter Sessions for stealing 7s 6d. But that was then half the weekly wage for a semi-skilled worker. Today's equivalent would be about £100-£150. Angelic little mite, or calculating criminal? (NP)

Would Hannah Martin look like 69 years old Elizabeth Wade after 57 years? Oundle magistrates gave her one month hard labour in 1871 for stealing a pair of galoshes. (NP)

Theft from the Leeds-London Mail Coach, Finedon 1812. Finedon cross-roads, looking up Irthlingborough Road, where the hill slowed the coach down, which enabled the mail bags to be taken from the rear mail box. Finedon Obelisk can be seen to the right.

such is the theft from the Leeds to London Mail Coach at Finedon in 1812.

In the early hours of Monday 26 October 1812, the Mail Coach from Leeds to Lonon set off from Kettering after its mail stop. Sixteen mail bags, together with the local mail bye-bags were locked into the mail box at the rear of the coach. Resuming its journey the coach drove southward along the road towards Burton Latimer (ie the present A6) with the guard sitting on top of the mail box. But between Burton Latimer and Finedon the guard clambered over the top of the coach and went to sit and talk with the driver at the front, thus leaving the mail box unguarded at the rear.

Just before Higham Ferrers, the guard resumed his proper place, and when the coach stopped at Higham, the mail box was found to have been forced and all 16 mail bags stolen. Because there was no local police force to contact, the coach continued to London where the matter was reported at the General Post Office.

Immediately, several Bow Street Runners were commissioned to investigate, and one, by the name of Lavender, was eventually to clear up the crime. Suspicion soon fell on two local petty crooks, Huffham White and Robert Kendall. Kendall was quickly arrested at his home in Wellingborough by Lavender, but White and his mistress Mary Howes had disappeared. However, they were at liberty for only two weeks, as eventually they too were arrested.

# General Post-Office,

*February* 9th, 1813.

# 200 POUNDS

## *REWARD.*

WHEREAS, HUFFEY WHITE is strongly suspected to have been concerned in the Robbery of the *Leeds Mail*, between *Kettering* and *Higham Ferrers*, on Monday Evening, the 26th of October last: whoever shall apprehend, or cause him to be apprehended, will be paid a Reward of ONE HUNDRED POUNDS upon his Commitment for Trial, and the further Reward of ONE HUNDRED POUNDS upon his Conviction.

*By Command of the Postmaster General,*

FRANCIS FREELING,

*Secretary.*

The said HUFFEY WHITE is a Native of *London*, by Trade a Cabinet-Maker, about 35 or 36 Years of Age, of good Appearance, 5-Feet 8 or 9-Inches high, stoutish made and stands very upright, has thin Legs, brown Hair, broad or full Forehead, Pale Complexion, light Grey Eyes, and little Eye Brows; is marked with the Small Pox in large Pits deep in the Skin, and at some distance from each other; his Nose turns up. He has a Squeaking Voice, is Mild in manners, and does not Talk much. He is well known at all the *Police Offices*.

He had formerly served some Years on Board the Hulks, and returned about 10 Years since.

About four Years ago he was capitally convicted at the *Old Bailey*, and ordered to be transported for Life, but afterwards made his Escape.

About twelve Months after this Conviction he was apprehended at *Stockport*, and tried and convicted at *Chester Assizes* for this Escape, and sent back to the Hulks, but again escaped.

He afterwards robbed the *Paisley Union Bank*, and immediately proceeded to *London* by the way of *Edinburgh*, in Post Chaises; and in two or three Days after his arrival, was apprehended in *Surry*, and tried and convicted at *Kingston Lent Assizes*, 1811, for being at large, and was sent to the Hulks.

From thence he again escaped, and has since been in the Counties of *Cambridge*, *Huntingdon*, and *Northampton*, passing by the Name of WALLIS, until the Robbery of the *Leeds* Mail the 26th of October last.

It is not known where he has been since, except that he was at the *Bull's Head* in *Bread-Street*, for two or three Days immediately afterwards, and then went to *Bath*. He slept at the *Swan* Inn in *Birmingham* on Sunday the 24th of January last, and proceeded the next Day in Company with Robert Brady, otherwise called Oxford Bob, in the *Shrewsbury* Mail to *Wolverhampton*, where Brady was apprehended, and White took the opportunity to quit the Coach, and has not since been heard of. He may probably be in the Company of two Persons herein described, viz.

One of them about 28 or 30 Years of Age, stout made, 5-Feet 9-Inches high, of a dark Complexion, black Hair, has fine black Eyes, and good Teeth, lisps in speaking, and has an Oval Visage.

The other about 35 or 36 Years of Age, 5-Feet 10-Inches high, sandy complexion, Hair and Whiskers, the Calves of his Legs thin, a little Pitted with the Small Pox, and looks like a Horse Dealer.

Theft from the Leeds-London Mail Coach, Finedon 1812. Reward Notice issued from the General Post Office in London, where the theft was reported, as at that time there was no local county police force. Note the confusing (and wrong) description of this as a Robbery. (NRO)

From the evidence given at the trial, it appears that White, using the alias of Wallis, was staying with Mary Howes at the Keyston Tollgate House, which Howes kept. Late on Saturday 25 October, Kendall collected White from Keyston in a horse and cart, and had driven through Thrapston to Finedon, where the London Road crosses the Wellingborough to Thrapston Road.

The theft was committed at Finedon Crossroads. The guard by then was sitting at the front of the coach, leaving unguarded the mail box, which would have been easy to break into and steal from, as the coach slowed to a crawling pace as it climbed up the long steep hill (now Irthlingborough Road, Finedon) on the way towards Higham Ferrers.

The small bye-bags of local only mail were discarded on the road near to the Finedon Obelisk, but the main mail bags were spirited away by White and Kendall to Wellingborough where Kendall lived. The next day, White returned to Howes', and they ran away to London to see if they could 'fence off' some of the negotiable bonds and bills of exchange contained in the mail bags.

No less than 40 witnesses appeared against White, Kendall and Howes at the trial. Howes was acquitted on a technicality, but White and Kendall were found guilty. They were both hanged on Northampton Racecourse on Friday 13 July 1813, in front of a large crowd.

**xii) Treason**

Historically, there have been two types of treason, High Treason and Petty Treason, with the death penalty for both. Under the Common Law of England, High Treason was for offences against the State and the King.

But in 1351, The Treason Act defined seven offences which constituted High Treason: 1) killing or attempting to kill the King, or the Queen, or their eldest son and heir; 2) violating the Queen, or the King's eldest unmarried daughter, or the wife of the King's son and heir; 3) waging war against the King; 4) giving help to the King's enemies; 5) counterfeiting the money of the realm or the Great Seal; 6) importing counterfeit money; 7) killing the Chancellor of the Exchequer or any Judge.

These definitions stood until the Treason Act of 1795 when High Treason was redefined under three offences; 1) killing, wounding, imprisoning or restraining the King, or any attempt to do these; 2) waging war against the King; 3) helping the King's enemies.

And in effect, these are the definitions still in use today. By Acts of Parliament in 1800 and 1945, the capital punishment for the offence was reaffirmed, and because these two Acts have not been rescinded, the death penalty for Treason still applies today.

Petty Treason was where a servant killed his master, a wife killed her husband or an ordained cleric killed his superior. In Northamptonshire we have had six cases of Petty Treason, all for wives killing their husbands, and all were burnt, the usual punishment. For these, see Chapter 6.

There have been four executions for High Treason in Northamptonshire, including the most famous one of all, Mary, Queen of Scots. Three were beheaded because they were of noble blood, but the first was hung because he was a commoner.

During the Parliament held at Northampton in July 1317, a certain John Poydras was tried on the charge of claiming to be the rightful king of England, instead of the then king Edward II. Poydras, in reality a tanner's son from Exeter, had been brought from Oxford where he had declared himself.

Poydras said that he had been changed at birth by a nurse in favour of the present king Edward, but could produce no evidence to support his claim. He had obviously been duped into being the stooge for others who had wanted to draw attention to the worsening political state of the country under Edward II, and for his pains was hung on Northampton Market Square.

Grafton Regis in Northamptonshire had been the home of the Woodville family for generations, but the family had never risen above the social status of Lords of the Manor. But on Tuesday 1 May 1464, Elizabeth Woodville became Queen of England when she had married king Edward IV, and within a year, she had arranged for most of her family to be married into the great noble families of England.

But all this empire building attracted potent enemies, the most powerful being the old 'Kingmaker' himself, the Earl of Warwick. Edward IV was Yorkist, Warwick was Yorkist, but the Woodvilles were Lancastrian, and Warwick felt himself increasingly alienated and snubbed by the Yorkist king on account of the Lancastrian upstarts.

Not wishing to appear involved himself, he engineered a rebellion in the north of England. Sir John Conyers, hiding under the nickname of 'Robin of Redesdale' marched south with an army, heading towards Northampton and Grafton Regis, the home of the hated Woodvilles.

On Wednesday 26 July 1469, a weak Royalist army under the joint command of William Herbert, Earl of Pembroke and his brother, Sir Richard Herbert, met in battle with Robin of Redesdale at Edgecote near to the village of Culworth in Northamptonshire. Defeat of the Royalists was inevitable as was the capture of the two Herbert brothers.

William and Richard Herbert were taken to Northampton, and without any trial or legal justification whatsoever, were both beheaded on the Market Square the next day, Thursday 27 July 1469. It was common knowledge that the Northampton executions (as well as those of Earl Rivers and Sir John Woodville, the queen's father and brother, soon afterwards at Kenilworth) were the direct orders of the Earl of Warwick for his own political purposes.

Queen of Scotland when she was six days old, queen of Scotland and France when she was 16 years old, queen of neither when she was 25. The story of Mary Stuart is so well known that it does not need to be repeated in full.

Escaping from the wrath of the Scots who had just deposed her, Mary fled to England in 1568, and quickly presented a threat to the Protestant Elizabeth of England. Mary was seen by the English Catholics as England's rightful queen, and became a focus for plots to set her upon the English throne in preference to Elizabeth. This Elizabeth could not tolerate, and so had Mary imprisoned, but resisted all the urging of her ministers to put Mary on trial.

However, faced with the evidence of Mary's involvement in the Babbington Conspiracy, Elizabeth had no choice. Mary was brought to Fotheringhay castle, near Oundle, and placed on trial in October 1586, charged with conspiring to bring about the death of the queen. She was found guilty and sentenced to death (reluctantly, if we believe the history books) by her cousin Elizabeth of England.

At 8am on Sunday 8 February 1587, Mary Stuart entered the Great Hall of Fotheringhay castle and mounted the newly erected platform. Despite crude attempts by the Dean of Peterborough (Richard Fletcher, later made Bishop of Bristol, Worcester and London by Elizabeth I) to get her to renounce her Catholicism, Mary resisted and died a Catholic. After taking three blows of the axe to sever her head, the executioner, a man called Bull, siezed her hair, but her famous auburn locks turned out to be a wig, and her head, with its prematurely greying hair (she was 44) fell to the ground. 'So perish all the Queen's enemies' yelled the Dean.

Mary's body was sealed in a lead coffin but was not buried for six months. Eventually she was given a (Protestant) burial in the south aisle of Peterborough Cathedral, where a plaque now marks the spot. In 1612, her son, who by then had been James I of England for nine years, had her body moved to her final resting place in the Henry VII Chapel in Westminster Abbey.

James, contrary to popular opinion, did not have the castle razed to the ground, but just let it fall into disrepair, when it was plundered for building material by local builders. Only the mound now remains. The stairs of the castle, down which Mary came to face her executioner, however, were built into the Talbot Hotel at Oundle, and are still in use to this very day.

### xiii) Vagrancy

Vagrancy, the Poor Law and the Workhouse are so bound up in English society that it would take a whole book to deal with it. The essence being however, that ever since Tudor times, English society has regarded the vagrant with a fear which is nothing short of paranoia.

The Tudors made the enlightened decision that poverty cannot be eradicated, but the paupers which resulted could be split into two groups, 'those who can't work and those who won't work'. The deserving poor were taken care of by leg-

Would you tangle with this man? Thomas Wragby had three convictions for sleeping rough, all at Oundle, together with two more for assault, one for drunkenness, and another for misconduct in Thrapston work house. He had sentences of between two weeks and one month in prison. (NP)

Begging by exposing wounds is an offence under the Vagrancy Act. Edward Vann alias William Smith received three weeks hard labour for begging in Northampton in February 1870. (NP)

islation, but the remainder felt the full weight of societal disapproval, being regarded as travelling criminals, and were treated as such.

Every village constable had to report to every Quarter Sessions how many wandering rogues and vagabonds his parish had dealt with over the last quarter, and the Sessions records are full of these reports. John Minor the village constable of Syresham, for example, told the 1630 Michaelmas Quarter Sessions that 'vagrants, as Agnes Smith born at Shels . . .? in the county of Oxford, and others have been whipped, whose names I know not'. And at the Epiphany Sessions of 1658, Robert Johnson, village constable, reported apprehending 'Ann Blackbourne begging who was legally punished and sent unto Tamworth in the county of Warwick being the place where she was born'.

This last refers to the legal requirement of sending wandering beggars and vagabonds back to their place of birth so that their native parish could support them. After suffering their punishment (whipping) they were given a 'pass' and escorted by the constable to the next parish in the right direction and handed over to its constable, who perhaps did not want them, and tried to stop his neighbouring parish from foisting off their vagrants on his parish. At the 1630 Michaelmas Sessions, Oundle had tried palming off William Wilton onto neighbouring Polebrook, who did not want him, and promptly appealed to Quarter Sessions, who sent him straight back to Oundle.

But the most important Act of Parliament on Vagrancy is the Vagrancy Act of 1824, parts of which are still in force. As well as the normal amount of wandering poor, the discharge from the army of soldiers from the Napoleonic Wars, poured thousands more homeless vagrants onto the streets of this country.

Vagrancy was regarded as serious by the old parish constables, and this continued even after the Northamptonshire and Northampton police forces were formed. In the county, during the years 1840 until 1857, arrests for vagrancy continually came second in the monthly totals of arrests (the highest was for larceny or theft), and averaged nearly 14 per cent of the monthly arrest rate.

Improving social conditions during the 19th and 20th centuries lessened the cause (and fear) of vagrancy, which today causes no problems. And although arrests under the Vagrancy Act can still be made, many of the offences contained in the old Act have been taken into other legislation. Comparisons therefore do not mean much, but for what it is worth, in 1852 there were 96 arrests for vagrancy in Northamptonshire with a population of 242,000 (.4 offences per 1,000 population) and in 1993, there were 46 arrests, with a population of 575,000, .08 offences per 1,000.

**xiv) Witchcraft**

Written in 1486 by two German theologians, Jacobus Sprenger and Heinrich Kramer, the great text book for the suppression of witchcraft, *Malleus Maleficarum* ('The Hammer of Witchcraft') effectively produced a model for the persecution of 'witches' for the next couple of centuries. Persecution in England, already fired by *Malleus Maleficarum*, was rigorously cultivated by William Perkins, a Cambridge University lecturer and divine, in his book, *A Disclosure on the Damned Art of Witchcraft.*

Of all the counties in England, Northamptonshire and Huntingdonshire, persisted in their belief in witches longer than in any other county in Britain. Indeed, Northamptonshire holds the honour(?) of holding the last witchcraft execution in the whole of England (Elinor Shaw and Mary Phillips in 1705).

In all, eight 'witches' (seven women and one man) were executed in Northamptonshire; five at once in 1612, one in 1674 and the two in 1705.

On Sunday 22 July 1612, five witches were hung together in Abington, near to Northampton: Agnes Brown and Joan Vaughan of Guilsborough; Arthur Bill of Raunds; Helen Jenkinson of Thrapston and Mary Barber of Stanwick.

Agnes Brown and Joan Vaughan were mother and daughter from

Guilsborough. Joan, it was alleged at her 'trial' at the Assizes in Northampton castle, had offended Elizabeth Belcher wife of the Lord of the Manor of Guilsborough, Dabridgecourt Belcher. Elizabeth Belcher had retaliated and struck Joan, apparently with no great force, but was immediately siezed with violent pains. Believing herself to be bewitched, she accused Joan and her mother of being witches.

The old superstition held that to purge a witch's curse, the witch herself must be scratched so as to draw blood. Elizabeth's brother visited the house of the two women with the express intention of scratching them, but 'as he came near the house he was suddenly stopped and could not enter . . . He tried twice or thrice after to go to the house but . . . he was still stayed'. A little while afterwards, the brother also suffered exactly the same pains as his sister, so consequently he also accused Joan Vaughan and her mother of being 'witches'.

The two women were arrested and clapped into Northampton gaol, and whilst there were visited by Elizabeth Belcher and her brother who still wished to scratch them. This they did and were 'Suddenly delivered of their pain Howbeite . . . they fell again into their old trances and were more violently tormented than ever'.

However, on the way back from Northampton in a horse drawn coach, the brother and sister noticed strange apparitions of a man and woman on horseback. The brother, 'noting many strange gestures from them . . . cried out . . . That either they or their horses should presently miscarry. And immediately the horses fell down dead'. Obviously thinking that this was the work of God triumphing over the Devil 'they both hyed them home, still praising God for their escape, and were never troubled after'.

In the light of this 'evidence', Joan Vaughan and Agnes Brown were found guilty of 'witchcraft'.

Arthur Bill of Raunds was also accused of being a 'witch' (apparently in those days, a witch could be either masculine or feminine). He and his parents were accused in that they bewitched to death a woman and some of her cattle. Having no direct 'proof', the Bills were subjected to the ancient 'Ordeal by Water'. Their thumbs were tied to their big toes and they were thrown into a pond. To float was to be guilty, to sink was to be innocent. All the Bills floated.

Arthur Bill was thrown into Northampton gaol to await execution. His father, for an unknown reason was neither gaoled nor hanged, and nothing more is known of his outcome. Arthur Bill's mother, however, unable to stand the mental torment, cheated the hangman by cutting her own throat.

Helen Jenkinson of Thrapston was accused of bewitching a child to death; and Mary Barber of Stanwick accused of bewitching an adult man to death. Nothing is known about either of these cases.

All five were hanged together on the permanent gallows in Abington village before a large crowd.

The sixth witch to be executed within the county, Ann Foster was described as 'an old woman who had long been observed muttering to herself'. She had been accused of witchcraft in that she bewitched horses and cattle and the flock of sheep belonging to Joseph Weedon, a rich farmer of Eastcote (which is about three miles north of Towcester) and with 'Satan her colleague, set his house and barns on fire'.

She was arrested and thrown into Northampton gaol, which apparently caused something of a stir. The anonymous book *Executions in Northampton* quotes a contemporary pamphlet describing her stay in gaol.

'The keepers caused her to be chained to a Post that was in the Gaol; but she had not been long so tied before she began to swell in all parts of her body, that her skin was ready to burst, which caused her to cry out in the most lamentable manner, insomuch that they were forced to Unchain her again, and to give her more Liberty that the Devil might come to suck her, the which he usually did, coming constantly about the dead time of night in the likeness of a Rat, which at his coming, made the most lamentable and hideous noise which affrighted the people which did belong to the Gaol, which caused many to come and see her during her abode there, and several hath been with her when the Devil hath been coming to her, but could see nothing but things like Rats, and heard a most terrible noise.'

Details of Ann Foster's 'trial' are lost, so we do not know what 'proof' there was. But she was found guilty of being a 'witch' and hanged at Northampton on Saturday 22 August 1674.

By being hanged at Northampton on Saturday 17 March 1705, Elinor Shaw and Mary Phillips both from Oundle, were the last two persons to be executed in the whole of England on the charge of witchcraft. They were both charged with: 'bewitching and tormenting in a Diabolical manner; the wife of Robert Wise, of Benefield, till she Died; as also by Killing by Witchcraft, and wicked Fascination, one Elizabeth Gorham, of Glapthorne, a Child of about four Years of age; as also for Bewitching to death one Charles Ireland, of Southwick; and also for Killing several Horses, Hogs and Sheep, being the Goods of Matthew Gorham, Father of the said Child aforesaid'.

The main 'evidence' against them was their own 'confession of witchcraft' which had been obtained by two constables by threatening them with death. The method used for bewitching Mrs Wise to death was apparently 'roasting her effigy in wax and sticking it full of pins . . . till it was all wasted.'

Not surprisingly, they were both found guilty. The sentence was that they be 'hanged till they are almost Dead, and then surrounded with Faggots, Pitch and other combustable matter, which being set on Fire, their bodies are to be consumed to Ashes', which had become the accepted method of execution of witches.

The eye witness account of the execution, contained in the book *Executions in Northampton* is quoted in full because of the historical interest.

'They were so hardened in their wickedness that they publicly boasted that their master (meaning the Devil) would not suffer them to be executed, but they found him a liar, for on Saturday morning, being the 17th inst., they were carried to the gallows on the north side of town, whither numerous crowds of people went to see them die, and being come to the place of execution the minister repeated his former pious endeavours, to bring them to sense of their sins, but to as little purpose as before; for instead of calling upon God for mercy, nothing was heard of them but damning and cursing; however, a little before they tied up, at the request of the minister, Elinor Shaw confessed not only the crime for which she dyed but openly declared before them all how she first became a witch, as did also Mary Phillips; and being desired to say their prayers, they both set up a very loud laughter, calling for the devil to come and help them in such a blasphemous manner as is not fit to mention; so that the sheriff seeing their presumptious impenitence, caused them to be executed with all the expedition possible, even while they were cursing and raving; and as they lived the devils true factors, so they resolutely dyed in his service to the terror of all the people who were eye witnesses to their dreadful and amazing exits. So that being hanged till they were almost dead, the fire was put to the straw, faggots and other combustible matter till they were burnt to ashes.'

As Northamptonshire and Huntingdonshire were (are?) the 'leaders' in witchcraft in the country, it is worth noting that five of the eight witches executed within Northamptonshire come from villages centred around Thrapston which is just a couple of miles from the Huntingdonshire border.

# CHAPTER 4

## 'WHEN CONSTABULARY DUTY'S TO BE DONE': THE POLICING OF NORTHAMPTONSHIRE

"Our feelings we with difficulty smother-
When Constabulary duty's to be done-
Ah, take one consideration with another-
A policeman's lot is not a happy one."

*The Pirates of Penzance*: W. S. Gilbert (1836-1911)

AFTER King Alfred the Great threw the Norse invaders out of southern England about the year 886, he set about giving his country safe defences to guard against any more attacks from the Norsemen. Amongst his reforms was a policing system. He divided the country into counties, or shires, for law keeping purposes, and in each shire placed a 'Shire Reeve' (later corrupted to 'sheriff') whose main occupation was to see that law and order were maintained, and that the shire enjoyed the peace that the King had provided for them: the 'King's Peace'.

The Shire Reeve was chosen from that land owning class of men from which also would eventually come the Lords of the Manors, and later on, the county Magistrates. The shire was split into smaller territorial groups which contained about ten families and their land, called Tithings (from the Saxon tithe, meaning ten), and large groups of ten Tithings, called, not unnaturally, Hundreds. Northamptonshire contained 20 Hundreds.

Every freeman of each Tithing who was 12 years of age or over, had to give an assurance, or pledge, that he would personally answer for the good behaviour of every other man in his Tithing. Every man therefore was a kind of policeman, and the pledge that he had given was called 'frankpledge'.

The man elected by each Tithing to be their spokesman at any court or official gathering was called the head 'borhoe' ('borhoe' being the Saxon word for pledge). The Headborough, or Tithingman, was therefore the spokesman for the settlement, and during the Saxon times, came to be seen as the chief person of the village. But after 1066, the Headborough or Tithingman came to be known by the new name the Norman conquerors gave him, and that name was

'Constable'. And it was to be the office of Parish Constable that was to form one of the two pillars of the policing system of this country until the 19th century. The other office was that of the Magistrate, and for a description of him, see Chapter 5.

To the Normans, the office of Constable was originally one of high state, given only to the most trustworthy, as the origin of the term betrays, 'comes stabuli', master of the stables. By the time of the Conquest however, the term had been downgraded somewhat, but still meant any trustworthy administrative officer, exactly the same qualities as needed by the Tithingman or Headborough.

And it was through the constable that the higher authorities could pass down orders. Thus he came to serve a much wider, even national, system of government. He was however, still an essentially local officer, chosen annually by the parish, as the smallest unit of local government had become by this time, superseding the tithing. And by a Statute of 1252, the task of keeping law and order (the 'King's Peace') in his parish, was placed fairly and squarely upon his shoulders. He was also part-time, as he was chosen from the village tradesmen, who naturally had their businesses to run during the day. He received no salary, apart from necessary expenses.

Possibly the greatest step in the development of the criminal law came with the Statute of Winchester, passed in 1285. This not only obliged every able bodied man between the ages of 15 and 60, to keep weapons for the maintenance of 'the King's peace', but made special provision for walled towns. During the nights, when the gates were shut, a Night Watch should be employed to arrest villains and suspected or suspicious persons. Thus the policing arrangements in the town (the 'Town Watch') evolved differently to that in the rural districts which used the Parish Constable system.

The Statute of Winchester made no mention of the system of Frankpledge, and so it is assumed that by then (1285), the Frankpledge system was obsolete. But, the Statute revived a technique of policing, the use of which obviously had been declining, but which was deemed to be good enough to be given another try. And that was the Hue and Cry.

The Hue and Cry was a very ancient custom. If a person was spotted who was believed to be guilty of a felony or serious wounding, either being committed there and then, or at any time in the past, and who was running away in an attempt to avoid capture, then it was lawful (indeed a legal requirement) for every person who could, to chase after him or her, shouting, and blowing horns if they had them, collecting a bigger and bigger crowd as they went, until the felon had been pursued and captured. All those who joined in the Hue and Cry were justified in capturing the fleeing criminal and using force if necessary, even though it should turn out that the person arrested was innocent.

Sometimes, however, the excitement of the chase became too much to control, and when the felon was caught, punishment was handed out there and then.

The Coroners' Rolls for Northamptonshire record the case of John of Ditchford on Wednesday 24 March 1322.

Henry Felip and his son were attacked by a gang of five footpads at Courteenhall. Henry was murdered, but his son escaped, and raised the Hue and Cry. All five of the murderers, including John of Ditchford, were captured.

But John escaped. He fled to sanctuary (see Appendix 1) into Wootton church, confessed to the Coroner, and was assigned to the port of Dover. However, John was obviously of no mind to leave England, and had no intentions of going to Dover. But he was to have his come-uppance in the most brutal fashion.

So long as sanctuary seekers kept to the main highways when on their way to their ports, no harm would come to them; but stray off the highway, and they were liable to be recaptured. When John left Wootton church two days later, instead of sticking to his assigned route, he thought he would take his chances, and he ran away towards the woods. He was observed by the parishioners of Wootton who were keeping an eye on him, and the Hue and Cry was raised to hunt him down.

Over the fields they chased him, getting nearer and nearer. Eventually he was caught in some fields in Collingtree parish, and was promptly beheaded. His body was left where it was, but his head was carried in triumph back to the Coroner in Northampton. No one was ever punished for his decapitation, because they had all acted inside the law.

Because it was so deep rooted in the depths of the English criminal justice system, the Hue and Cry took a long time to die out. At the Northamptonshire Easter Quarter Sessions of 1687, we read that a Mr John Haslewood of Kettering was granted £10 compensation for having his horse shot dead beneath him when pursuing a Hue and Cry against three robbers who had been discovered drinking in the Swan Inn at Kettering. Not only was the horse killed, but one of the robbers was shot dead as well.

At the same Sessions, Thomas Edy of Harrowden was also granted 'fifty shillings ... reimbursing him such charges as he hath lately been putt to upon the occasion of his killing a certain Theefe or high-way man near Sywell ... upon the pursuit of a Hue and Cry against the said high-way man and his fellowes for a robbery by them lately committed'. And note that, in both these incidents, although two men had been killed, no criminal charges were brought against their killers, because it was a genuine Hue and Cry.

Incidents of raising the Hue and Cry continued spasmodically over the years. James Blinco the Farthingstone parish constable paid out 2d for sending the Hue and Cry to Charlton in April 1704, and in February 1742, John Bellamy the Brigstock constable, paid 4d for a Hue and Cry from Brigstock to Gretton.

Gradually, the Hue and Cry petered out, and when the 18th turned into the 19th century, it had virtually disappeared altogether. As a policing method however, it certainly lasted a long time, well over 1,000 years. So it must have been effective. Perhaps we should revive it today.

So in 1285, in the Statute of Winchester, we have a very neat encapsulation of the basic principle of the English policing system: that it is the duty of *every able bodied* citizen to maintain the King's peace, and that they must arrest offenders and present them to a constable in order to bring them before a court. In other words, *every* man is a policeman. And that is exactly the same as it is today. And because it is exactly the same, it is breathtaking to realise that the Statute of Winchester of 1285 was the only important public legislation that regulated the policing of this country until the Metropolitan Police Act gave a police system to London in 1829, an incredible 544 years later.

Gradually parish constables had more and more duties placed upon them, especially in Tudor times, many of them more concerned with civil administration than criminal behaviour. The Tudors also introduced oaths of office for parish constables, which thus completely subordinated the parish constables to the magistrates, and in effect made them primarily local government officers rather than policemen.

This watering down of the original purpose of the parish constable continued, and thus by the 18th century, he had ceased being the representative of the people of the parish to the local landowner, but had done a complete about turn, and was now the representative of the local landowner to the parish. However, he never completely lost sight of his original use, because he was still chosen by the parishioners themselves for the administration of law and order in the parish. As such, he had the power of arrest for offenders, and the power to detain prisoners until they could be brought before a magistrate.

At the Northamptonshire Record Office several Parish Constables' account books are preserved. The earliest is Burton Latimer starting in 1631. Few however, record things past the 1830s or 1840s, as by the then parish constables were in decline, being replaced by the Northamptonshire County Constabulary.

An examination of these accounts reveals the tasks that the parish constable had to do. He had to keep prisoners in his own home, if there was no village lock-up, until he could present them before a magistrate. He was responsible for all public complaints; for example, unrepaired bridges, short measures of local tradesmen, bastardy orders, persons not going to church, and so on. All these had to be presented to the magistrates at the Quarter Sessions every three months, meaning time lost from his normal occupation to attend court.

Is it therefore any wonder that men tried not to be elected parish constables, and those who were unfortunate enough to be saddled, actually paid a deputy to undertake their year of office for them? These deputy constables were normally of the lowest intelligence, semi-literate, and as criminal as the thieves they were duty bound to catch. They were all of these, because no better calibre of person wanted the job.

With the attention of the parish constable diverted more and more to civil administration rather than crime fighting, coupled with the dubious qualities of the majority of the constables themselves, then it is small wonder that criminal behaviour was running wild and was going virtually unchecked, with the whole of the criminal justice itself coming under severe strain. It was this fact that led some people in taking steps to protect themselves. There were two main initiatives, the private police forces, and the private prosecution associations, which are sometimes known as felons' associations, or catch-criminal societies.

The best known private police force was the 'Bow Street Runners'. Much misunderstanding has arisen over the years about these. Only in the later years (1800s onwards) were police patrols organised from Bow Street, and then only in London, and certainly not as far north as Northamptonshire.

Originally, however, the 'Bow Street Runners' were a pool of detectives who could be hired by anyone who could afford the necessary fees. As such, these detectives were for a time the only detecting force in the country, and so were

Henry Goddard, first Chief Constable of Northamptonshire, and an ex 'Bow Street Runner'. (NP)

hired by people all over the country. There are instances of the 'Runners' clearing up crimes in Northamptonshire, notably the Finedon Mail Coach 'Robbery' in 1812 (see Chapter 3).

However, Northamptonshire has a special interest in the 'Runners', because an ex 'Runner', Henry Goddard, became the first Chief Constable of Northamptonshire in 1840. Goddard's memoirs have been printed, and interesting reading they make as well.

The second private initiative of the 18th century was the private prosecution association. Contrary to opinion, these associations were not private police forces, but were groups of prosperous people pooling their money so as to combat the exorbitant court costs of the time. The earliest known is probably the Bradfield Association in Yorkshire, started in 1737, followed by the Dore and Tetley Association in Derbyshire, started in 1742.

During the early 18th century the system of bringing criminals to justice in the law courts was getting more and more haphazard because of the continuing deterioration of the parish constable system. If the offender was caught (and it was a big 'if'), then the victim had to pursue his own claim through the court because there was no official body to do it for him, which meant paying all expenses. Sometimes, because of this, deals were struck between the criminal and victim, for the return of property intact in return for assurance of no prosecution. This was obviously completely unacceptable to right thinking people.

Each association member paid an annual subscription which went into the central fund. Two basic services were offered, firstly to circulate reward notices for the return of the property or for information, and then secondly, to pay any ensuing court costs from the central fund. And of course, the associations only provided this service to their own members, in other words, those who had something worth losing in the first place, and who could afford the annual subscription.

This made them totally out of the reach or interest of the average common working man, and as such, the associations were never very efficient as crime fighting institutions, or as a deterrent against crime. And as soon as the county police forces started appearing in the 1840s, where criminal prosecutions before the court cost the victim nothing, then the associations declined quite quickly.

As the Northampton Borough Police was founded in 1835, and the County Constabulary in 1840, the Northamptonshire associations went into decline from the early 1840s and eventually petered out. Some did hang on, however, and surprisingly enough, there are still five in existence today (Gretton; Higham Ferrers; Rothwell; Weekley, Warkton and Kettering; and Wellingborough) but these exist mainly as dining clubs.

Not much written material from the Northamptonshire associations has survived. The surviving associations still have their records of course, but of the others, the minute books of only four are preserved in the Northamptonshire

# TERMS, or PROPOSALS,

FOR THE

# MANAGEMENT

OF THE FOLLOWING

# SUBSCRIPTIONS,

TO PREVENT

# HORSE and SHEEP STEALING,

## In the County of NORTHAMPTON;

And to Profecute OFFENDERS.

---

I. THAT every Subfcriber pays Ten Shillings for the Year, (to wit) from the firft Day of *January*, 1781, to the firft Day of *January* following; and that fuch Subfcriptions be paid to Mr. JOHN HODSON, Attorney at Law, at *Wellingborough* in the faid County, who is to continue Agent for the faid Year.

II. THAT every Subfcriber will keep proper Defcriptions of his or her Horfes Marks and Ages; and that on lofing any, which are fufpected to be ftolen, he or fhe fhall immediately give Notice to the faid JOHN HODSON, in Perfon, or by Letter unfealed, when fuch Horfe was firft miffing—the Place from whence loft—the Age and Defcription of the Horfe—and what Road they may have Reafon to think fuch Horfe is gone, that Meffengers may be fent in Purfuit.

III. THAT every Subfcriber fhall mark his or her Sheep with his or her ufual Sheep-Brand; and on paying the Subfcription-Money, deliver to the faid JOHN HODSON the Mark or Form of the Brand he or fhe fhall make Ufe of, and alfo on what Part of the Sheep placed; and that on lofing any Sheep, which are fufpected to be ftolen, he or fhe fhall immediately give Notice to the faid JOHN HODSON, in fuch Manner as is mentioned in the fecond Article.

IV. THAT

( 2 )

IV. THAT whenever any Perſon is apprehended on Suſpicion of ſtealing a Horſe or Sheep of a Subſcriber in the ſaid County, the Owner thereof ſhall go or ſend to the Place where ſuch ſuſpected Perſon ſhall be apprehended, to own the Horſe or Sheep, and ſwear to the Property before a Magiſtrate, and to enter into Recognizance to proſecute the Offender; and on Neglect or Refuſal thereof, to be excluded any Benefit from the Subſcription: And that the Perſon ſo going to claim the Horſe or Sheep, and attending at the Aſſizes to proſecute the Offender, be paid his reaſonable Expences out of the Subſcriptions.

V. THAT the ſaid JOHN HODSON ſhall agree with proper Perſons to go in Purſuit of any Horſes or Sheep that ſhall be ſtolen, or of the Offenders, and pay the Purſuers out of the Subſcriptions; as alſo for all Advertiſements and printed Bills, or other neceſſary Expences in carrying on any Proſecutions; and all Proſecutions to be carried on by the ſaid JOHN HODSON.

VI. THAT a Book be kept by the ſaid JOHN HODSON, of the Names of all the Subſcribers, and alſo of an Account of all Diſburſements, for the Inſpection of any Subſcriber, at any ſeaſonable Time of the Day; and that the annual Account be ſettled, ſtated, and adjuſted, at *Wellingborough*, before ſuch Subſcribers as ſhall think proper to attend, on *Thurſday* the 27th Day of *December*, 1781, between the Hours of Twelve and Two in the Day.

VII. THAT in Caſe any Horſe or Sheep ſhall be ſtolen, as aforeſaid, and not reſtored to the Owner in eight Months, the Owner of ſuch Horſe or Sheep, being a Subſcriber, ſhall be paid out of the Subſcription Half the Value thereof, to be aſcertained by two ſubſtantial Neighbours of the Place from whence the ſame was ſtolen, or of ſome other near Place: The Value of any one Horſe not exceeding Twenty-five Pounds, and the Value of any one Sheep not exceeding One Pound Ten Shillings.

VIII. THAT whatever Sum the Subſcriptions for this Year amount to more than Fifty Pounds, ſhall be placed out at Intereſt, at the Rate of Four Pounds per Cent. per Annum, by the ſaid JOHN HODSON, on the Perſonal Security of Mr. ARCHIBALD RODDICK, of *Wellingborough* aforeſaid, to anſwer theſe Terms and Propoſals; and that no greater Sum be left in his Hands; and that in Caſe the ſaid JOHN HODSON ſhall pay or expend any more Money than he ſhall, at any Time, have received from the Subſcriptions, that the ſaid JOHN HODSON ſhall be allowed legal Intereſt for the ſame and be repaid the ſame by the Subſcribers.

IX. THAT no Perſon, who is reputed to be a Horſe-Dealer, or Sheep-Jobber, ſhall be permitted to ſubſcribe to theſe Terms and Propoſals.

X. THAT if any Subſcriber ſhall be ſuſpected of having any fraudulent Intention of taking the Advantage of theſe Terms and Propoſals, by giving Notice of his or her having loſt (ſuppoſed to have been ſtolen) any Horſe or Sheep; ſuch Perſon ſhall be excluded the Benefit hereof, until he or ſhe jointly, with his or her Shepherd, or other creditable Servant or Perſon, ſhall make Oath thereof before a Magiſtrate, or a Commiſſioner for taking Affidavits, in either of the Courts at *Weſtminſter*.

XI. THAT

( 3 )

XI. THAT the ſaid JOHN HODSON ſhall bring in his Bill for his Trouble, Journies, Attendances, and Diſburſements, to be allowed by the Majority of the Subſcribers that ſhall be preſent on the ſaid 27th Day of *December*, 1781, whereof public Notice ſhall be given.

XII. That any Subſcriber loſing any Horſe or Sheep (ſuppoſed to have been ſtolen) may, in Order to ſave Time, take ſuch Meaſures for the apprehending the Offender, as he or ſhe ſhall, in his or her Diſcretion, think proper, without previouſly giving Notice thereof to the ſaid JOHN HODSON; and his or her Expences, after having been examined and allowed by the Majority of the Subſcribers that ſhall be preſent on the ſaid 27th Day of *December*, 1781, ſhall be paid by the ſaid JOHN HODSON out of the Subſcription-Money.

XIII. That the Day, Month, and Year, be put down, to denote the Time of Subſcription, from whence the Subſcriber will be intitled to the Benefit of theſe Subſcriptions.

☞ Any Proprietor of Horſes or Sheep, inclined to favour the Subſcription, may ſend the Subſcription-Money to the ſaid JOHN HODSON, who will receive the ſame, and have Books of the Terms at length, wherein to enter Subſcribers Names.

The Wellingborough private prosecution association was the first in Northamptonshire, established on New Year's Day 1781. (NRO)

Record Office: Broughton and Cransley 1823-1867; Corby 1813-1829; Cranford 1818-1837 and Harlestone 1815-1834. There is a small collection of Reward Notices at the Northamptonshire Record Office, but these are mainly of the associations in the north of the county, because of the preservation of the archives of Henry Lamb, who was the Kettering based solicitor to them.

The very first association to be formed in Northamptonshire was 'The Wellingborough Association for protecting the persons and property of the several subscribers against Incendiaries, Housebreakers, Horse and Sheep Stealers, Thieves and Depredators of every description' formed on Monday 1 January 1781, followed rapidly by several others, which lost no time in starting to operate. During 1783, for instance, eight different associations placed a total of 30 notices in the *Northampton Mercury*, six of which were reward notices.

Despite the associations in their titles offering protection for more than property crime, the main bulk of the reward notices concern killing, maiming and theft of livestock, especially sheep. Out of a grand total of 130 reward notices for the period 1835 to 1860, sheep notices account for 69, or 53 per cent, and only two concern violence to persons, robberies in 1835 and 1837.

But to be fair, the whole concept of the prosecution associations had never been designed as a total law enforcement or policing system. The associations

**Rowell Association.**

**15 GUINEAS**

**REWARD.**

***WHEREAS,***

Some Person or Persons, did, late on SATURDAY Night, or early on SUNDAY Morning last, Slaughter, in a Close, in ROWELL, in the County of *Northampton*, commonly called *Hobb's Hill Close*, adjoining the Road leading to Kettering,

**ONE EWE SHEEP,**

*THE PROPERTY OF MR. WILLIAM ROE,*

the whole of which was left in the said Close. The Person or Persons who committed the Offence, attempted, as appeared from the state in which the Carcase was found, to cut off a Leg, but did not succeed.

Whoever will give Information, so that the Offender or Offenders may be Apprehended and Convicted of the said Offence, shall, on his, her, or their Conviction, receive a Reward of FIVE GUINEAS, to be paid by the *Treasurer* of the above Association; and a further Reward of TEN GUINEAS will be paid by the said WILLIAM ROE, on such Conviction.

***HENRY LAMB,***

KETTERING, MARCH 10, 1818.

Solicitor and Treasurer.

*N. B. Persons desirous of becoming SUBSCRIBERS to the above ASSOCIATION, are requested to signify the same to Mr. LAMB, of Kettering.*

DASH, PRINTER, KETTERING.

Rowell (Rothwell) Association reward poster for sheep theft, 1818. (NRO)

# *Harleston Association,*

FOR

## PROSECUTING ROBBERS, THIEVES, &c.

FEBRUARY 24th, 1812.

AT a Meeting held this Day, at the Sign of the *Fox-and-Hounds*, in *Harleston*, in the County of Northampton, of the Members of the ASSOCIATION for APPREHENDING and PROSECUTING ROBBERS, THIEVES, &c. by Subscription,

*It was (amongst other Things) resolved,*

That the following Rewards should be paid by the Treasurer of this Association, out of the public fund of the said society (over and above the Rewards allowed by Act of Parliament or otherwise howsoever), to any person or persons who should apprehend, or cause to be convicted, any one guilty of the following offences against any member of this society, such Rewards to be paid on conviction of the offender or offenders, viz.

| Offence | £. | s. | d. |
|---|---|---|---|
| For wilfully setting Fire to any Dwelling-house, Warehouse, Barn, Stable, or other Out-building, Stack or Rick of Corn, Grain, Hay, Straw, or Bark, or to any Stack of Wood, Furze, or other Fuel or Property, a Reward of Fifty Pounds, provided the Committee, or the major part of them, or any five or more of them, shall think the offence of that magnitude as to merit such a Reward; and if not, then such lesser sum (not less than Six Guineas) as they shall think proper to allow. | | | |
| Stealing or killing any Sheep or Lamb (not a sucking Lamb) | 25 | 0 | 0 |
| Stealing or killing a sucking Lamb | 5 | 5 | 0 |
| Stealing, killing, or maiming, any Horse, Mare, or Gelding, Ox, Cow, Calf, or other Neat Cattle | 5 | 5 | 0 |
| Burglary or House-breaking | 5 | 5 | 0 |
| Highway or Footpad Robbery | 5 | 5 | 0 |
| Stealing Goods from any Shop, Warehouse, Storehouse, Building, or other place; or any Corn, thrashed or unthrashed, or Hay, or other thing, out of any Barn, Hovel, Rick-yard, or other place | 2 | 2 | 0 |
| Buying or receiving any Stock, Goods, or Effects, the property of a subscriber, knowing the same to have been stolen | 2 | 2 | 0 |
| Stealing or maliciously killing Pigs or Poultry | 2 | 2 | 0 |
| Breaking or stealing any Doors, Window-Shutters, Bars, Locks, Bolts, or any Hedges, Gates, Stiles, Pens, Hurdles, Fleaks, Stakes, Posts, Rails, or any Iron-work belonging thereto, or any Fire-wood | 1 | 1 | 0 |
| Robbing or maliciously damaging any Garden, Orchard, or Fish-pond; or cutting down, barking, or destroying any Timber, Fruit, or other Trees, Underwood, or Quicksets, growing | 1 | 1 | 0 |
| Stealing any Corn, Grass, or Hay, either growing, or in Shocks or Cocks in the Field | 1 | 1 | 0 |
| Stealing or damaging any Waggon, Cart, Plough, Harrow, or other Implement in Husbandry | 1 | 1 | 0 |
| Cutting the Mane or Tail of any Horse, Mare, or Gelding, or the Tail of any Bull, Ox, or Cow, or otherwise disfiguring them | 1 | 1 | 0 |
| Stripping or pulling Potatoes, Cabbages, [illegible] Gardens, or Orchards | 1 | 1 | 0 |

*And for every other offence*, not before specified, such Reward as the Committee, or any five of them, shall think proper to allow.

### List of the Members of this Association.

Right Honourable EARL SPENCER,

Andrew Robert, Esq. Harleston Park
Adams Joseph, Bugbrook
Adams Richard, Upper-Heyford
Andrew Thomas, Harleston

BouverieEdward, Esq. Delapre Abbey
Blencowe Rt. Willis, Esq. Dallington
Baker Elizabeth, Harpole
Barnett Thomas, Weedon-Beck
Bliss Thomas, Stow-nine-Churches
Bliss John, Thrup Grounds, Norton Parish
Boswell John, Upton
Briggs Jeremiah, Northampton
Britten William, Weston-Favell
Brown Benjamin, Long-Buckby
Bull John, Preston-Deanry
Butcher Thomas, Northampton
Buswell Richard, Ditto

Causer Francis, Kingsthorpe
Chamberlain James, Northampton
Clarke John, East-Haddon
Clarke Joseph, Quinton
Cleaver William, Chapel-Brampton
Coleman William, Long-Buckby
Collis Samuel, Murcott in Watford
Cooch John, Harleston
Coxe Joseph, Northampton
Crofts Edward, Long-Buckby

Dames William, Ravensthorpe
Danes William, Kingsthorpe
Daniel William, Dodford
Dickens William, Dodford Mill
Dunkley James, Northampton
Dunkley John, Ditto
Dunkley William, Kislingbury
Dunkley William, Northampton
Dunkley Robert, Dodford
Dunkley Samuel, Rotherstborpe

Earl Robert, Dallington
Edmonds Samuel, West-Haddon
Evans Francis, Wootton
Evans Martha, Ditto

Fitzhugh Charles, Kingsthorpe
Flavell Thomas, Ditto

Garrett William, East-Haddon
Gulliver William, West-Haddon
Gurden Richard, Dodford

Harris William, Esq. Wootton House
Hunter Rev. Christopher, Gayton
Hughes Rev. R. Barnston, Kislingbury
Harris Richard, Ditto
Harris William, Welton
Hawkes Stephen, Abington
Hewitt Richard, Dodford
Hilliard Sarah, Northampton
Hillyard Clarke, Ditto
Howes Mark, Rotherstborpe

Ireson John, sen. Nether-Heyford
Ireson John, jun. Weston-Favell

Jackson George, West-Haddon
Jakeman William, Floore
Jeffery Moses, Northampton
Jones Thomas, Little-Billing

Knight Rev. Robert Harvey, Weston-Favell
Kay John, sen. Newnham
Kilsby Robert, West-Haddon
Kilsby William, Ditto
Knight Robert, Walgrave

Lansbury Thomas, Weston-Favell
Linnell Richard, Stow-nine-Churches
Loe John, Dodford
Love Thomas, Harpole
Lovell Isaac, Paulerspury
Lumley Mary, Harleston

Main William, East-Haddon
Malsbury Richard, Bugbrook
Manning John, Harpole
Manning William, Ditto
Marriott William, Preston-Deanry
Marriott John, Floore
Marston William, Great-Brington
Miller Bartlett, Chapel-Brampton
Montgomery Joseph, Ashby-Ledgers
Mountfort Mrs. Snoscomb
Mumford Richard, Rotherstborpe

Palmer Thomas, Norton
Pell William, Little-Billing Lodge
Pell Samuel, Overston
Perkins Edward, Northampton
Perkins John, East-Haddon
Perkins Thomas, Long-Buckby
Phillips Abraham, jun. Welton
Potterton Thomas, Boughton

Roe Thomas, Preston-Deanry
Roddis Samuel, Floore
Russell James, Dodford
Russell William, Ditto

Samwell T. S. W. Esq. Upton
Sawbridge Wm. Esq. East-Haddon
Smith Thomas, Esq. Great-Houghton
Standert Osborne, Esq. London
Slade Rev. James, Dodford
Stanton Rev. John, Scaldwell
Stockdale Rev. William, Walgrave
Saddington Thos. Church-Brampton
Sanders Henry, Harleston
Scriven Edward, Harpole
Scriven Richard, Ditto
Smith Michael, Northampton
Stanton Thomas, Upper-Heyford
Stanton Samuel, Dallington
Stubbs Matthew, Braunston Wharf

Thursby John Harvey, Esq. Abington
Tarry Samuel, Weedon-Beck
Tucker Charles, Dodford
Turland Thomas, Bugbrook

Vyse R. W. Howard, Esq. Boughton
Vigoreux Rev. Lewis John, Great-Brington
Vialls John, Harleston
Vialls Joseph, Ditto

Wrighte Miss Ann Barbara, Gayhurst
Wadsworth John, Long-Buckby
Walker John, Great-Brington
Walker Thomas, Bugbrook
Walker Wm. White-Hall, Heyford
Walker James, Newnham
Walton John, Chapel-Brampton
Walton Thomas, Harleston
Watts John, Kislingbury
Watts James, Ditto
Webb John, Great-Brington
West Richard, Dallington
White Thomas, East-Haddon
White John, Overston
White James, Great-Brington
Whiting Charles, Harleston
Wilkins George, East-Haddon
Wilson Samuel Burditt, Northampton
Wood John, Moulton Park
Worley John, Great-Brington
Worcester R. jun. Long Buckby Wharf
Wykes William, Great-Brington

Yorke John, Northampton

And it was also resolved (amongst other things), that a proper number of hand-bills, specifying the rewards offered by this Association for apprehending and prosecuting offenders, and containing the names of all the members of this society, be printed, and posted up in such parishes or places, and at such time or times, as the subscribers shall think proper.

RICHARD BUSWELL, Treasurer and Solicitor.

[FREEMAN, PRINTER, &c, NORTHAMPTON.]

The Harleston Association List of Rewards and Members in 1812. Note that Rick burning had £50 reward, sheep stealing £25, but highway robbery only £5 5s. (NRO)

# KETTERING ASSOCIATION,

***For prosecuting Felons, Thieves, and Depredators of every Description;***

PARTICULARLY

***HORSE and SHEEP STEALERS, STOCK CATTLE, &c.***

ALSO FOR THE MORE EFFECTUALLY PROTECTING THE

**Gardens, Orchards, Field Barns, Turnips, Fences, &c.**

OF THE SEVERAL SUBSCRIBERS.

*Kettering*, **16*th May*, 1814.**

At a **MEETING** of several of the Inhabitants of the Parish of Kettering, in the County of Northampton, held this Day, at the **GEORGE INN**, pursuant to Public Notice given, to consider of and adopt a **Plan**, for forming a Society or Association for prosecuting **Robbers**, Thieves, and Felons, of every Denomination, for Offences that may be committed on the Persons or Property of any of the Members,

***The following Rules, Orders, and Regulations, were agreed upon:***

IMPRIMIS. It is resolved, that a Society, or Association, be immediately formed and entered into, to be stiled, THE KETTERING SOCIETY, OR ASSOCIATION.

II. That a Meeting of the Society shall be held at the GEORGE and WHITE HART Inns, in Kettering, alternately, on the Day hereafter named, at Twelve of the Clock at Noon, when a Committee of Seven, or such Number as may be thought proper, shall be chosen, to manage the Business of the Society for the Year ensuing.

III. That at every such Annual Meeting, a Treasurer and Solicitor be appointed by the Majority of the Members then present, to receive the Subscriptions, prosecute Offenders, and transact the Business of the Society; and to make Entries in a Book or Books, provided for that purpose, of all his Receipts and Disbursements, which Book or Books shall be produced at every of the Annual Meetings, for the Inspection of the Members then present, and be then and there settled and allowed by the Committee.

IV. That, for the Provision of a Fund for the carrying on the Business of this Association, every Person desirous of becoming a Member, shall forthwith pay into the Hands of Thomas Marshall, of Kettering aforesaid, Solicitor, (who is hereby appointed the present Treasurer,) the Sum of Ten Shillings and Sixpence; and shall over and above, at the Annual Meeting, or within Fourteen Days after, pay or cause to be paid into the Hands of the Treasurer such Sum as shall be agreed upon at each such Annual Meeting to be paid by such Subscriber, or be excluded all Benefit from the Society: and no Person shall be entitled to any Benefit in respect of any Offence committed before Payment of his or her Subscription.

V. That every Member not being present at the Annual Meeting shall pay over and above the Call then made, the Sum of Two Shillings and Sixpence.

VI. That the Expenses of the Annual Meeting, and all Expenses of advertising, apprehending to Conviction any Offender who shall rob, steal from, or otherwise feloniously defraud, or injure, any Member of the Society, shall be defrayed out of the Common Fund of the Society; and in case any Member shall at any Assizes or Quarter Session be ordered or allowed by the Court any Sum towards his or her Expenses of prosecuting any Offender or Offenders, and any Reward shall be paid him for convicting any such Offender or Offenders, then, and in each and every of the said Cases, the said Sums respectively shall be paid over by such Member so prosecuting as aforesaid, into the Hands of the Treasurer, to be by him placed to the General Fund of this Society.

VII. That if any Member of this Society shall be robbed, or otherwise injured in his or her Person or Property, he or she shall use his or her utmost endeavours to apprehend the Offender or Offenders, (for which he or she shall be allowed such Expenses as the Committee or the Major Part of them shall think reasonable,) or give immediate Information to the Treasurer, who shall take such Steps as he shall think proper for the apprehending and prosecuting to Conviction the Offender or Offenders; but in case it shall appear that any Cattle or Effects supposed to have been stolen shall have only strayed or been misplaced, then the Owner of such Cattle or Effects, supposed to have been stolen, shall pay or reimburse the Treasurer all such Sum and Sums of Money as he shall have expended on that Account.

VIII. That when any Person or Persons shall be apprehended on suspicion of any Felonious Offence towards any Member of this Society, such Member shall on reasonable Notice appear before the Magistrate before whom such Felon or suspected Person shall be brought, (he or she being allowed their reasonable Expenses of such Attendance, to be paid by the Treasurer,) and if required, enter into Recognizance to prosecute the Offender; and on his or her refusing or neglecting to appear, to be excluded the Benefit of the Subscription, and to be expelled the Society.

IX. That if any Member of this Society shall compound any Felony or Felonies, or neglect to prosecute, or shall stop any Prosecution when commenced for any Offence against him or herself, (without the Consent of a Majority of the Committee for the Time being,) then such Members shall pay all such Expenses which shall have accrued, and be excluded the Society.

X. That the Executors or Administrators of any Members of this Society who shall happen to die, be entitled to such Benefit therefrom as such Members would have been entitled to if they had been then living.

XI. That the Treasurer for the Time being shall always be considered one of the Committee, and in case there shall be an equal Number of Votes, either at a Committee or a General Meeting, for or against any Question, the Treasurer shall have a Casting-vote.

XII. That the following Rewards be paid by the Treasurer of this Society, out of the Public Fund, over and above the Rewards allowed by Act of Parliament, to any Person not being a Member thereof, who shall apprehend, or cause to be convicted, any Person guilty of the following Offences against any Member of the Society, to be paid on Conviction of the Offender or Offenders: viz.

| | By the Society. | | | By Act of Parliament. | | |
|---|---|---|---|---|---|---|
| | £. | s. | d. | £. | s. | d. |
| For Burglary | 5 | 5 | 0 | 40 | 0 | 0 |
| Highway or Footpad Robbery | 5 | 5 | 0 | 40 | 0 | 0 |
| Stealing or Maiming any Horse, Mare, or Gelding | 5 | 5 | 0 | 40 | 0 | 0 |
| Stealing or Maiming any Ox, Cow, Calf, Sheep, Lamb, or Neat Cattle | 5 | 5 | 0 | 10 | 0 | 0 |
| Stealing or Killing of Pigs, Hogs, or Poultry | 2 | 2 | 0 | | | |
| Shooting or otherwise Killing of Pigeons | | | | | | |
| Robbing any Garden, Orchard, or Fishpond, or destroying any Fruit | [illegible] | | | | | |
| For Stealing any Out-houses, or any Warehouses, Storehouses, Shops, Buildings, or other Places | 5 | 5 | 0 | | | |
| Breaking, Stealing, or Carrying away, any Doors, Window Shutters, Bars, Locks, Bolts, or any Gates, Stiles, Pens, Fleaks, Posts, Rails, Pales, Fences, or any Iron-work thereto belonging | 2 | 2 | 0 | | | |
| Stealing Turnips, Potatoes, or Cabbages | 1 | 1 | 0 | 0 | 10 | 0 |
| Stealing Corn, or Grain, thrashed or unthrashed, or any Poultry, or other Things, out of any Field Barn, or any other Barn, Hovel, Rick Yard, or other Place | 1 | 1 | 0 | | | |
| Stealing any Corn, Grain, Grass, or Hay, growing, or in Shocks, or Cocks; or Stealing or Damaging any Waggons, Carts, Ploughs, Harrows, or other Implements of Husbandry | 1 | 1 | 0 | | | |
| Cutting Horses' Manes, or Tails, or otherwise disfiguring them | 2 | 2 | 0 | | | |
| For wilfully setting Fire to any Dwelling-House, Warehouse, Barn, Stable, or other Out-buildings, or any Stacks, or Ricks, of Corn, Grain, or Hay | 5 | 5 | 0 | | | |
| For wilfully setting Fire to any Stack of Straw, Wood, Furze, or Fuel | 2 | 2 | 0 | | | |

And for every other Crime, or Felonious Act, not before mentioned, such Rewards as the Majority of the Committee shall think proper.

That in Order to carry the Intention of this Society effectually into Execution, the Major Part of the Committee from Time to Time shall have full Power to alter and amend the foregoing Resolutions, and to make such further Rules and Orders as to them shall seem and appear most proper, so as no such Rules, Orders, or Amendments, shall continue in force longer than till the next General Meeting, unless then ratified and confirmed by the Majority of the Members then present.

That the whole of the Members be, and they are hereby appointed, a Committee till the next General Meeting; and that Four of the Committee, with the Treasurer, (if no more attend,) be competent to transact the Business of this Society.

That Thomas Marshall of Kettering aforesaid be appointed the Solicitor to this Society.

That the Annual Meeting be held on the First Thursday in January next; and that the Members then dine together at the George Inn in Kettering, at Three o'Clock in the Afternoon.

ORDERED LASTLY, That the Rules and Resolutions of this Society and List of the present Subscribers be printed and distributed to the Subscribers, and stuck up and circulated in the Town and Neighbourhood.

FULLER, PRINTER, KETTERING.

LIST OF PRESENT SUBSCRIBERS.

The Kettering Association List of Rewards in 1814. This time straw burning is bottom of the list. (NRO)

# Burglary & Robbery.

## SCALDWELL,

NORTHAMPTONSHIRE.

## *Kettering Association.*

# 20 GUINEAS

## *REWARD.*

WHEREAS some evil-disposed person or persons did on *Monday* night last, or early on *Tuesday* morning, enter the Dwelling-house of Mr. WILLIAM MANNING, of *Scaldwell* (a Member of this Association), by breaking a pane of Glass in the Window of the Parlour, adjoining the Garden, and forcing the Window Shutters, and feloniously steal, take, and carry away the following articles, viz.---

From the first Parlour---6 silver tea spoons, marked W. L. M. 1 other silver tea spoon, marked A. M. 2 silver table spoons, one marked T. or I. S. M. 2 silver salt spoons (unmarked), 2 plated salt frames, 2 bottles of rum, 2 bottles of currant wine, 1 or 2 bottles of gin, and a mahogany portable writing desk, which desk was afterwards found in the garden.

From the second Parlour---(out of a Bureau, which was forced open) 2 or 3 one pound notes (supposed to be Percival's bank), 1 plain silver hunting watch, with roman figures, 1 other old-fashioned silver watch, with italic figures, and from the chimney-piece from a Derbyshire time piece, 1 other silver seconds watch, double cased, roman figures, with gilt chain and 2 keys affixed thereto.---In this parlour was found a twitch stick, with a hole burnt through the top, left by the Depredators.

Any person giving information of the offender or offenders, or if more than one concerned either impeaching his accomplice, shall on conviction receive a reward of FIFTEEN GUINEAS of the said Mr. WILLIAM MANNING, and a further reward of FIVE GUINEAS of the Treasurer of this Association.

THOMAS MARSHALL,
*Treasurer and Solicitor to the Association.*

KETTERING, April 13th, 1824.

DASH, PRINTER, KETTERING.

Kettering Association reward poster for a burglary at Scaldwell. (NRO)

# Harleston Association,

## *For Prosecuting Robbers, Thieves, &c.*

## ARTICLES,

OR

# *Rules and Orders*

## OF THE ABOVE ASSOCIATION.

I. THAT every person, on becoming a Member of this Society, shall pay into the hands of the Treasurer the sum of 11s 6d. for the first year's subscription, commencing from the 8th day of February in the year in which he shall become a Member, and the sum of 5s. yearly for every subsequent subscription.

II. That a general Annual Meeting, for the purpose of transacting the business of this Association, shall be held at the Sign of the *Fox-and-Hounds*, in *Harleston*, in the County of Northampton, some day in the month of *February* in every year, at Eleven o'Clock in the Forenoon; of which previous notice shall be given in the *Northampton Mercury* twice.

III. That every Member who shall not pay his annual subscription to the Treasurer on or before the General Annual Meeting, or within fourteen days then next following, shall be excluded all benefit of this Association, and be no longer considered as a Member thereof; consequently liable to pay his subscription as a new Member on re-admission to the Society, pursuant to the terms of the first Resolution: and no person shall be intitled to receiving any benefit from this Society for any offence committed before the payment of his subscription money.

IV. That the Treasurer of this Society shall enter the names of the several Subscribers in a book to be provided for that purpose; wherein he shall also fairly transcribe and enter an account of all his receipts and disbursements respecting the business of this Association; which accounts shall be audited and passed annually at the General Meeting, by a Committee then to be appointed for that purpose, consisting of five or more of the Subscribers.

V. That at such Annual Meeting a Committee of 33, or such other number of the Members as may be approved of by a majority of the Subscribers then present, shall be chosen to regulate the business of this Society for the year ensuing, who shall be empowered to hold meetings for that purpose as occasion may require; and that the attendance of any five of the Committee shall constitute a meeting, which shall be attended by the Treasurer or his sufficient deputy, who shall enter the minutes and proceedings thereof in a book to be kept for that purpose, and defray the expences then incurred, provided no greater sum than Ten Shillings be expended, or charged to this Society, at any one such meeting.

VI. That if any Member of this Society shall be robbed, or otherwise feloniously defrauded, or injured in his or her person or property, he or she shall use his or her utmost endeavours to apprehend the Offender or Offenders, (for which he or she shall be allowed such charges and expences as the Committee shall think reasonable,) or shall give immediate notice thereof to the Treasurer, or to one or more of the Committee, who shall take such methods as he and they shall think proper for apprehending and prosecuting to conviction the Offender or Offenders. But in case it shall happen that any Cattle or effects, supposed to have been stolen, shall have strayed or been misplaced, then the owner of such Cattle or effects shall pay and reimburse to the Treasurer of this Society all such sums of money as shall have been by him expended on such account. And it is resolved that no person residing out of Northamptonshire be admitted a Member of this Association, and that no Member having stock or property out of Northamptonshire shall receive any benefit from this Society on account of the loss thereof.

VII. That when any person or persons is or are apprehended on suspicion of being guilty of any felonious offence against any Member or Members of this Society, such Member or Members shall, on notice given him, her, or them, by the Treasurer or any one of the Committee, appear as speedily as possible, before the Magistrate (before whom such suspected person or persons shall be taken) in order to prove the offence, and enter into recognizances to prosecute the Offender or Offenders; for which he shall be intitled to receive of the Treasurer, for expences incurred by such attendances, such sum as the said Committee shall think reasonable; and on his, her, or their neglecting or refusing to appear as aforesaid, he, she, or they shall be excluded the benefit of this Association.

VIII. That if any Horse, Mare, or Gelding, shall be stolen from any Member of this Society, immediate notice thereof shall be transmitted to the Treasurer, or to one of the Committee, as aforesaid, describing the colour, age, and marks, as nearly as possible, of the Horse, Mare, or Gelding so stolen, (of which every Member is requested to keep an accurate account), and also describing the place from whence stolen, the person or persons suspected, and what road he or they are supposed to have taken; whereupon hand-bills shall be immediately dispersed, and proper persons dispatched in pursuit of the Offender or Offenders, and descriptions both of them and the Horse, Mare, or Gelding stolen, shall be transmitted to the Public-office, Bow-street, London.

IX. That the expences of advertising, apprehending, and prosecuting, any person or persons who shall rob, steal from, or otherwise feloniously defraud or injure, any Member of this Society, shall be paid and defrayed out of the fund in the hands of the Treasurer, so far as the same will extend.

X. That the following Rewards shall be paid by the Treasurer of this Association, out of the public fund of the said Society, to any person or persons who shall give such Information as shall lead to the detection of any one guilty of the following offences against any Member of this Society, such Rewards to be paid on conviction of the Offender or Offenders:—

| | £. | s. | d. |
|---|---|---|---|
| For wilfully setting Fire to any Dwelling House, Warehouse, Barn, Stable, or other Out-building, Stack or Rick of Corn, Grain, Hay, Straw, or Bark, or to any Stack of Wood, Furze, or other Fuel or Property, a Reward of Fifty Pounds, provided the Committee, or the major part of them, or any five or more of them, shall think the Offence of that magnitude as to merit such a Reward; and if not, then such lesser sum, (not less than Six Guineas), as they shall think proper to allow. | | | |
| Stealing or killing any Sheep or Lamb, (not a sucking Lamb) | 15 | 0 | 0 |
| Stealing or killing a sucking Lamb | 3 | 5 | 0 |
| Stealing, killing, or maiming any Horse, Mare, or Gelding, Ox, Cow, Calf, or other Neat Cattle | 5 | 5 | 0 |
| Burglary or House-breaking | 5 | 5 | 0 |
| Highway or Footpad Robbery | 5 | 5 | 0 |
| Stealing Goods of the Value of forty Shillings or upwards, from any Shop, Warehouse, Storehouse, Building, or other Place | 5 | 5 | 0 |
| Stealing Goods under the Value of forty Shillings, from any Shop, Warehouse, Storehouse, Building, or other Place | 2 | 2 | 0 |
| Stealing any Corn, thrashed or unthrashed, or Hay, or other thing, out of any Barn, Hovel, Rick-yard, or other Place | 2 | 2 | 0 |
| Buying or receiving any Stock, Goods, or Effects, the Property of a Subscriber, knowing the same to have been stolen | 2 | 2 | 0 |
| Stealing or maliciously killing Pigs or Poultry | 2 | 2 | 0 |
| Breaking or stealing any Doors, Window-Shutters, Bars, Locks, Bolts, or any Hedges, Gates, Stiles, Pens, Hurdles, Fleaks, Stakes, Posts, Rails, or any Iron-work belonging thereto, or any Fire-wood | 1 | 1 | 0 |
| Robbing or maliciously damaging any Garden, Orchard, or Fish-pond; or cutting down, barking, or destroying any Timber, Fruit, or other Trees, Underwood, or Quicksets growing | 1 | 1 | 0 |
| Stealing any Corn, Grass, or Hay, either growing, or in Shocks, or Cocks in the field | 1 | 1 | 0 |
| Stealing or damaging any Waggon, Cart, Plough, Harrow, or other Implement in Husbandry | 1 | 1 | 0 |
| Cutting the Mane or Tail of any Horse, Mare or Gelding, or the Tail of any Bull, Ox, or Cow, or otherwise disfiguring them | 1 | 1 | 0 |
| Stripping or pulling Wool from any Sheep | 1 | 1 | 0 |
| Stealing any Turnips, Potatoes, Cabbages, Green Peas, or other Vegetables, from the fields, Gardens, or Orchards | 0 | 10 | 6 |

And for every other Offence, not before specified, such Reward as the Committee, or any five of them, shall think proper to allow.

XI. That any person who shall buy any Stock, Goods, or Effects, the property of a Subscriber, knowing the same to have been stolen, shall be prosecuted at the expence of this Society.

XII. That the benefit of this Association shall not be extended to Co-partners in any trade or business, unless such Co-partners shall severally be Members of this Society.

XIII. That the Treasurer of this Society shall pay to the Member or Members thereof such sum or sums of money as the Committee at the annual meeting of this Society shall think proper to allow for the loss of time and expences of any such Member or Members, incurred in attending at any Assize or Sessions, in order to prosecute any person or persons for any of the offence or offences before mentioned, or for any other offence or offences not before mentioned, in which the Committee shall think proper to make allowance.

XIV. That the Treasurer of this Society shall pay to the Member or Members thereof such sum or sums of money as the Committee at the annual meeting of this Society shall think proper to allow for the expences of any such Member or Members incurred in removing or causing to be removed any Gypsies or Vagrants from the lordships or parishes in which such Member or Members respectively reside.

XV. That if any Member or Members of this Society who shall be robbed or otherwise feloniously defrauded or injured in his, her, or their person or property, persons or properties, shall not apply to the Solicitor of this Association for the purpose of having the offence or offences advertised or otherwise made public, such Member or Members shall not be allowed any expence or expences which he, she, or they, may be put to in advertising, or otherwise making public such Offence or Offences.

XVI. That the following Subscribers be, and they are hereby appointed a Committee for the ensuing year (ending on the 8th day of February, 1826,) for the conducting and managing the business of this Association, viz.

Right Honourable EARL SPENCER.
Right Honourable LORD ALTHORP.
Sir WILLIAM WAKE, Bart.

[illegible] Esq. Thomas Samwell Watson Samwell, Esq. William Sawbridge, Esq. John Harvey Thursby, Esq. Richard William Howard Vyse, Esq. Rev. Roger Barnston Hughes. Rev. Robert Harvey Knight. Rev. Thomas Lockton. Rev. John Stanton. Rev. Lewis John Vigoreux. Messrs. Henry Bailey, John Brettell, William Britten, John Cooch, Joseph Cooper, John Dix, William Dunkley, Robert Earl, Thomas Emery, Robert Fascutt, Thomas Grose, Richard Harris, Robert Kilsby, John Manning, sen. John Mawle, Thomas Potterton, James Russell, Richard Scriven, John Walton, James White, and John Worley.

And that they have power to increase the number of the Committee, by adding such other Subscribers as they shall think proper.

XVII. That Mr. *William Buswell*, Attorney, of Northampton, (with whom the Agreement of this Association, is deposited), shall be and is hereby appointed Treasurer and Solicitor to this Society; by whom all subscriptions are to be received, and all prosecutions to be conducted. And in case the Treasurer's necessary disbursements shall at any time exceed the amount of subscriptions in his hands, he shall be allowed legal interest for what he advances until he is reimbursed.

XVIII. That in order to carry the intentions of this Society effectually into execution, the major part of the Committee shall have power from time to time to alter and amend the foregoing Rules and Orders, and to make and substitute such others as to them shall appear most proper for the purposes intended; so that no such alterations, amendments, or new rules or orders, enlarge or alter the subscriptions for the time being, or the several rewards before specified, or continue in force longer than until the next General Annual Meeting, unless the same shall be then ratified and confirmed by the majority of the Members present.

XIX. That every Member of this Association who shall not attend and dine at the General Annual Meeting, shall forfeit 3s. 6d. which shall be paid into the hands of the Treasurer at the time such absentee pays his annual subscription: and the Treasurer shall, at such Annual Meeting, advance the forfeiture of each such absentee, which shall be applied towards discharging the dinner bill and expences at such meeting. But in case any such absentee shall withdraw himself from this Society, and shall not after such annual meeting, within the time before limited, pay his annual subscription, and also such forfeiture, then the said Treasurer shall be reimbursed out of the fund of this Society all such forfeitures as he shall so advance for such absentees respectively.

XX. That a proper number of hand-bills specifying the Rewards offered by this Association for apprehending and prosecuting Offenders, and containing the names of all the Members of this Society be printed, and posted up in such parishes or places, and at such time or times, as the Subscribers shall think proper.

XXI. That the Members of this Society may derive all possible advantage and protection from the present Association, it is resolved, that a list of their names and places of abode shall (if thought necessary) be inserted in the *Northampton Mercury*, within the space of one month from each General Annual Meeting; and also that each Subscriber shall be furnished with a printed copy of these Resolutions.

WILLIAM BUSWELL,
March 8th, 1825. Treasurer and Solicitor.

CORDEUX, PRINTER, NORTHAMPTON.

The Harleston Association Rules and Orders in 1825. Always one of the richest because of the Spencer involvement, the Harleston Association could, by 1825, afford more flamboyant posters, and bigger rewards. (NRO)

**CRANFORD**
**ASSOCIATION,**
***FOR PROSECUTING FELONS.***

**FIVE**
***GUINEAS***
**REWARD.**

**WHEREAS**

Some Person or Persons did, on Thursday Night last, steal from the STABLE of Mr. JOHN LINNELL, at WOODFORD, near THRAPSTON,

**A Saddle, & 3 Bridles.**

Whoever will give Information that will lead to the discovery, and conviction of the Person or Persons, guilty of this Felony, shall receive a Reward of FIVE GUINEAS from

**HENRY LAMB,**
*Solicitor and Treasurer to the above Association.*

◀ Cranford Association rewards poster, 1829. (NRO)

***Cranford Association***
FOR
**PROSECUTING FELONS.**

**Two Guineas**
**REWARD.**

WHEREAS on *Thursday Night* last, between 9 and 10 o'Clock, some malicious and evil disposed person or persons did break the Kitchen Window of the RECTORY HOUSE, at *Cranford St. Andrew*, by throwing a large Stone, with great force, through the same, and did thereby endanger the lives of the persons who were within.---And did also break several Panes of Glass in a Frame in the Rectory Garden, and commit other Acts of wanton Mischief.

Whoever will give Information that will lead to the discovery and conviction of the person or persons guilty of the above offences, shall receive a Reward of

***Two Guineas.***

**HENRY LAMB,**
*Solicitor & Treasurer to the above Association.*

☞ As similar Acts of malicious Depredation have, at former periods, been committed in the Garden and Shrubberies of the above Premises,

**SPRING GUNS & TRAPS**
*Will, for the future, be set in them.*

KETTERING, June 3rd, 1826.

DASH, PRINTER, KETTERING.

Cranford Association reward poster, for damage in 1826. Note the dire warning of what will happen next time — the house, remember — is the Rectory. (NRO) ▶

# Arson.

## *Thrapston Association.*

SIXTY GUINEAS REWARD.

**WHEREAS** some evil-disposed **Person** or **Persons did**, on the Night of **SATURDAY** the **24th INSTANT, WILFULLY** and **MALICIOUSLY**

**SET FIRE**

*TO A RANGE OF*

**HOVELS OR SHEDS,**

***Partly covered with Beans, and partly with Straw,***

STANDING IN A FARM YARD IN THE

**PARISH OF RINGSTEAD,**

*In the County of Northampton.*

*Now in the Occupation of Mr. WM. COLEMAN.*

Notice is hereby given, That whoever will discover the Offender or Offenders, so that he, she, or they may be brought to Justice, shall, on his, her, or their Conviction, receive a Reward of FIFTY GUINEAS from the COUNTY FIRE OFFICE, and TEN GUINEAS from Mr. BENJ. LEETE, of Twywell, the Treasurer to the Thrapston Association.

If two or more were concerned, the above Rewards will be paid, on Conviction as aforesaid, to any one (except the Person who actually set Fire to the Premises), who shall discover his or her Accomplice or Accomplices.

SHERARD & ARCHBOULD,
Solicitors to the said Association.

THRAPSTON, APRIL 26TH, 1824.

DICEY & SMITHSON, PRINTERS, PARADE, NORTHAMPTON.

Thrapston Association reward poster for arson in 1824. Sixty guineas in 1824 was a substantial sum. The 'Captain Swing' rioters of 1830, remember, wanted 2s 3d per day wages. Sixty guineas, therefore, would have paid their wages for two years. (NRO)

**BROUGHTON AND CRANSLEY**

ASSOCIATION.

**3 GUINEAS**

**REWARD.**

**Whereas, on THURSDAY NIGHT, the 5th of December instant, upwards of**

**30 YOUNG FOWLS**

**were Stolen from the Farm Yard of Mr. THOMAS PULVER, in the Village of Broughton, near Kettering.**

**Whoever will give information so that the Offender or Offenders may be apprehended and convicted shall receive a reward of One Guinea from the Treasurer of this Association, and a further reward of Two Guineas will be paid by the said Thos. Pulver.**

**HENRY LAMB,**

*Solicitor and Treasurer to the above Association.*

Kettering, December 6th, 1850.

DASH, PRINTER, KETTERING.

Broughton and Cransley Association reward poster of 1850, which is fairly late in the day for the associations. (NRO)

The Broughton Association
To
Geo W Lamb

| Date | Item | £ | s | d |
|---|---|---|---|---|
| 1863. May 7 | Making up Accounts for the year - entering same in Book and attending the Annual Meeting at Broughton when usual business transacted | - | 10 | 6 |
| June 15 | Attending the Rowell + Broughton Policemen taking down particulars of a Charge of Fowl stealing from Mr John Wiggins in Sept last - Bollard of Rowell in whose house the Fowls were found having absconded immediately after the robbery and having now been apprehended at Liverpool on his way to America - advising on the evidence and instructing the Policemen as to the Witnesses whose attendance would be required at the Magistrates Meeting | - | 6 | 8 |
| 17 | Examining Witnesses before the Magistrates when Prisoner committed for Trial | - | 10 | 6 |
| | Making Copy of Depositions foll | - | 5 | 0 |
| 21 | Letter to the Clerk of the Peace with instructions for indictment | - | 3 | 6 |
| | Instructions for Brief - Drawing same and Copy - 4 Brief Sheets | 2 | 0 | 0 |
| July 2 | Attending Quarter Sessions at Northampton delivering Brief to Counsel, obtaining indictment and certificate of previous conviction - Attending in Court during Trial when Prisoner convicted and sentenced to three years penal servitude - afterwards attending taxing Costs + obtaining County allowance | 1 | 1 | 0 |
| Oct 28 | Magistrates Clerks Fees on Conviction of | | | |
| | Forward £ | 4 | 17 | 2 |

| Item | £ | s | d |
|---|---|---|---|
| Forward £ | 4 | 17 | 2 |
| William Jones for stealing growing Turnips from Mr Manton | - | 12 | 0 |
| | 5 | 9 | 2 |
| Cr By County Allowance on Mr Wiggins Prosecution | 1 | 1 | 0 |
| | £4 | 8 | 2 |

Solicitor's account to the Broughton Association, 1863, showing costs incurred in a crime of theft right through to conviction. (NRO)

had no machinery to cope with the 'street crime' of vagrancy, 'sturdy beggars' and public drunkenness, nor could they cope with riots and public disorder.

The county magistrates who were extremely concerned about the crime in the county in the mid to late 1830s, were also well aware of the minimal contribution made to the suppression of crime by the associations. So when the opportunity arrived in 1839 to establish a police force and thus try to do something about county crime, the magistrates did just that, ignoring the associations completely.

But in any case, the associations were privately run and subscribed, which put them 'outside' the official county jurisdiction. As such they could not be interfered with, and so were left to their own devices. Their subsequent decline in Northamptonshire after 1840 emphasised that, although there had been a small place for them previously, their usefulness evaporated when faced with a more effective means of placing offenders before a court, and they were never to be taken under the umbrella of 'official' law enforcement.

Although the parish constable system was creaking by the late 18th century, the real death blow was the 'Industrial Revolution', which provided the country with social conditions and environment which were totally alien to those which had existed when the system was created. The one essential ingredient of the parish constable system which had made it work for well over 500 years, was that the people lived in little, almost self-contained, settlements, where everybody knew everybody else's business.

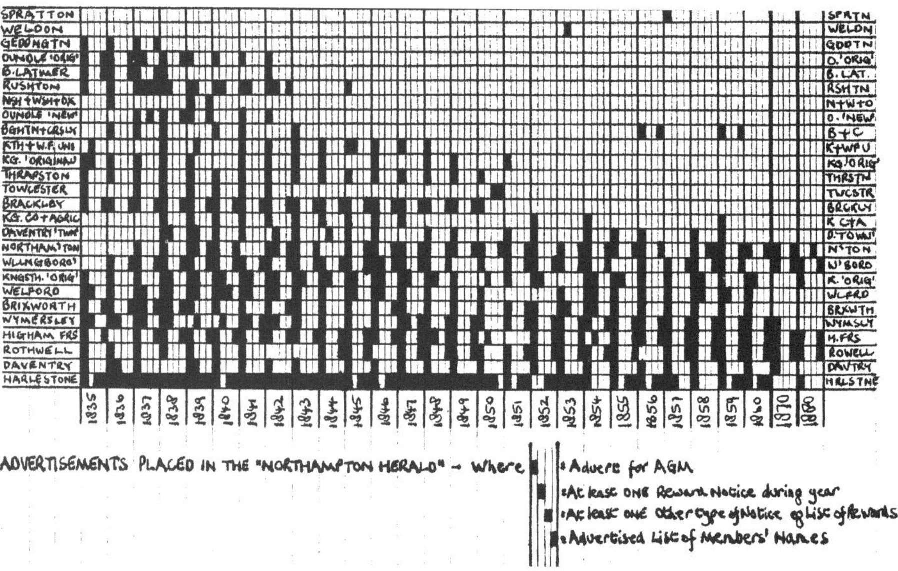


The decline in activity of the Northamptonshire private prosecution associations, based on advertisements in the *Northampton Herald*, 1835-1860, and 1870 and 1880

It is always amusing to read in the newspapers of country villages being described as 'sleepy', as the person who could write such rubbish has obviously never lived in one, because 'sleepy' is the very *last* thing they are. Everybody knows everybody else's business. And as such, if an offence occurred then everybody in that settlement, including no doubt, the parish constable himself, would know the culprit. It was thus an easy task for the constable to 'feel his collar' and transport him to the local magistrate.

However, with the coming of 'The Industrial Revolution', where villages grew and grew and met up with their neighbours doing exactly the same, then the one essential ingredient of the parish constable system was lost; everybody did not know everybody else's business. Crime thus became undetected, buried inside slums teeming with humanity, and spiralled even more out of control.

And no more so, of course, than in London itself, where at the turn of the 18th and 19th centuries, according to contemporary sources, petty crime was rampant. The result was the Metropolitan Police founded in 1829, which introduced the new concept of full-time professional police officers, rather than part-time, unpaid amateurs.

PC Robert Kitchen, Northamptonshire County Constabulary, showing the uniform of 1860

A PC of the Northampton Borough Police, 1840s. (NP)

Because of the major social changes going on at that time, the Municipal Corporation Act was passed in 1835, which gave the boroughs of the country the chance to elect a town council for their own governance. That was the main thrust of the 1835 Act, but it also said that the boroughs must elect a sub-committee, called the Watch Committee, from the main town council, and into its hands placed the responsibility of forming a full time police force for their borough along the lines of the Metropolitan Police.

In Northamptonshire, Northampton, Daventry and Higham Ferrers were the only boroughs affected by the 1835 Act. Thus, Northampton set up its force in January 1836, as did Daventry.

Daventry, however, almost overnight it seems, lost its economic livelihood and consequently never enlarged. The newly built railways took all the road trade away from the goods hauliers and passenger coaches which used the A5, on which Daventry stood. Daventry's police force therefore remained very small (only two or three men at most) until it was forcibly amalgamated with the county force in 1889.

Higham Ferrers never seems to have set up a police force at all, as no trace can be found of one. But in 1874, Higham lost its self policing powers anyway,

St Giles Square, Northampton, the County Constabulary buildings 1846-1881. The Chief Constable's house is on the right, and police headquarters on the left. The small porch in between was built in 1877.

so was subsequently policed by the County Constabulary.

The reasons for the establishment of the County Constabulary are too complicated and too lengthy to be described here. At the present time, historians are divided as to exactly *why* county police forces were set up, and there are 'for' and 'againsts' for each argument.

Suffice it to say, that the County Police Act was passed in 1839, which gave county magistrates the power to form a police force for their county if they so wished. This Act was not made mandatory because of the political situation in the country at that time (and was therefore termed the 'permissive' Act) but nevertheless, no fewer than 28 out of 56 English and Welsh counties eventually elected to establish a force under this legislation. Northamptonshire was amongst these pioneering counties, when its force was founded on Saturday 25 January 1840, with its first Chief Constable being Henry Goddard, an ex 'Bow Street Runner'.

Things however, were not smooth running, and in the first nine years of exis-

The uniform of the Northampton Borough Police c1900

tence of the county police force, numerous attempts were made to disband it, mainly on the grounds of the enormous cost to the ratepayers. The main abolitionist campaigner was the Reverend Francis Litchfield, who was Rector of Farthinghoe from 1838 until 1876. All the abolitionist attempts failed, but in any case, county police forces were eventually made compulsory by the County and Borough Police Act of 1856.

We cannot leave the subject of policing without mentioning the enormous contribution in formulating Victorian policing policy made by a Northamptonshire man. The 1856 County and Borough Police Act in making police forces compulsory, also established the Inspectorate of Constabulary, which had the task of inspecting every police force in the country to see whether or not it was 'efficient' as a police force. If it was thought to be, then central government would pay 25 per cent (later 50 per cent) of the yearly pay and clothing bill of that force.

William Cartwright, of the old Northamptonshire family from Aynho was the very first Inspector to be chosen, in August 1856. Although not a policeman, it was Cartwright who was by far and away the most influential of the first three

County police officers at Wellingborough c1900, showing style of uniform.

Farthinghoe Rectory, near Brackley, March , 1842.

REVEREND SIR,

A notice which, in consequence of no magistrate more influential than myself in property and station having taken the matter up, I have been induced to give relative to the Police Force in this county, will come under discussion at the ensuing Quarter Sessions. The main question involved in that notice must, it is obvious, refer to the method best calculated to effect the prevention and detection of crime. A more important public question, or one more deeply interesting to the clergy, can scarcely be imagined. I trust, therefore, I shall not be deemed presumptuous in the hope I entertain, that my Reverend Brethren will favour me with their kind and cordial co-operation, in an endeavour to throw light on so momentous a subject as the ***present state of crime*** in Northamptonshire, its probable *causes* and proper *remedies*. It is with that hope that I have framed a number of queries intended to elicit what would, I believe, if extended to its full and farthest limits, constitute a mass of invaluable statistical information. Such information has never before been obtained, or perhaps asked for, nor could it be got, I am inclined to think, more effectually, than by some such appeal as I now make to the good sense, sympathy and assistance of the parochial Clergy. In proportion as they consent to aid this enquiry shall I be able to profit by the opportunity now presenting itself, of advancing a cause about which they ever show themselves most warmly anxious. The opinions of intelligent Gentlemen known to be solicitous for the public morality and peace will thus be collected from every Parish in the county. Facts as the groundwork of those opinions will also be acquired, by which something like a safe general conclusion may be arrived at, respecting the *causes* which may have rendered additional protection necessary at this time, the expediency of a Police as that protection, the efficiency and adequacy to its object of the Force now in existence, the propriety of a change, whether reaching to an entire discontinuance of the Force or to a partial or extensive alteration, as well as the desirableness and means of substituting in its stead a system of paid parochial, or district constabulary. It will of course be desirable that I should be able to substantiate the facts communicated to me by quoting my authority if occasion require it. Should, however, objections exist to the authority being made known, any expression of your wishes to that effect will be strictly attended to.

I take the liberty, therefore, Reverend Sir, of requesting, that, after communicating with such Rate-payers, Proprietors of Land, and others as you may deem most capable of giving useful suggestions and information, you will have the goodness to reply to the queries annexed, to the best of your judgment and at your earliest leisure. Your compliance with this request will greatly oblige,

Reverend Sir,

Your faithful and obedient Servant,

FRANCIS LITCHFIELD.

P.S. The Queries to which this circular refers have become more necessary and more numerous in consequence of Mr. Goddard's refusal to let me inspect his books previous to the ensuing Quarter Sessions, or to allow his men to convey these Queries to the Clergy in the course of their walks through the Parishes of their Districts.

Circular letter sent to fellow clergymen (the majority of whom would be magistrates) by Rev Francis Litchfield, Rector of Farthinghoe. He was the most vociferous of the campaigners to abolish the county constabulary, which had been established in 1840. (NRO)

# PUBLIC NOTICE,

# POLICEMEN WANTED.

The very extensive remodelling of the Police Force of this County, and the Irish Military Rule established,— Reduction of Pay,— Increase of duty, No fixed time, Perpetual Motion,— and the total subversion of respectability in the force, has caused a great Number of Vacancies.

## WE THEREFORE GIVE NOTICE,

That all who are strong enough to perform 24 hours duty, daily, do it for nothing! maintain Themselves, their Wives, and Families respectably !! keep out of Debt !!! and submit to undergo the following DEGRADATIONS, may probably be successful candidates.

To have their BEDS!! their Own, and their WIVE'S LINEN examined!! should the HUSBAND be absent during the time the house is being rummaged, the WIFE will be required to hold her HUSBAND'S MASTER'S HORSE.

They must also submit to have it Published in the Newspapers, and posted in every PUBLIC HOUSE that they are drunkards.

They must submit to be Watched by every Thief and Blackguard in the Country, who may report them, and upon such testimony they must suffer Punishment without Murmuring.

Those who possess the above qualifications (without hope of promotion or reward) may make Application to the Head Police Office, Northampton, or to a Rector on the borders of Oxfordshire.

Sign'd,

TRUTH.

Northampton Sep. 8th. 1849

A spoof recruiting poster probably issued by disgruntled policemen because of the shake up and reorganisation of the force by the new Chief Constable, Henry Bayly, who was Irish and had served in the para-military Irish Constabulary. The Rectory on the borders of Oxfordshire, is, of course, Farthinghoe. (NRO)

The County Constabulary uniform, just prior to the Great War.

Inspectors, and a lot of his recommendations are still recognisable in the police force of today, nearly 150 years later.

For the first few years, the county police were a supplement to, and not a replacement for, the old system of parish constables. But as time progressed the parish constables, being unpaid amateurs could not hope to compete with the full-time professional policemen, and so by the 1850s, their influence and contribution to the criminal justice system of the county was waning seriously, along with the private prosecution associations.

Thus by the 1860s, the policing of the county was effectively in the hands of the Northamptonshire County Constabulary and the Northampton Borough

William Cartwright, a Northamptonshire man, from the Aynho family. He was the first Inspector of Constabulary in 1856, and arguably, the most influential. (NRO)

Police. These two forces remained side by side in the county until 1966 when they were (forcibly) amalgamated by the Home Secretary to form the Northampton and County Constabulary, which in turn was renamed the Northamptonshire Police in 1974. A list of all Chief Constables is given in Appendix 4.

If anyone wants to know the full history of the Northampton Borough Police and the Northamptonshire County Constabulary, then by far and away the best (indeed, the only) book to look at, is *Policing Northamptonshire 1836-1986*, by an author whose name escapes me.

# CHAPTER 5

## 'THE ONLY PLACE TO LEARN THE WORLD IN': TRIALS AND COURTS IN NORTHAMPTONSHIRE

"Courts and army camps are the only place to learn the world in."
The Earl of Chesterfield (1694-1773)
Letter to his son, 2 October 1747:

THE end product of a policing system is the accused person, who then has to be examined to see whether or not he, or she, has broken the rules laid down by society, and thus punished or released. And it was quickly found out that a standard procedure and a set of rules governing these examinations had to be evolved so that both sides of the argument could be heard fairly. So the trial and courts system grew up as a result of the needs of the time, and not vice-versa.

Thus every hundred held a hundred court every month, which was presided over by the county sheriff, or his bailiff acting as deputy. The county sheriff, remember, was the man directly responsible to the king for the King's Peace in his county.

And as well as overseeing the hundred court, the sheriff also visited every tithing twice every year at Easter and Michaelmas, to see if, in his view, the system of frankpledge was working. His court, therefore, touring round each tithing, came to be known as the court tourn, or the alternative name, the view of frankpledge. It is doubtful whether any written records were ever made of these courts, but if they were, not one has survived, either for Northamptonshire, or anywhere else.

After the Norman Conquest under the system known as feudalism, the unit of local government came to be called the manor rather than the tithing. Rather than take the cases to the hundred courts every month, or wait for the court tourn to visit every six months, it was expedient, and cheaper, to try the petty criminal cases there and then in the manor. These courts came to be known, not surprisingly, as manorial courts, or an alternative name, the court leet, where leet was

COUNTY OF NORTHAMPTON.

# A CALENDAR OF PRISONERS

FOR TRIAL AT THE

# ASSIZES,

TO BE HOLDEN AT NORTHAMPTON,

ON THURSDAY, THE FOURTH DAY OF DECEMBER, 1856.

BEFORE THE HONORABLE SIR JAMES SHAW WILLES, KNIGHT,

*One of the Justices of our Lady the Queen of Her Court of Common Pleas.*

OSCAR WILLIAM HAMBROUGH, ESQUIRE, HIGH SHERIFF.
HENRY PHILIP MARKHAM, GENTLEMAN, UNDER SHERIFF AND CLERK OF THE PEACE.

N.B.—(N.) signifies neither read nor write; (R.) read only; (Imp.) read and write imperfectly; (Well) read and write well; (Sup.) superior education.

INDEX.



T. E. DICEY, PRINTER, MERCURY OFFICE, NORTHAMPTON.

The Calendar for the 1856 Winter Assizes, issued after the Assizes had finished, and giving the Verdict and Sentence. See pages 138 to 140. (NRO)

| No. | NAME. | Age. | TRADE. | Degree of Instruction. | Name and Address of Committing Magistrate. | Date of Warrant. | When received into Custody. | Offence as charged in the Commitment. | When tried. | Before whom tried. | Verdict of the Jury. | Sentence or Order of the Court. |
|---|---|---|---|---|---|---|---|---|---|---|---|---|
| | | | | | IN THE COUNTY GAOL AT NORTHAMPTON. | | | | | | | |
| 1 | JOSEPH IRESON . . . Once before convicted of felony. | 20 | Labourer . | R. | W. S. Rose, Esq., Cransley, Kettering; J. B. Robinson, Esq., Cranford, Thrapston. | 13th Aug., 1856 . | 13th Aug., 1856 . | Wilfully setting fire to a barn and a stack of straw, the property of Thomas Jennaway, at Sibbertoft, on the 4th August, 1856. | 4th Dec., 1856 | Mr. Justice Willes . | Guilty of arson. | Transportation for life. |
| 2 | JOHN DUNLEERY . . . | 18 | Private in the 98th Regt. Foot | N. | C. C. Elwes, Esq., Great Billing, Northampton. | 22nd Sept., 1856 | 22nd Sept., 1856 | Stealing one sovereign and a pair of boots, the property of Charles Fordyce, from his person, at Floore, on the 16th September, 1856. | 4th Dec., 1856 | Ditto . . . | John Dunleery, guilty of highway robbery; James Crawford, acquitted of highway robbery; William Winwood, guilty of highway robbery. | John Dunleery to be imprisoned, with hard labour, for One Year, in the House of Correction at Northampton; William Winwood to be imprisoned, with hard labour, for Six Calendar Months, in the House of Correction at Northampton. |
| 3 | JAMES CRAWFORD . . and | 20 | Ditto . | Imp. | | | | | | | | |
| 4 | WILLIAM WINWOOD . . | 19 | Ditto . | Imp. | | | | | | | | |
| 5 | HENRY HARRIS . . . Twice before convicted of felony. | 17 | Labourer . | Imp. | Thos. Tryon, Esq., Bulwick; John Yorke, Esq., Thrapston. | 29th Sept., 1856 . | 30th Sept., 1856 . | Carnally knowing a certain ewe sheep, at Harringworth, on the 20th September, 1856. | 5th Dec., 1856 | Ditto . . . | Guilty of an attempt at buggery. | Imprisonment, with hard labour, for Two Years, in the House of Correction at Northampton. |
| 6 | JOSEPH WRIGHT . . . Three times before summarily convicted. | 32 | Labourer . | Imp. | T. B. Robinson, Esq., Cranford, Thrapston. | 1st Oct., 1856 . | 3rd Oct., 1856 . | Stealing 11s. 6d., the property of Jabez Smith, from his person, at Kettering, on the 29th September, 1856. | 4th Dec., 1856 | Ditto . . . | Guilty of highway robbery. | Imprisonment, with hard labour, for Six Calendar Months, in the House of Correction at Northampton. |
| 7 | (On Bail.) JOHN LANGLEY . . . Four times before for poaching. and | 30 | Labourer . | Imp. | . . . . . . | Rendered . . | 4th Dec., 1856 . | For having, in the night time of the 7th October, 1856, at the parish of Gretton, with other persons, entered certain enclosed land, armed, for the purpose of taking game. | 4th Dec., 1856 | Ditto . . . | Severally pleaded guilty of night poaching. | Imprisonment, with hard labour, for Six Calendar Months each, in the House of Correction at Northampton. |
| 8 | EDMUND SNOWDEN . . Four times before for poaching. | 25 | Labourer . | N. | W. B. Stopford, Esq., Drayton House, Thrapston. | 8th Oct., 1856 . | 10th Oct., 1856 . | | | | | |
| 9 | ROBERT JONES . . . Four times before for assaults. | 35 | Drover . | Imp. | C. C. Elwes, Esq., Great Billing, Northampton. | 11th Oct., 1856 . | 11th Oct., 1856 . | Wounding Thomas Herbert Hart, at Dallington, on the 6th October, 1856, with intent to do him some grievous bodily harm. | 5th Dec., 1856 | Ditto . . . | Guilty of unlawfully wounding. | Imprisonment, with hard labour, for Twelve Calendar Months, in the House of Correction at Northampton. |
| 10 | WILLIAM WHITE . . . Once before convicted of felony. | 27 | Bootcloser . | Imp. | C. Markham, Esq., Mayor of Northampton; Wm. Hollis, and Wm. Dennis, Esqrs., Northampton. | 3rd Oct., 1856 . | 3rd Oct., 1856 . | Assaulting Martha Appleby, at Dallington, on the 8th February, 1854. | 5th Dec., 1856 | Ditto . . . | Guilty of an indecent assault. | Imprisonment, with hard labour, for Eighteen Calendar Months, in the House of Correction at Northampton. |
| 11 | JONATHAN GOODMAN . . | 52 | Labourer . | R. | P. E. Hicks, Esq., Gent., Coroner, Northampton. | 29th Oct., 1856 . | 29th Oct., 1856 . | Manslaughter of William Payne, at Ravensthorpe. | 4th Dec., 1856 | Ditto . . . | Acquitted of manslaughter. | |

| | | | | | | | | | | | | |
|---|---|---|---|---|---|---|---|---|---|---|---|---|
| 12 | THOMAS ONLEY | 12 | Labourer | Imp. | J. Nethercoat, Esq., Moulton Grange, Northampton. | 15th Nov., 1856 | 15th Nov., 1856 | Wilfully and maliciously placing a slab of wood on the railway of the London and North-Western Railway Company, at the parish of Heyford, on the 4th November, 1856. | 4th Dec., 1856 | Ditto | Pleaded guilty to placing a piece of wood on a railway. | Imprisonment, with hard labour, for 14 days, in the House of Correction at Northampton, and at the expiration thereof to be taken to the Reformatory School at Tiffield, in this county, and there be detained for the further term of Five Years. |
| 13 | (On Bail.) JOHN CLEAVER | 38 | Labourer | Imp. | | Rendered | 4th Dec., 1856 | Stealing certain pieces of wood, the property of William Cole, at Sulgrave, on the 17th November, 1856. | 4th Dec., 1856 | Ditto | Severally acquitted of larceny. | |
| 14 | WILLIAM WRIGHT. Twice before summarily convicted. | 38 | Labourer | Imp. | A. J. Empson, Clerk, Eydon Rectory, Daventry. | 24th Nov., 1856 | 25th Nov., 1856 | | | | | |
| 15 | ALFRED HARRIS | 20 | Shopman | Well | W. M. Dolben, Esq., Finedon Hall, Wellingborough. | 24th Nov., 1856 | 25th Nov., 1856 | Stealing a quantity of new clothes and other articles, the property of Edwin Dunmer, at Wellingborough, in the month of November last. | 4th Dec., 1856 | Ditto | Pleaded guilty of larceny as a servant. | Imprisonment, with hard labour, for Twelve Calendar Months, in the House of Correction at Northampton. |
| | | | | | | | | Also with having, on the 18th November last, feloniously embezzled certain sums of money which he had received in the name and on the account of the said Edwin Dunmer, his master. | | | Pleaded guilty of embezzlement. | |
| 16 | (On Bail.) WILLIAM EDWARDS | 28 | Builder | Imp. | | Rendered | 5th Dec., 1856 | Assaulting Ann Matthews, at Long Buckby, on the 10th August, 1856. | 5th Dec., 1856 | Ditto | Acquitted of rape. | |
| 17 | JAMES ALDRIDGE | 25 | Tailor | Imp. | The Right Hon. the Earl Pomfret, Easton Neston, Towcester. | 29th Nov., 1856 | 29th Nov., 1856 | Stealing 4lb. of bacon, value 3s., the property of Joseph Blythe Stevens, at Towcester, on the 27th November, 1856. | 4th Dec., 1856 | Ditto | Guilty of larceny. | Imprisonment, with hard labour, for Six Calendar Months, in the House of Correction at Northampton. |

JOHN GRANT,
Governor of said Gaol.

## IN THE BOROUGH GAOL AT NORTHAMPTON.

| | | | | | | | | | | | | |
|---|---|---|---|---|---|---|---|---|---|---|---|---|
| 18 | (On Bail.) RICHARD PEARSON | 43 | General dealer | Imp. | | Rendered | 5th Dec., 1856 | Wounding William Smith, at Northampton, on the 24th July, 1856, with intent to do him some grievous bodily harm. | 5th Dec., 1856 | Ditto | Guilty of unlawfully wounding. | To enter into his own recognizance in the sum of £100, and two sureties in the sum of £50 each, to keep the peace towards all Her Majesty's subjects for twelve calendar months, and to come up for judgment whenever called upon. |

GEO. ARKESDEN,
Governor of said Gaol.

possibly a corruption of an older word 'lathe' meaning division of a county.

Manorial courts, or courts leet, were therefore the sessions for trying the petty criminal cases of each manor (and then of the parish, as the manor would eventually be called) and are the forerunners of today's magistrates' courts. It was the court leet which also chose the constable for the ensuing year. The courts leet only tried the petty crimes. More serious crimes occurring in the manor had to be referred onwards and upwards to the court tourn.

A written record (called rolls) of these manorial courts was taken down at the time, by a scribe writing in Latin. A few manorial rolls survive for Northamptonshire, mainly from the late 15th century onwards, but one of the earliest is that from Weedon Bec in 1248.

However, when we read the cases recorded in this roll, they are depressingly familiar. If you go into any criminal court today, you will find exactly the same old offences, excuses and judgements as are recorded in the Weedon Bec manorial roll. For instance, at the Weedon Bec court held on the Feast of Saint Peter in Chains (Saturday 1 August) 1248, Hugh of Stanbridge complained that William of Stanbridge and the wife of Gilbert the Vicar's son, beat and unlawfully struck him and dragged him by his hair out of his house, by which he suffered damage to his house worth 40s, and loss of dignity to the tune of 20s.

Obviously finding the blame equal between all three, the court's decision was that they all be bound over to keep the peace towards each other in the sum of 6s 8d, which they will forfeit to the lord of the manor if they are found guilty of any offence against each other again. The bind over to be of good behaviour after a Breach of the (King's/Queen's) Peace is still in use today, see Chapter 3.

But courts leet only tried the petty stuff. More serious criminal cases were sent to the courts tourn, but eventually came to be sent to an even higher court, which was slowly evolving.

Soon after the Conquest which gave him his nickname, king William of England needed to impose a strong government to subjugate his new country, so he collected together administrators and judges learned in both civil and criminal law into one body. This was called the King's Court, or in Latin, Curia Regis, and because of the superior competence of the judges in it, this eventually came to be regarded as the senior court of the country. It was the Curia Regis for instance, which administered the commissioners who compiled the Domesday Book in 1086.

But eventually, the Curia Regis, because it became too big, had to split into separate courts, each dealing with a specific set of cases. Thus the courts of the King's Bench, the Common Pleas and The Exchequer came into being. The story of this is fascinating, but it does not concern us at this moment.

Because of the difficulty that coming to London posed for some people, it became easier and acceptable for the judges of the Curia Regis to go to the cases, rather than the cases go to the judges. Curia Regis judges therefore made regu-

COUNTY OF NORTHAMPTON.

A

# CALENDAR OF PRISONERS

FOR TRIAL AT

# THE ASSIZES,

HOLDEN AT NORTHAMPTON

On Monday, the Seventeenth, Tuesday, the Eighteenth, and Wednesday, the Nineteenth, Days of January, 1881,

BEFORE

THE HONOURABLE GEORGE DENMAN,

*One of the Justices of the Common Pleas Division of the High Court of Justice;*

AND

JOHN PATRICK MURPHY, ESQUIRE,

*One of Her Majesty's Counsel learned in the Law.*

HENRY VANE FORESTER HOLDICH HUNGERFORD, ESQUIRE, HIGH SHERIFF.
ARTHUR DUKE COLERIDGE, ESQUIRE, CLERK OF ASSIZE.
HENRY WILLIAM KENNEDY MARKHAM, GENTLEMAN, UNDER SHERIFF.

N.B.—(N.) signifies neither read nor write (Imp.) read and write imperfectly; (Well) read and write well; (Sup.) superior education.

INDEX.

| NAME. | No. | NAME. | No. |
|---|---|---|---|
| Cadd, Frederick | 14 | Hawkes, Joseph | 4 |
| Cadd, Maria | 15 | Jones, Ellen | 2 |
| Dainty, John | 1 | Smart, William | 10 |
| Drage, Thomas | 9 | Stanton, Benjamin | 5 |
| Edmunds, Fletcher Euston | 7 | Thornton, Robert | 13 |
| Flynn, Edward | 6 | Willis, George | 11 |
| Gray, William | 12 | Wilson, Fred | 8 |
| Hawkes, George | 3 | | |

BUTTERFIELD AND SON, HERALD STEAM PRINTING WORKS NORTHAMPTON.

The 1881 Winter Assizes Calendar. Each prisoner's criminal record is now included. Note the number of assaults on police by George Hawkes, and still only 22. See pages 138 to 140. (NRO)

## IN HER MAJESTY'S PRISON AT NORTHAMPTON.

| No. | NAME. | Age. | TRADE. | Degree of Instruction. | Name and Address of Committing Magistrate. | Date of Warrant. | When received into Custody. | Offences as Charged in the Commitment. | When Tried. | Before whom Tried. | Verdict of the Jury. | Particulars of Previous Convictions charged in the Indictment and proved in Court. | Sentence or Order of the Court. |
|---|---|---|---|---|---|---|---|---|---|---|---|---|---|
| 1 | JOHN DAINTY............... | 18 | Labourer ... | Imp. | G. H. Capron, Clerk, Southwick Hall, Oundle. | 1880. Nov. 2nd. | 1880. Nov. 2nd. | Maliciously placing upon a certain Railway, called the Northampton and Peterborough Line, a certain piece of wood, to wit, a fence rail, with intent to endanger the safety of certain persons travelling upon the said Railway, at Thorpe Achurch, on the 18th October, 1880. | 1881. ............... | ............................ | ..................... | ................................... | Removed to Berry Wood Asylum, Nov. 25, 1880, by order of the Secretary of State, he having been certified to be insane. True bills are now found against him, but he is confined in a Lunatic Asylum; the trial is therefore postponed. |
| ... | The Same. JOHN DAINTY............ | ... | ............... | ... | G. H. Capron, Clerk. | Nov. 2nd. | Nov. 2nd. | Stealing eleven brace-bits, of the value of 6s., the property of Samuel Warner, at Titchmarsh, on the 19th October, 1880. | | | | | |
| ... | The Same. JOHN DAINTY............... | ... | ............... | ... | G. H. Capron, Clerk. .. | Nov. 2nd. | Nov. 2nd. | Stealing certain brasses of cart-horse harness, to wit, eleven pieces of brass, and also certain pieces of leather, of the value together of £1, the property of Robert Joseph Chew, at Wigsthorpe, on the 19th October, 1880. | | | | | |
| 2 | ELLEN JONES ............... | 18 | Single Woman | Well | C. J. Strong, Esq., Peterborough. | Nov. 10th. | Nov. 10th. | Wilful murder of her illegitimate female child, at Peterborough, on the 9th October, 1880. | Jan. 18th. | J. P. Murphy, Esq., Commissioner. | Not guilty ......... | ................................... | To be discharged. |
| 3 | GEORGE HAWKES ........ Wellingborough:—Dec. 20, 1878, assaulting police, fined 19s. 6d.; Sept. 13, 1878, poaching, fined 29s. 6d.; Oct. 16, 1877, assaulting police, 2 calendar months, hard labour; Sept. 15, 1876, poaching, 1 month, hard labour; Sept. 15, 1876, assaulting police, 6 weeks, hard labour; Nov. 26, 1875, assaulting police, one month, hard labour. | 22 | Shoemaker ... | Imp. | H. W. Beauford, Esq. Sudborough House, Thrapston. | Nov. 25th. | Nov. 26th. | Feloniously wounding one George Wilfrid Currin, he being a police-constable, and in the due execution of his duty, with intent to do him some grievous bodily harm, at Twywell, on the 19th August, 1880. | Jan. 19th. | Mr. Justice Denman ... | Guilty ............ | ................................... | Seven years penal servitude. |
| 4 | and JOSEPH HAWKES ........... Northamptonshire January Sessions, 1877, stealing two tame rabbits, 21 days, hard labour, and 5 years Reformatory. | 18 | Labourer ... | Imp. | ............................ | ........... | ........... | ............................................................ | Jan. 19th. | Mr. Justice Denman ... | Guilty ............ | ................................... | Five years penal servitude. |
| 5 | BENJAMIN STANTON...... (Bailed Dec. 2, 1880.) | 47 | Shoemanufacturer | Well | R. Derby, Esq., Mayor, Northampton. | Dec. 1st. | Dec. 1st. | Forging and uttering the acceptance of one James Earl to a certain bill of exchange, for the payment of £16 8s. 6d., with intent thereby to defraud, at Northampton, on the 22nd November, 1880. | Jan. 19th. | J. P. Murphy, Esq., Commissioner. | Not guilty ......... | ................................... | To be discharged. |
| 6 | EDWARD FLYNN ........... | 26 | Labourer ... | R. | Capt. E. Stopford, R.N., Falconer's Hill, Daventry. | Dec. 8th. | Dec. 8th. | Feloniously setting fire to a stack of straw, the property of John Hands, at Welton, on the 1st December, 1880. | Jan. 18th. | J. P. Murphy, Esq., Commissioner. | Not guilty ......... | ................................... | To be discharged. |

| | | | | | | | | | | | | | |
|---|---|---|---|---|---|---|---|---|---|---|---|---|---|
| 7 | FLETCHER EUSTON EDMUNDS | 26 | Clerk ... | Well | R. Derby, Esq., Mayor. | 1880. Dec. 29th. | 1880. Dec. 29th. | Receiving and taking into his possession three several sums of money, amounting to £28 10s., being employed in the capacity of Clerk to Messrs. Phipps, and feloniously and fraudulently embezzling the same, at Northampton, on the 19th June, 1880, and within six months thereafter. | 1881. Jan. 18.... | J. P. Murphy, Esq., Commissioner. | Pleaded guilty ... | ............ | 15 calendar months, hard labour. |
| ... | The Same. FLETCHER EUSTON EDMUNDS | ... | ............ | ... | R. Derby, Esq. ...... | Dec. 29th. | Dec. 29th. | Being employed in the capacity of Clerk to Messrs Phipps, stealing £1,060, the moneys of the said Messrs. Phipps, at Northampton, on the 19th October, 1880. | Jan. 18 ... | J. P. Murphy, Esq., Commissioner. | Pleaded guilty ... | ............ | |
| 8 | FRED WILSON ............ (On Bail.) | 23 | Rivetter ..... | Imp. | The Right Honourable the Lord Henley, Watford Court, Rugby. | Nov. 3rd. | ......... | Burglariously breaking and entering the dwelling-house of George Moore, and therein feloniously stealing the sum of £3 5s. 0d., his monies, at Long Buckby, about the hour of twelve in the night of the 23rd October, 1880. | Jan. 18.... | Mr. Justice Denman ... | Not guilty ........ | ............ | To be discharged. |
| 9 | THOMAS DRAGE ........... (On Bail.) | 27 | Labourer ... | N. | H. M. Stockdale, Esq., Mears Ashby Hall, Northampton. | Dec. 10th. | ......... | Breaking and entering the shop of Johnson Kilsby, and therein stealing twelve pairs of boots, nine pairs of boot tops, and three pairs of soles, of the value of £5, the property of the said Johnson Kilsby, at Wollaston, on the 12th November, 1880. | Jan. 18.... | J. P. Murphy, Esq., Commissioner. | Pleaded guilty ... | ............ | Four calendar months, hard labour. |
| 10 | and WILLIAM SMART ... ..... | 22 | Shoemaker... | Imp. | F. U. Sartoris, Esq., Rushden Hall, Higham Ferrers....... ....... | 1881. Jan. 14th. | 1881. Jan. 14th. | ............ | Jan. 18.... | J. P. Murphy, Esq., Commissioner. | Pleaded guilty ... | ............ | Four calendar months, hard labour. |
| 11 | GEORGE WILLIS .......... | 24 | Shoemaker... | Imp. | Capt. E. Stopford, R.N. | Jan. 12th | Jan. 12th | Burglariously breaking and entering the dwelling-house of George Moore, and therein feloniously stealing the sum of £3 5s. 0d., of the monies of the said George Moore, at Long Buckby, about the hour of twelve in the night of the 23rd October, 1880. | ............ | ............ | No true bill ...... | ............ | To be discharged. |
| 12 | WILLIAM GRAY ........... | 50 | Labourer ... | Imp. | H. W. Beauford, Esq. | Jan. 14th. | Jan. 14th. | Committing wilful and corrupt perjury at Thrapston, on 11th January, 1881. | Jan. 19.... | Mr. Justice Denman ... | Not guilty ........ | ............ | To be discharged. |

| | | | | | | | | | | | | | |
|---|---|---|---|---|---|---|---|---|---|---|---|---|---|
| 13 | ROBERT THORNTON ...... Northampton, July 10, 1880, drunkenness, fined 20s.; Leicester, 1879, assault, fined 32s. 6d.; Northampton:—Feb. 12, 1876, drunkenness, fined 30s. 6d.; Feb. 27, 1875, drunkenness, fined 19s. 6d.; Dec. 12, 1874, game trespass, 21 days, hard labour; Dec. 27, 1873, game trespass, fined 30s. 6d. Daventry:—Jan. 11, 1871, poaching, fined 49s. 6d.; Nov. 13, 1867, wilful damage, 2 months, hard labour. and | 36 | Plumber...... | Imp. | H. O. Nethercote, Esq., Moulton Grange, Northampton. | 1881. Jan. 15th. | 1881. Jan. 15th. | Stealing eight tame fowls, the property of John William Cattell, at Duston, on the 8th January, 1881. | 1881. Jan. 18.... | J. P. Murphy, Esq., Commissioner. | Pleaded guilty ... | ................................ | Two calendar months, hard labour. |
| 14 | FREDERICK CADD... ...... Northampton:—Sept. 4, 1880, keeping dog without license, 1 calendar month, hard labour; July 17, 1880, game trespass, 1 calendar month, hard labour; March 13, 1880, neglecting to send child to school, order made; Aug. 23, 1879, poaching, 1 calendar month, hard labour; April 19, 1879, keeping dog without license, fined 19s. 6d.; March 15, 1879, game trespass, 14 days, hard labour; June 13, 1873, embezzling leather, 6 months, hard labour; Northamptonshire October Sessions, 1869, stealing wheat, 9 calendar months, hard labour. Northampton:—Aug. 22, 1864, damaging work, 14 days, hard labour; Jan. 7, 1863, embezzling leather, 3 calendar months, hard labour. | 35 | Shoemaker... | Imp. | ........................ ... | ............ | ............ | ........................................................ | Jan. 18.... | J. P. Murphy, Esq., Commissioner. | Pleaded guilty ... | Northamptonshire Quarter Sessions, October, 1869, stealing wheat, 9 calendar months, hard labour. | Nine calendar months, hard labour. |
| 15 | MARIA CADD ............... Northampton, July 29, 1873, larceny, 3 months, hard labour. | 35 | Married Woman | Imp. | H. O. Nethercote, Esq. | Jan. 15th. | Jan. 15th. | Receiving four tame fowls, the property of John William Cattell, well-knowing them to have been stolen, at Duston, on the 8th January, 1881. | Jan. 18.... | J. P. Murphy, Esq., Commissioner. | Guilty ........... | Northampton, July 29, 1873, larceny, 3 months, hard labour. | Six calendar months, hard labour. |

J. HOWE,

Governor of the said Prison.

lar tours throughout the counties of England during the Norman period.

It was then just a short step to the next development, royal judges making regular and set journeys round each county in turn, for the purposes of trying suspected criminals accused of major offences. Thus were born the county Assizes.

The administering of the law was strict during Norman times, as an alien ruling house had to impose their wills on a conquered country. But it was left to that most charismatic of early kings, Henry II, to add the next vital ingredient.

By the Assizes of Clarendon in 1166, and of Northampton in 1176 (Assize is Norman French for the gathering together of important people for the purposes of law making, and this emphasises the importance of Northampton during that period) it was decreed that a jury consisting of 12 representatives of each hundred of each county had to present to the authorities any person they suspected of serious crime within their hundred. These 'presentments' were first made to the county sheriff in the court tourn after being passed on by the courts leet, who because of the seriousness of the crime, felt it outside their competence.

The court tourn was given power to try the lesser offences, but for the greater offences (such as murders, serious assaults and the like, which were coming to be known as 'felonies') the alleged offenders had to be kept in custody, and the hundred jury had to present them to the Curia Regis/Assize judge when next he came visiting to the county, as it was also decreed that from then on, felons could only be tried by Assize judges.

The Assizes also had the power to try civil as well as criminal cases. The civil cases were obviously heard separately, in a court called the 'Nisi Prius'. All civil cases had to be tried before the Curia Regis in London, and the sheriffs were directed to bring the cases to London on a certain day, 'unless before that day' (Latin = 'nisi prius') the Assize judge visited the county, which, of course, they always did.

In the earliest days of the Assizes however, jurisprudence was still in the rudimentary stages, and for about 60 years after the Assize of Clarendon, alleged felons presented before the Assize by the hundred jury, still had to undergo the trial by combat or trial by ordeal.

In those God fearing times, it was thought that an appeal to the judgement of God was the best determination of guilt or innocence, rather than the tedious and lengthy job of weighing up the ascertainable facts. The trials by combat and ordeal had therefore been used since the year dot to just that.

When a person was accused of a crime, his accuser had to come along to the court and accuse him to his face in front of the open court. The court could then rule that a judicial duel be fought between the two parties, the winner of the duel obviously being regarded as the innocent one. Not surprisingly, few of these offers were taken up, especially if the accused was bigger and stronger. If this happened, or the accuser was still too badly injured or ill, then the trial by ordeal was resorted to. If the accused was a free man, then he was tried in the ordeal by hot iron. If he was a villain, then he was tried by water.

The ordeal by hot iron was either holding a red hot plough share in the hand, or walking barefoot over them. If the person was unhurt, he was innocent; if he was injured, he was guilty.

The ordeal by water was either hot or cold. The hot water type of ordeal had the alleged offender plunging his arm in boiling water: no injury meant innocence, scarred for life meant guilty. The cold water ordeal consisted of throwing the alleged offender into a pond or river. If he sank, he was innocent, if he floated, he was guilty. The Northamptonshire Assize roll of 1203 records two cases of trial by ordeal by cold water, but unfortunately, not their result.

But in 1215, by the Lateran Council, the Church decreed that it could no longer uphold the truths of these ordeals as being 'judgements of God'. Trials by ordeal therefore quickly fell into obsolescence. This new development then presented the authorities with a question. If there was to be no more trial by ordeal, how is guilt to be determined? It is this precise point in time, that has been called 'the moment of extreme importance in the history of the English criminal law'.

Had the judges themselves decided guilt or innocence, then our criminal justice system would have become 'inquisitorial', similar to that of France with its examining magistrate determining guilt or innocence. English sense prevailed however on this question, and eventually the system of bringing in another jury, quite separate and distinct from the hundred or grand jury, came into being.

This second jury was called the petty jury (Norman French again, petty meaning lesser, modern French, petit = small). And because of the possible and obvious danger of a person from the accusing jury (the grand jury) sitting on the determining jury (the petty jury), in 1351 a Statute was passed forbidding members of the grand jury from sitting on the petty jury.

Before the trial by ordeal finally petered out however, there were some alleged felons who wanted to be tried by ordeal rather than by jury. These people were kept in prison and 'persuaded' (which meant torturing, of course) to be tried by jury. This practice actually survived into later times, where a person who refused to plead before a court, was tortured in an attempt to make him plead one way or the other. In Northamptonshire, we actually have an example of this, as late as the 17th century, where a prisoner was 'pressed' to death when he refused to enter a plea before a court, but see Chapter 6 for more details on that one.

There only remained one more development in the criminal justice system of the country. This was the coming of the Justices of the Peace, otherwise called Magistrates, during the 14th century, and the evolvement of their court of Quarter Sessions.

Richard the Lionheart, king of England, in 1195 commissioned knights in every shire of the land to take surety from everyone over the age of 16 to ensure that they 'kept the peace'. This arrangement continued, and by the 13th century, these selected knights were known as 'custodes pacis', or keepers of the peace.

COUNTY OF NORTHAMPTON.

# A CALENDAR OF PRISONERS

FOR TRIAL AT THE

GENERAL QUARTER SESSIONS OF THE PEACE,

TO BE HOLDEN AT NORTHAMPTON,

ON WEDNESDAY, THE FIRST DAY OF JULY, 1857.

THE RIGHT HON. THE LORD SOUTHAMPTON, CHAIRMAN.

WILLIAM HARCOURT ISHAM MACKWORTH DOLBEN, ESQUIRE, HIGH SHERIFF.
HENRY PHILIP MARKHAM, GENTLEMAN, UNDER SHERIFF, AND CLERK OF THE PEACE.

N.B. N., signifies neither read nor write; R., read only; Imp., read and write imperfectly; Well, read and write well; Sup., superior education.

INDEX.

| Name | No. | Name | No. |
|---|---|---|---|
| Atkins, William | 4 | Newitt, John | 7 |
| Balderson, Richard | 10 | Norton, William | 1 |
| Bird, Thomas | 5 | Smith, James | 13 |
| Chambers, Herbert | 11 | Surridge, Prudence | 14 |
| Gill, Joseph | 12 | Thompson, William | 9 |
| Hamson, William | 3 | Wakefield, John | 2 |
| Hill, William | 6 | Wills, William | 8 |

JAS. BUTTERFIELD, PRINTER, NORTHAMPTON.

The Calendar for the July Quarter Sessions 1857. This also has the results of the cases, the majority of which are theft. See pages 138 to 140. (NRO)

IN THE COUNTY GAOL AT NORTHAMPTON.

| No. | NAME. | Age. | TRADE. | Degree of Instruction. | Name and Address of Committing Magistrate. | Date of Warrant. | When received into Custody. | Offence as charged in the Commitment. | When tried. | Before whom tried. | Verdict of the Jury. | Sentence or Order of the Court. |
|---|---|---|---|---|---|---|---|---|---|---|---|---|
| 1 | WILLIAM NORTON ......... Once before convicted of felony. | 20 | Shoemaker.. | N. | Charles Hill, Esq., Wollaston Hall, Wellingborough; John Young, Esq., Stanwick, Wellingborough. | 13th April, 1857.. | 14th April, 1857.. | Stealing a quantity of leather, and several Shoemaker's tools, the property of Thos. Mills, at Earl's Barton, on the 10th April, 1857. | 2nd July, 1857 | John Yorke, Esq., Thrapston, Second Chairman. | Pleaded guilty of larceny. | Four Years' Penal Servitude. |
| | | | | | | | | Also stealing one waistcoat, and divers others articles, the property of Edward Hilton, at Earl's Barton, on the 9th of April, 1857. | Ditto ............ | Ditto ...................... | Pleaded guilty of larceny. | Not to be now sentenced. |
| | | | | | | | | Also stealing four pairs of soles, and one pair of welts, the property of Thomas Smith, at Earl's Barton, on the 10th of April, 1857. | Ditto ............ | Ditto ...................... | Pleaded guilty of larceny. | Not to be now sentenced. |
| | | | | | | | | Also stealing one pair of boots, and divers other articles, the property of William Weed, at Earl's Barton, on the 9th of April, 1857. | Ditto ............ | Ditto ...................... | Pleaded guilty of larceny. | Not to be now sentenced. |
| | | | | | | | | Also stealing one pair of soles, and other articles, the property of Josiah Mills, at Earl's Barton, on the 9th April, 1857. | Ditto ............ | Ditto ...................... | Pleaded guilty of larceny. | Not to be now sentenced. |
| | | | | | | | | Also stealing one pair of shoes, and other articles, the property of Samuel Underwood, at Earl's Barton, on the 9th of April, 1857. | Ditto ............ | Ditto ...................... | Pleaded guilty of larceny. | Not to be now sentenced. |
| 2 | JOHN WAKEFIELD ......... | 40 | Drover ..... | Imp. | J. Yorke, Esq., Thrapston | Ditto ............... | Ditto ............... | Embezzling £1. 4s. 6d., which he had received for his master, John Jones, at Thrapston, on the 17th March, 1857. | Ditto ............ | The Right Hon. the Lord Southampton, Whittlebury, Towcester, Chairman. | Guilty of embezzlement as a servant. | Imprisonment, with Hard Labour, for Six Months, in the House of Correction at Northampton. |
| 3 | WILLIAM HAMSON ......... Once before transported, once besides convicted of felony, once convicted of coining, and once acquitted of felony. | 32 | Labourer ... | Imp. | R. Lee Bevan, Esq., Brixworth. | 15th April, 1857.. | 15th April, 1857.. | Stealing one lamb, the property of William Watts, at Scaldwell, on the 12th April, 1857. | Ditto ............ | John Yorke, Esq. ......... | Guilty of stealing one lamb. | Six Years' Penal Servitude. |
| 4 | WILLIAM ATKINS ......... | 20 | Labourer ... | R. | W. S. Rose, Esq., Cransley, Kettering. | 17th April, 1857.. | 18th April, 1857.. | Stealing £6. 15s. 6d., the monies of Andrew Browitt and John Cannon, as trustees of the Wilbarston Benefit Society, at Wilbarston, on the 8th October, 1854. | Ditto ............ | Lord Southampton ...... | Acquitted of larceny. | |
| 5 | THOMAS BIRD ............... | 32 | Labourer ... | R. | J. Yorke, Esq., Thrapston | 22nd April, 1857. | 22nd April, 1857. | Stealing one draining tool, the property of William Abbott, at Great Addington, on the 26th January, 1857. | Ditto ............ | John Yorke, Esq......... | Guilty of larceny | Imprisonment, with Hard Labour, for Two Months, in the House of Correction, at Northampton. |
| | | | | | | | | Also stealing a shovel, the property of Joseph Abbott, at Great Addington, on the 26th January, 1857. | Ditto ............ | Ditto ...................... | Acquitted of larceny. | |

| | | | | | | | | | | | |
|---|---|---|---|---|---|---|---|---|---|---|---|
| 6 | WILLIAM HILL.......... Alias HENRY CORBETT. Once acquitted of felony. | 33 | Labourer ... | Imp. | C. J. Vernon, Clerk, Grafton Underwood, Kettering. | 7th May, 1857 ... | 8th May, 1857 ... | Stealing one coat, one pair of boots, one pair of shoes, and other articles, value £4, the property of Samuel Patrick, at Burton Latimer, on the 6th December, 1856. | 2nd July, 1857 | Lord Southampton ...... | Pleaded guilty of larceny. | Imprisonment, with Hard Labour, for Three Months, in the House of Correction at Northampton. |
| | | | | | | | | Also stealing a silver watch, value £3, the property of Samuel Hull, at Burton Lattimer, on the 6th December, 1856. | Ditto ........... | Ditto ..................... | Pleaded guilty of larceny. | Imprisonment, with Hard Labour, for Three Months, in the House of Correction at Northampton, to commence at the expiration of the first sentence. |
| 7 | JOHN NEWITT .............. (Bailed 16th May, 1857.) Once before convicted of felony. | 40 | Shoemaker.. | Imp. | Geo. Norman, Esq., Mayor of Daventry. | 12th May, 1857... | 14th May, 1857... | Stealing a pig, the property of John Kennard, at Daventry, on the 9th May, 1857. | Ditto ........... | John Yorke, Esq......... | Acquitted of larceny. | |
| 8 | WILLIAM WILLS ........... Once before transported. | 29 | Labourer ... | Imp. | Geo. Stone, Esq., Blisworth. | 28th May, 1857... | 28th May, 1857... | Stealing 4s. 4½d., the property of William Talbot, at Slapton, on the 26th May, 1857. | Ditto ........... | Lord Southampton ...... | Acquitted of larceny. | |
| 9 | WILLIAM THOMPSON...... | 27 | Baker ...... | Imp. | R. Isham, Clerk, Lamport, Northampton. | 29th May, 1857... | 30th May, 1857... | Stealing seventeen fowls, value £1. 14s., the property of William Garratt, at Cransley, on the 6th January, 1853. | Ditto ........... | John Yorke, Esq......... | Guilty of larceny as a servant. | Imprisonment, with Hard Labour, for Six Calendar Months in the House of Correction at Northampton. |
| 10 | (On Bail.) RICHARD BALDERSON ... | 42 | Farmer ...... | N. | ............................ | Rendered ........ | 2nd July, 1857 .. | Stealing three trusses of hay, value 6s., the property of Willingham Franklin, at Spratton, on the 16th May, 1857. | Ditto ........... | Lord Southampton ...... | Acquitted of larceny. | |
| 11 | HERBERT CHAMBERS...... | 13 | Labourer ... | Imp. | J. W. Smith, Esq., Oundle | 29th June, 1857... | 23rd June, 1857... | Attempting to commit an unnatural offence with a certain ewe sheep, at Deenthorpe. | Ditto ........... | John Yorke, Esq. ........ | Pleaded guilty of an attempt to commit an unnatural offence with an ewe sheep. | Imprisonment, with Hard Labour, for Six Months, in the House of Correction at Northampton. |
| 12 | JOSEPH GILL .............. | 36 | Groom ...... | Imp. | G. Palmer, Esq., Carlton Park, Rockingham. | 6th June, 1857 ... | 29th June, 1857... | Uttering false and counterfeit coin, at Cottingham, on the 14th June, 1857. | Ditto ........... | Ditto ..................... | Guilty of uttering counterfeit coin. | Imprisonment, with Hard Labour, for One Year, in the House of Correction at Northampton. |
| 13 | JAMES SMITH .............. Once before summarily convicted. | 22 | Hawker ... | Imp. | R. T. Clarke, Esq., Welton Place, Daventry. | 1st July, 1857 ... | 2nd July, 1857 ... | Stealing two tame ducks and three hen's eggs, the property of Daniel Darnell, at Welton, on the 13th of June, 1857. | Ditto ........... | Ditto ..................... | Acquitted of larceny. | |
| 14 | PRUDENCE SURRIDGE ... Twice before convicted of felony and once summarily convicted. | 31 | Wife of Richard Surridge, labourer. | N. | J. Nethercoat, Esq., Moulton Grange, Northampton. | 29th May, 1857... | 6th June, 1857 ... | Want of sureties in a breach of the peace towards Mary Baily, at Kingsthorpe, on the 6th June, 1857. | Ditto ........... | Lord Southampton ...... | .................. | Discharged for want of prosecution. |

BENJAMIN RUST, Governor *pro tem.*

We cannot get away from this expression 'the peace', which keeps cropping up time and time again throughout the history of the English criminal law, and even today is still legally defined as 'the normal state of society', with any breach of this normal state being a 'Breach of the Peace'. So it was with the law givers and policy makers of medieval England, they always desired to live in 'the peace', and went to some lengths to achieve it.

In the remarkably short space of 40 years between 1327 and 1368, the office and duties of the magistrates was assembled by various acts of Parliament. And by the 1370s the magistrates had come to be chosen by the king only from the land owning classes, which obviously made them of higher social rank than the constable, who then became attributable to the magistrates.

It was because they were chosen only from the land owning upper classes, that the magistrates soon came to be seen as a self-perpetuating socially superior elite, which indeed they were, and in Northamptonshire, more so than in many other counties. In the 1830s for example, on the Northamptonshire bench of magistrates were ten peers of the realm with large estates, and 37 landed gentry with estates, five being Baronets, as well as a large number of professional gentry and clergymen.

When they were established, the magistrates were given powers to hold sessions of a court, which because it was held every three months became known as the Quarter Sessions, and these Quarter Sessions were also given the power of 'oyer and terminer' over criminal cases (Norman French again: 'oyer', to hear [the town crier's cry 'Oyez, Oyez', 'hear this, hear this'] and 'terminer' to de'termine' or decide the outcome).

The magistrates in Quarter Sessions were thus empowered to summons before them, try, and to pass sentence, on any criminals brought before them by the parish constables via the courts leet. They were obliged, however, to pass the really serious criminal cases straight to the Assizes.

Because of the need for a single spokesman to speak for the whole body of justices, it became the custom to elect a Chairman of Quarter Sessions. Originally the chairman was elected annually, but gradually it came to be the norm that the chairman, once elected, held his office for life. Also, the justices needed secretarial help, so in 1361, the office of Clerk of the Peace was established to do just that. All the actual 'nuts and bolts' of the paperwork and administration fell directly on him and his staff.

So successful and more efficient did the Quarter Sessions become, that they soon superseded the courts tourn and the hundred courts, both of which soon fell into disuse. So much so, that in 1461 an act of Parliament officially transferred to the Quarter Sessions all cases formerly heard before the hundred and courts tourn.

It was during Tudor times, that the Quarter Sessions had also come to be the court through which the county was civilly administered; not only were crimi-

COUNTY OF NORTHAMPTON.

# CALENDAR OF PRISONERS

FOR TRIAL AT THE

## GENERAL QUARTER SESSIONS OF THE PEACE,

HOLDEN AT NORTHAMPTON,

**On WEDNESDAY, the FIFTH day of JANUARY, 1881.**

HENRY MINSHULL STOCKDALE ESQUIRE CHAIRMAN.
SACKVILLE GEORGE STOPFORD SACKVILLE, ESQ., SECOND CHAIRMAN.

HENRY VANE FORESTER HOLDICH HUNGERFORD, ESQUIRE, HIGH SHERIFF.
HENRY WILLIAM KENNEDY MARKHAM, GENTLEMAN, UNDER SHERIFF.
HENRY PHILIP MARKHAM, GENTLEMAN, CLERK OF THE PEACE.

N.B.—(N.) signifies neither read nor write; (R.) read only; (Imp.) read and write imperfectly; (Well) read and write well; (sup.) superior education.

INDEX.

| NAME. | No. | NAME. | No. |
|---|---|---|---|
| Brown, Charles | 1 | Read, Sands | 7 |
| Carpenter, Robert | 4 | Smith, Lewis Thomas | 8 |
| Earl, Richard | 6 | Stafford, John | 3 |
| Gibbs, David William | 5 | Tack, John | 9 |
| Limbrey, James | 10 | Thomas, John | 2 |

BUTTERFIELD AND SON, HERALD OFFICE, NORTHAMPTON.

The Calendar for the January Quarter Sessions 1881. As with the Assizes Calendars, criminal records are now also given. See pages 138 to 140. (NRO)

## IN HER MAJESTY'S PRISON AT NORTHAMPTON.

| No. | NAME. | Age. | TRADE. | Degree of Instruction. | Name and Address of Committing Magistrate. | Date of Warrant. | When Received into Custody. | Offence as Charged in the Commitment. | When Tried. | Before whom Tried. | Verdict of the Jury. | Particulars of Previous Convictions Charged in the Indictment and proved in Court. | Sentence or Order of the Court. |
|---|---|---|---|---|---|---|---|---|---|---|---|---|---|
| 1 | CHARLES BROWN ......... Kettering, May 12, 1880, stealing mutton, 42 days' hard labour; Nottingham, June 24, 1880, stealing clock, two months, hard labour. | 61 | Painter ...... | Imp. | Hon. C. J. Vernon, Clerk, Grafton Underwood, Kettering. | 1880. Oct. 27th.. | 1880. Oct. 27th.. | Feloniously stealing one coat, of the value of £1 2s. 0d., the property of William Wells and William Levett Wells, at Kettering, on the 26th October, 1880. | 1881. Jan. 6th... | H. M. Stockdale, Esq. | Pleaded guilty ... | Nottingham, June 24, 1880, stealing clock, two months, hard labour. | Four calendar months, hard labour. |
| 2 | JOHN THOMAS............... | 46 | Labourer ... | Imp. | F. U. Sartoris, Esq., Rushden Hall, Higham Ferrers. | Nov. 5th... | Nov. 5th... | Stealing from the person of Eliza Austin the sum of 10½d. in money, the monies of her, the said Eliza Austin, at Wellingborough, on the 3rd November, 1880. | Jan. 6th... | H. M. Stockdale, Esq. | Guilty ........... | ........................... | Six calendar months, hard labour. |
| ... | The Same. JOHN THOMAS............... | ... | .............. | ... | F. U. Sartoris, Esq. ... | Nov. 5th... | Nov. 5th... | Attempting to feloniously steal from the person of Sarah Ann Gascoyne, at Wellingborough, on the 2nd of June, 1880. | ............ | ............ | ............ | ............ | No evidence offered. |
| 3 | JOHN STAFFORD........... Oakham, July 2,1846, misdemeanour, 12 months; Stamford, June 27, 1857, misdemeanour, six months; Oakham: July 5, 1862, larceny, 7 years' penal servitude; June 29, 1865, larceny, six months; February 29, 1872, misdemeanour, six months, and three years' police supervision; Sept. 9, 1879, assault, 14 days; July 17, 1877, misdemeanour, 12 months, and three years' police supervision. | 59 | Labourer ... | N. | G. Cayley, Esq., Wothorpe, Stamford. | Nov. 5th... | Nov. 5th... | Obtaining, by certain false pretences, from James Porter Greenwood, the sum of 2s. in money, the monies of the said James Porter Greenwood, with intent to defraud, at Easton, on the 23rd October, 1880. | Jan. 6th... | H. M. Stockdale, Esq. | Pleaded guilty ... | July 17, 1877, Oakham, misdemeanour, twelve months, and three years' police supervision. | Twelve calendar months, hard labour, and three years police supervision. |
| 4 | ROBERT CARPENTER...... | 50 | Shoemaker... | Well | H. O. Nethercote, Esq., Moulton Grange, Northampton. | Nov. 6th... | Nov. 6th... | Stealing one engine cloth, of the value of 15s., the property of John S. Smith, at Quinton, on the 16th October, 1880. | Jan. 6th .. | S. G. Stopford Sackville, Esq. | Guilty ........... | ........................... | Six calendar months, hard labour. |
| ... | The Same. ROBERT CARPENTER... .. | ... | .............. | ... | C. Smyth, Esq., Little Houghton, Northampton. | Nov. 6th... | Nov. 6th... | Stealing twelve fowls, of the value of 18s., at Duston, on the 27th October, 1880. | Jan. 6th... | S. G. Stopford Sackville, Esq. | Guilty ... ........ | ........................... | Six calendar months, hard labour, to commence at the expiration of another sentence of even date herewith. |
| 5 | DAVID WILLIAM GIBBS... Northamptonshire Sessions, Oct. 17, 1879, stealing watch and chain and 12s., three calendar months, hard labour. | 24 | Labourer ... | Imp. | Sir R. Knightley, Bart., Fawsley Park, Daventry. | Nov. 17th. | Nov. 17th. | Burglariously breaking and entering the dwelling-house of Thomas Inns, with intent to steal the goods and chattels of the said Thomas Inns, at Preston Capes, about the hour of five in the morning of the 15th November, 1880. | ............ | ............ | No true bill ...... | ........................... | To be discharged. |
| 6 | RICHARD EARL............... Wellingborough, December 8, 1876, threatening language, paid costs, 2s.; Sept. 4, 1877, stealing a silver watch, three months' hard labour; May 3, 1878, drunk and riotous, fined 14s. 6d.; March 19, 1880, stealing a bottle of brandy, one month hard labour; June 4, 1880, drunk, fined 19s. 6d. | 25 | Labourer ... | Imp. | F. U. Sartoris, Esq. ... | Dec. 3rd... | Dec. 4th... | Obtaining, by certain false pretences, of and from George Manning, three pints of beer, of the value of 9d., with intent to defraud, at Wellingborough, on the 29th November, 1880. | Jan. 6th... | H. M. Stockdale, Esq. | Pleaded guilty ... | ........................... | One calendar month, hard labour. |

| | | | | | | | | | | | | |
|---|---|---|---|---|---|---|---|---|---|---|---|---|
| 7 | SANDS READ.................. | 20 | Labourer ... | N. | The Most Noble the Duke of Grafton, Wakefield Lodge, Stony Stratford. | 1880. Dec. 28th. | 1880. Dec. 29th. | Feloniously attempting to commit an unnatural offence with a cow, at Deanshanger, on the 24th December, 1880. | 1881. Jan. 6th... | H. M. Stockdale, Esq. | Guilty ............ | .................................. | Nine calendar months, hard labour. |
| 8 | LEWIS THOMAS SMITH... | 42 | Blacksmith... | Imp | H. W. Beauford, Esq., Sudborough House, Thrapston. | Dec. 31st.. | Dec. 31st.. | Obtaining, by a certain false pretence, from Mary Ann Russell, the sum of 9d. in money, the monies of the said Mary Ann Russell, with intent to defraud, at Brigstock, on the 30th December, 1880. | Jan. 6th... | S. G. Stopford Sackville, Esq. | Pleaded guilty ... | .................................. | One calendar month, hard labour. |
| 9 | JOHN TACK .................. (On Bail.) | ... | .................. | ... | F. U. Sartoris, Esq. ... | Dec. 3rd. | .............. | Indecently assaulting Elizabeth Cox, at Rushden, on the 22nd November, 1880. | .............. | ........... .... .......... | No true bill ...... | .................................. | To be discharged. |
| 10 | JAMES LIMBREY ............ Northampton, Oct. 25, 1877, stealing a moulding plane, 14 days, hard labour; Newport Pagnel, May 26, 1880, stealing a coat, 21 days, hard labour. | 34 | Labourer ... | Imp. | H. O. Nethercote, Esq. | 1881. Jan. 1st... | 1881. Jan. 1st... | Stealing four knives and four forks, of the value of 3s., the property of Richard Knight, at Hackleton, on the 9th December, 1880. | Jan. 6th... | H. M. Stockdale, Esq. | Guilty ............ | Newport Pagnel, May 26, 1880, stealing a coat, twenty-one days, hard labour. | Six calendar months, hard labour. |

J. HOWE,

Governor of the said Prison.

NORTHAMPTONSHIRE, TO WIT. } TAKE NOTICE that you Lawrence Turner of Rowell in the County of Northampton are bound in the Sum of Ten Pounds, to appear at the next General Quarter Sessions of the Peace, to be holden for the County of Northampton, at the *County Hall*, in *Northampton*, on the Eighth Day of January next, to give Evidence before the Grand Jury upon a Bill of Indictment to be preferred against Mary Ann Coleman by John Meadows for Felony and also to give Evidence on the Trial of the said Mary Ann Coleman if the said Bill should be found a true Bill, and unless you personally make your appearance accordingly, the recognizance entered into by you will be forthwith levied on you. Dated this twentieth Day of November One Thousand Eight Hundred and Forty five

W. Wetherell *Justice of the Peace.*

For Witness to give Evidence.

County of Northampton to wit. } TAKE NOTICE, That you John Meadows of Kettering in the said County are bound in the Sum of Twenty Pounds, to appear at the next Quarter Session of the Peace for the County of Northampton to be holden at Northampton on the eighth day of January next, to prosecute Mary Ann Coleman for Felony and unless you personally make your appearance accordingly, the Recognizance entered into by you will be forthwith levied on you. Dated this 20th Day of November One Thousand Eight Hundred and Forty five

W. Wetherell Justice of the Peace.

Recognizance Notice, No. 5. Printed and sold by Shaw & Sons, 136, 137, & 138, Fetter-lane, London.
For Prosecutor to Prosecute.—Sessions. Notice 3 Geo. IV. Chap. 46, Sec. 6.

Printed Bail forms supplied to magistrates to bail both accused and witnesses to Quarter Sessions. See page 138. (NRO)

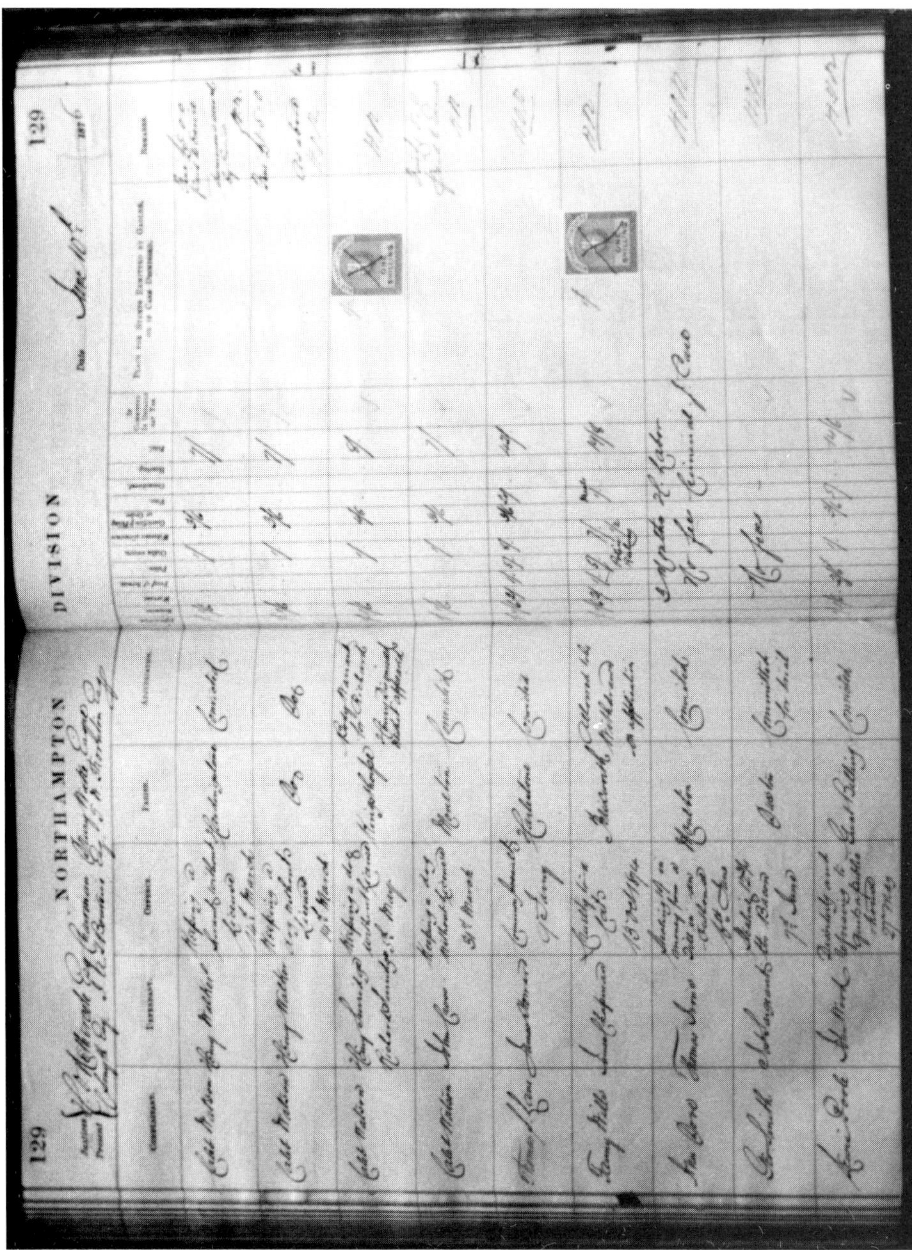

The Register of the Northampton Borough Petty Sessions, June 1876. Every case appearing at the Petty Sessions (magistrates' court) was recorded. The stamps are receipts for payment of gaoler's dues. (NRO)

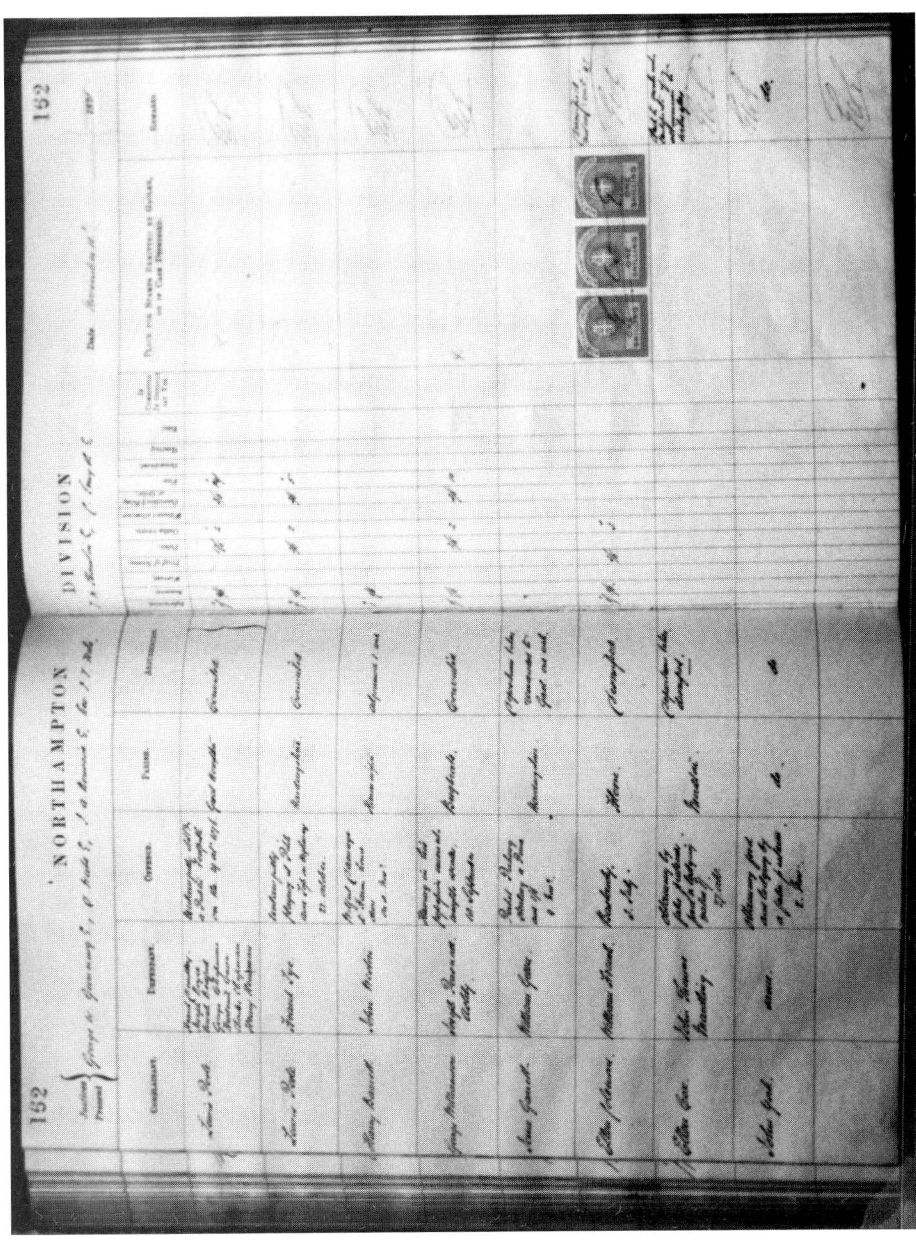

Northampton Borough Petty Sessions Register for November 1876. (NRO)

The plaster ceiling in the criminal court of Northampton Sessions House, containing the 'Devil's Mask'. This has a moveable tongue which is supposed to wag every time a lie is told in the court.

nals tried at the Sessions, but the affairs of the county were attended to as well, roads, bridges and so on. But when the Local Government Act of 1888 set up the politically elected County Councils, the civil administration was taken away from the non elected Quarter Sessions and given instead to the new democratically elected County Council.

So by the early 14th century, England had in place a sophisticated criminal justice system. And it is amazing to think that this structure for bringing criminal cases before a court remained virtually the same until half way through the 19th.

First of all, the person arrested either on warrant, or without a warrant by a constable or a private individual, was taken before the nearest local magistrate for a preliminary examination as to whether or not to allow bail. If bail was refused by the magistrate, which would obviously be for the more major crimes destined for the Assizes rather than Quarter Sessions or Petty Sessions, then he had the power to remand the alleged offender straight to gaol to await trial, and it was the responsibility of the parish constable to escort him there.

If bail was granted, however, the alleged offender was bailed either to the next Petty Sessions, or to the next Quarter Sessions, and normally, on someone else's surety for his appearance there. Also, any witnesses to the incident were also bailed to the court as well, but these would be on their own recognizance. During the 18th and 19th centuries, magistrates were supplied with printed bail forms,

The Sessions House, George Row, Northampton. From a post card of 1912. (Northampton Libraries and Information Service)

The Sessions, House, George Row, Northampton. From a post card of 1912. The County Hall, which contained the county police headquarters from 1881 to 1950 is on the extreme right.

Brackley combined police station and magistrates' court. It dates from 1851, and was the first to be built under the county's first programme for such buildings. It is the sole survivor of the programme, but is not now used either for police or court use.

which they could fill in, one copy going to the person concerned, and one copy going to the Clerk of the Peace for the county. The Clerk of the Peace could then keep a register of all the accused persons and witnesses who would be appearing at the next Assizes or Quarter Sessions. The County of Northampton has a full run of these Recognizance books, preserved at the County Record Office, which stretch from 1672 until 1846.

From these Recognizance books, and from the register of gaol prisoners, a list of the people appearing at the next Assizes or Quarter Sessions could be made by the Clerk of the Peace. This list would be printed and published, and would be called a Calendar. Northamptonshire has a fair few surviving Assize and Quarter Sessions Calendars preserved at Wootton Park.

On the actual day of the trial, there was a strict procedure to follow. First of all, the accused person was charged ('arraigned') before the open court. He would then be charged again, but this time in private, and before the grand (accusing) jury. The grand jury (remember, the direct descendant of the hundred jury) would be assembled from the non-magistrates of the county, but were still men of substantial financial and social standing. The grand jury then heard the

Thrapston combined police station and magistrates' court. Built in 1860 in the second county building programme, it is now a hotel.

Oundle combined police station and magistrates' court. Built in 1877 under the second county building programme, it occupies the site of the old Oundle Bridewell, on Stoke Hill. It is now converted for office use.

prosecution evidence, also in private.

If the grand jury found a 'prima facie' case against the accused, then the words 'True Bill' would be written on the Indictment, and the case would then go back into open court, and be tried normally, but this time before the petty (determining) jury, the jury made up from the rate payers of the county, much as today's juries are.

But if the grand jury thought there was not sufficient evidence against the accused, then 'No True Bill' (or sometimes, 'Ignoramus', Latin, again, meaning 'we know not') would be written on the Indictment, and the accused person would then be allowed to walk free out of the court. The system of two juries survived until 1933, when by the Administration of Justice Act of that year, the grand jury was abolished, leaving just the one jury to determine guilt or innocence in open court.

The only major addition to the system, came in 1848 when the power of summons, as opposed to arrest, was introduced by the two pioneering Acts of that year, the Summary Jurisdiction Act, and the Indictable Offences Act. Thereafter, greater emphasis was placed on summary jurisdiction, and an increasing number of cases went before the magistrates' courts.

This system of Assizes and Quarter Sessions survived intact until quite recently. By the Crown Courts Act 1971, the Assizes and the Quarter Sessions, were abolished, and replaced by just the one higher criminal court, the Crown Court.

At the county Assizes, it was the custom for the county police to provide the court ushers, and as a young police officer, I well remember being present at the Northampton Sessions House during the last sitting of the Northamptonshire Assizes in 1971. I did not know it then, although I do now, that I was part of an historic moment, the last session of a court that had been held continuously for nigh on 800 years.

Northamptonshire has a fine surviving set of court buildings. The gem of the collection is the Sessions House, in George Row, Northampton, which sadly is now no longer used for its original purpose, and is standing empty awaiting a bright idea for its future. A new Court House has just been opened in Lady's Lane.

Up to 1570, the Assizes and Quarter Sessions for Northampton and Northamptonshire were held in the old Northampton castle, which also doubled as the county gaol. However, in that year, because the castle was so dilapidated, the courts were moved to a temporary structure in the middle of the town, and the gaol moved to George Row.

Work was eventually started to provide a permanent building, but in the great fire of Northampton in September 1675, this partly completed Sessions House was burnt to the ground, together with the gaol. So in 1676 work was started again on a new Sessions House in George Row. It is this building that is the one still there today, and a wonderful building it is too, especially the plasterwork ceiling, which features a Devil's Mask with a loose fitting tongue, which is supposed to wag every time a lie is told within the court.

Two court rooms were provided, which gave space for the criminal and nisi prius courts, as well as offices and judges' chambers. A complete network of underground passages enabled the prisoners to be brought straight up into the dock from the cells underneath.

The criminal courtroom contains the grand jury gallery into which the grand jury would file when they brought their verdict back into the court. Because there were no stairs down into the main court, the Indictment (with its inscription of either 'A True Bill' or 'No True Bill'/'Ignoramus') would be fastened

'Anging Orkins'. Judge Henry Hawkins was a frequent judge at the Northamptonshire Assizes in the 1880s. 'Orkins' never deserved his nickname, and never passed the death sentence in any of the five cases of homicide that he tried in Northampton. When ennobled in 1899, he chose the title Lord Brampton, as he did not want to be called Lord 'Enry 'Awkins of 'Itchin, 'Erts. (Popperfoto)

onto a spring clip at the end of a long fishing rod and poked over the side of the gallery so that the Clerk of the Court could reach it.

He would then read it, and in a hushed court would look up into the gallery and ask the grand jury to confirm their verdict. Apparently when this happened, no matter what was going on then in court, everything stopped, so everybody could enjoy the spectacle of the fishing rod being dangled over the side of the gallery.

During the very first building programme undertaken by the Northamptonshire County Constabulary starting in 1851, police stations with magistrates' court rooms attached were built at Towcester, Brackley and Kettering. Of these three, only the building at Brackley still stands, although not now used as either police station or court. More police stations and courtrooms were built over the years, but the magistrates' courts in use at the present are all fairly modern.

So after all the developments and experiments and tinkering with the criminal law, we arrive at the system we have today; one crime fighting agency (The Northamptonshire Police), and two tiers of courts (The Magistrates' Courts and The Crown Courts). It has taken over 1,000 years to arrive at this, and this is the system that we will take into the new millennium. Will it be adequate? Will it cope with ever more sophisticated crime as new technology, unheard of until yesterday, helps the criminal? We cannot answer that question, that will have to be left to future legal and social historians.

# CHAPTER 6

## 'HANGING, BEHEADING, BURNING AND PRESSING': CAPITAL PUNISHMENT IN NORTHAMPTONSHIRE

THE beheading of a crowned queen; the hanging of the last two 'witches' in the whole of Britain, and the burning of a Christian martyr: all these judicial executions have taken place in Northamptonshire.

There are lots of ways to execute people, but in Northamptonshire only four of them have been used; hanging, beheading, burning and pressing.

Beheading, of course, has been quite common in British history, but because it was the method of execution reserved exclusively for those of noble blood, it has only been used in Northamptonshire on three occasions, the two Herbert brothers in 1469, and Mary, Queen of Scots in 1587. Beheading as a means of execution was abolished after 1747, the last person suffering this fate being Lord Lovat, who had been found guilty of rape and forceful abduction to secure succession to his title.

Thankfully, there has only been one recorded case of 'pressing to death' in Northamptonshire, when in 1630, an unknown person was pressed to death in the New Pastures (now Spencer Parade) in Northampton. This means of execution was reserved for those who on being charged with a felony, refused to plead. This is not so idiotic as appears at first glance.

Had the prisoner pleaded to the felony he was charged with, he obviously thought that the chances of being found not guilty were slim, and therefore he knew he was going to hang anyway. But worse than that, in those days, a convicted felon's belongings and property would have been confiscated, and his next of kin would have been left with nothing and would probably have faced destitution. By refusing to plead, and therefore face trial, he would not have died as a convicted felon, and would thereby assure that his surviving relatives inherited his property.

The naked prisoner was laid on his back on the bare floor so that there could be placed upon his body 'so great a weight of iron as he could bear, and more'. In this position the prisoner was given only a mouthful of bread on one day and

Northampton Racecourse, at the junction of Kettering Road and Kingsley Road, the site of the gallows for the majority of Northamptonshire hangings, until the erection of the permanent 'new drop' at Angel Lane in 1819.

three sips of water on the next. This alternating daily diet continued until either the prisoner died or he pleaded to the charges against him.

Death by burning was normally only used for heresy and for a crime called Petty Treason. Of Northamptonshire's seven burnings, one has been for heresy, and six for Petty Treason.

The burning of John Kurde in 1557 for 'heresy' has been the only martyrdom in the county. The queen, 'Bloody' Mary Tudor, had revived *de Heretico Comburendo* which had legalised the burning of heretics, but which had been repealed in 1547 by the Protector Somerset. Burning for heresy was finally abolished by Queen Elizabeth in 1559.

The crime of Petty Treason, which was considered more serious than 'ordinary' murder, was committed when a master was murdered by his servant, or a clergyman by his inferior, or, as was more common, when a wife murdered her husband. The six burnings for Petty Treason in Northamptonshire all come under this last category, because the punishment for a woman was to be burnt at the stake. Men convicted of the offence were merely hung, no equal rights or 'Women's Lib' in those days. Juliann de Murdak was the first to be burnt in

1316, followed by Mrs Lucas in 1631, two unknown women in 1645 and 1655, Elizabeth Trasler in 1715, and Elizabeth Fawson in 1735. Burning as a punishment was abolished in 1790, and Petty Treason in 1820. Thereafter these crimes were treated as murder, with hanging as the punishment.

By far the commonest form of capital punishment was, of course, by hanging. This had always been the favourite English means of judicial execution, but it was given extra impetus in 1723 by the infamous piece of legislation which came to be known by the sinister nickname of the 'Black Act'. In that year, some poachers who had blacked their faces so as to make their identification difficult, had been hung under powers given by a new Act of Parliament which had just been passed to discourage lawlessness. This legislation, which then came to be nicknamed after the poachers, is famous for introducing that most notorious of penal codes in the entire history of this country, the 'Bloody Code'. Lasting for over 100 years, the 'Bloody Code' would eventually list nearly 230 criminal offences as punishable by death.

The obvious crimes were included of course, murder, theft, rape, arson and so

The site of the 'new drop', in Angel Lane, at the rear of the old county prison, the large building in the centre being the men's block. The actual gallows were on the site of the gatekeeper's lodge, just behind the largest notice. Between 1819 and 1852, 18 men and two women were hanged on this spot.

on, but you could also be hung, for example, for writing a threatening letter, or consorting with gypsies, or perhaps the most evil crime of all time, impersonating a Chelsea Pensioner. Such was the savagery of the penal code in the 18th century that there were at least two occasions in London when 40 people were hanged on one day. And it was also estimated that a staggering 90 per cent of these were under the age of 21. As far as is known, however, only two teenagers were hanged in Northamptonshire, John Lavendar in 1750 for arson at Kettering aged 17, and William Love for theft at Wellingborough in 1754 who was just 16.

In the ancient times, gallows were set up anywhere as and when needed, but eventually 'permanent gallows' were erected which came to be used for all the executions in the county. The first recorded permanent gallows in Northamptonshire were in Abington village just a couple of miles north east of Northampton. It was to Abington that five 'witches' were brought in 1612 and where 24 years later the triple execution of the Barker household took place for the murder of the illegitimate baby of the woman concerned.

Arthur Bett in 1638 appears to be the last person hanged at Abington, because in 1651 when a 'knot of thieves broke into' Northampton, the leader of the gang, Leonard Bland, was hanged at Northampton 'on a new gallows made for him'. These gallows were somewhere near to Northampton Heath, or Northampton Racecourse as it is now called. However, in 1779, when Northampton's fields were enclosed, in order that these gallows should not be included in a private person's allotment of land, the Commissioners ordered that the gallows be moved. The site chosen was on the Racecourse in the corner between the Northampton to Kettering and the Kingsthorpe to Abington roads, which today is just a few yards over the Kingsley Road from the White Elephant public house.

The Northampton gallows had been used to hang every person sentenced to death within the county. However, there was a thought prevalent at the time which dictated that criminals convicted of particularly brutal, sickening or gruesome crimes be hanged at, or their bodies hanged at, the scenes of their crime. Four men were given this 'honour'. In 1611 Stephen Preston was hung at Kingsthorpe for murder; in 1739 John Cotton's body was hung in an iron cage on Paulerspury Common after he had been hanged at Northampton for the murder of his daughter (he had swung her by the legs and had dashed her brains out against a wall); the body of Brian Connell was hung in chains for several months in 1741 on Weedon Common within sight of his mother's house after he had been hung at Northampton for a murder where the victim had been decapitated; and in 1785 John Roberts was hung at Boughton for a particularly brutal robbery.

The Racecourse gallows lasted until 1818 when Cobbett and Wilkin were the last to be hung there. This spectacle however, convinced the authorities that something must be done, because the crowd attending the drive of the condemned from the gaol to the gallows through the streets of Northampton, and at the Racecourse itself, had become far too large and unruly for comfort. So in 1819 a new gallows was commissioned at the rear of the County gaol in Angel Lane.

This was a permanent fixture, and was set up high in the air so the spectacle would still be public for crowds assembling in Cow Meadow. And being permanent, a new arrangement could be made. Instead of having the culprit stand on the back of a cart, which then drove away from underneath him, leaving him dangling, a trapdoor mechanism was made on which the condemned stood. This was then opened suddenly so causing him to drop downward, and which led to these new gallows being nicknamed the 'new drop'.

The 'new drop' was a large structure, so big in fact, that it was said that it could hang '20 at once, quite comfortably'. Only a quarter of its capacity however, was used on its first public outing in 1819 when five burglar colleagues were hung together.

Altogether, 20 people were hung on the 'new drop', including Thomas Gee for arson in 1834, and Elizabeth Pinckard for murder in 1852. Thomas Gee was the last person to be executed in the county for a non-homicide offence, and

The site of the gallows at the Northamptonshire county prison in Angel Lane, 1868 to 1879. The brick course where the platform went can clearly be seen, as can the steps up to the platform from the condemned cell door. The rear wall and gate to the garden of the Judges' Lodgings is to the left.

The location of the platform of the gallows, and the steps up to it, can still clearly be seen. Only two men were hung here, Richard Addington in 1871 and Thomas Chamberlain in 1874. The gallows were dismantled when the county prison was closed in 1879.

Elizabeth Pinckard's was the last public execution inside Northamptonshire.

The social feeling that had caused the introduction of the 'Bloody Code' had been changing for a long time. Society was becoming more tolerant, civilised and educated. No longer was it acceptable to hang people for theft or any other non-homicide offence for that matter. This trend had been emerging since the turn of the 18th and 19th centuries, and although the Judges still by law had to give a mandatory death sentence, this, more often than not, was commuted to imprisonment except in the very worst cases. For instance, in 1831, 1601 people were sentenced to death throughout the country, but only 52 were actually hung.

The great champion for the abolition of the 'Bloody Code' was a Member of Parliament, Sir Samuel Romilly. Although he died in 1818, the campaign continued after his death and resulted in Acts of Parliament being passed in 1823 and 1827 which took several offences off the 'Bloody Code'. But it was not until 1837 that the Home Secretary, Sir Robert Peel, could report that the death penalty had been completely abolished for all offences, except murder, treason, piracy and arson in royal dockyards.

So Thomas Gee in 1834 was the last to be hanged for a non-homicide offence in Northamptonshire. After that, every judicial execution within the county would be for murder, the next being in 1852. There *was* a murder in the meantime, in 1840, but the killers of William Dunkley, the Yardley Hastings gamekeeper, chose transportation instead, which at that time they could do, see Chapter 8.

It was Elizabeth Pinckard who was hanged for the murder of her mother-in-law in 1852. And once again the hanging was in public. But little did those who witnessed it realise they would never see the like again. In 1868, after a long campaign and a report of a Select Committee, public hangings were finally abolished. Thereafter all hangings (plus the burial) were to be inside prison walls.

Becoming now redundant, the 'new drop' was therefore dismantled, but in any case it had not been used for 16 years. The site of the 'new drop' is now occupied by the porter's lodge, at the rear of the old County Hall in Angel Lane, Northampton.

The door of the condemned cell, showing the bell which was rung when the executioner was ready.

So not only was Elizabeth Pinckard the last woman to be hanged in Northamptonshire, hers was also the last public execution as well. The next two, Richard Addington in 1871 and Thomas Chamberlain in 1874, were both held in private in a specially constructed shed in the prison yard of the County gaol in Angel Lane, Northampton, just a few yards from the site of the 'new drop'.

This shed has obviously been dismantled long since, but the remains are still visible. The wooden door leading from the condemned cell to the hanging shed is still there, and it is quite easy to see where the steps leading up to the hanging platform went. The line of the floor of the hanging platform is clearly visible, as are the remains of the four beams that supported it.

It turned out, however, that the executions of Addington and Chamberlain were destined to be the very last held in the County gaol. By the time there was another prisoner for execution for a murder committed within the county as opposed to within the borough, the County gaol had ceased operating, which meant that Richard Sabey had to be hanged at the Borough gaol, in 1893. All the last seven executions within the county therefore took place at the old Northampton Borough gaol on the Mounts, the very last one being John Eayrs for murder of his wife at Peterborough in 1914.

By 1922 however, the Mounts gaol had long since passed its useful purpose, and was considered of no further use by the Home Office. Consequently it was closed and demolished in 1931, with the site being used for a new swimming pool, fire station, and the headquarters for the Northampton Borough Police, which is now Campbell Square county police station.

But the 1868 Act which had made hangings private, also dictated that the burial should be inside the prison as well. So the bodies of the seven murderers hanged at the gaol (Byrne, MacRae, Sabey, Parker, Claydon, Rowledge and Eayrs) had to be moved. During the night of Wednesday/Thursday 22/23 April 1931 therefore, all seven bodies were exhumed. It is interesting to know, though perhaps somewhat macabre, that because the bodies were buried in quicklime, when their execution hoods were removed, the facial features were found to be perfectly preserved, looking as though they were merely asleep. All seven were then re-buried in a communal grave at the Towcester Road Cemetery in Northampton, where they rest to this day.

There were several murders in Northamptonsire after 1914, but only one, Arthur Rouse, required the death sentence and he was hung in Bedford gaol in 1931. The rest were either imprisoned, found insane or had their sentences commuted by reason of age.

## Postscript

In 1949 a Royal Commission was established to look at the whole issue of capital punishment, and for a time the death sentence was held in abeyance. However, after a heated debate in Parliament it was re-introduced. The Member

The north eastern corner of the Towcester Road Cemetery, Northampton. The bodies of the seven murderers (Byrne, MacRae, Sabey, Parker, Claydon, Rowledge and Eyres) were reinterred here in 1931 after the Northampton Borough Gaol was closed. The actual grave, in unconsecrated ground, is under the far hedge, to the right of the centre of the picture.

of Parliament, Sidney Silverman began campaigning for permanent abolition and established the National Campaign for the Abolition of Capital Punishment in 1955. It was partly because of this campaign coupled with disquiet about some famous cases, not the least of which were the Craig and Bentley and Timothy Evans cases, that the Homicide Act was passed in 1957.

The Homicide Act split the crime of murder into two groups, capital and non-capital murder. Capital murder was defined as any of the following circumstances: murder in the course of, or furtherance of theft; murder by shooting or causing an explosion; murder done in resisting a lawful arrest; murder done in escape from legal custody; murder of a police officer on duty or of a person assisting; and murder by a prisoner of a prison officer. Under the Act, capital murder received the death penalty, but non-capital murder received life imprisonment.

The agitation for the total abolition of capital punishment did not diminish however, and in 1965 the Murder (Abolition of Death Penalty) Act was passed. This provided for a trial period of five years without the death penalty.

In 1969, capital punishment for murder was totally abolished. Only the crime of treason now remains where the penalty is death by hanging.

# CHAPTER 7

## 'AND THE WARDER IS DESPAIR': THE GAOLS OF NORTHAMPTONSHIRE

"The vilest deeds like poison weeds
Bloom well in prison air
It is only what is good in man
That wastes and withers there
Pale Anguish keeps the heavy gate
And the warder is Despair"
*The Ballad of Reading Gaol:* Oscar Wilde (1854-1900)

NORTHAMPTONSHIRE has no gaols today. In the past it has had two, plus two bridewells and several lock-ups, but these are all gone now. Gaols (or prisons) are for long term sentences, which, surprisingly, as a punishment is a comparatively modern concept. In the olden days, gaols were merely places where prisoners could be kept until they faced trial, after which they were either executed or punished — if found guilty, of course.

Bridewells (named after the original, at St Bride's Well in London) were houses of correction used only for very short term sentences, but big enough to require a permanent keeper. In Northampton, both the gaols also doubled as bridewells, but there were two more in the rest of the county, at Oundle and Kettering.

The Oundle bridewell was on the site of the old police station on Stoke Hill, now offices of the Social Services Department. It had several rooms, but hardly any security, and the only way to keep prisoners in was to chain them in leg irons. In 1742, the keeper, John Southwell, was allowed 6d per day to feed each prisoner. In 1840, the headquarters of the Oundle division of the newly formed Northamptonshire County Constabulary started occupying the same site, and the bridewell virtually ceased to function.

Weldon lock up.

Weldon lock up.

Kettering's bridewell was built in 1747, not surprisingly in a lane that came to be known as Bridewell Lane, which runs down the side of what is now *Henry's* public house in the Horsemarket. There were separate rooms for men and women, each 18ft by 16ft and an exercise yard 17ft square. The first Keeper was Joseph Warden at a salary of £12 per year. As with Oundle bridewell, when the new County Constabulary arrived in 1840 with Kettering as a main divisional headquarters, Kettering bridewell stopped functioning, and was subsequently demolished.

Lock-ups were single rooms where prisoners were kept for just a few hours (or overnight) in a secure place before escorting them before a magistrate, or until they had sobered up. Every village must have had access to a lock-up, or at least a secure room, but at Brackley, Daventry and Weldon, special places were built. The Brackley lock-up was a room 4ft square under the stair case of the Town Hall, and by 1851 had ceased to be used. Daventry lock-up was similar, and in January 1776, the great penal reformer, John Howard, reported that there was no exercise yard, no running water — and no prisoners. Although there may be more, the only surviving village lock-up seems to be in Weldon. It is a round stone building, and can still be seen from the old Stamford Road.

Northampton Town Hall in 1864. Standing on the corner of Wood Hill and Abington Street, the ground floor of this building was the Borough gaol from 1584, until a new Borough gaol was built in Fish Street in 1792. (Northamptonshire Libraries and Information Service)

What is believed to be a cell door, the only surviving part of the Borough gaol in Fish Street, Northampton. It is at the rear of the *Beamhouse* public house.

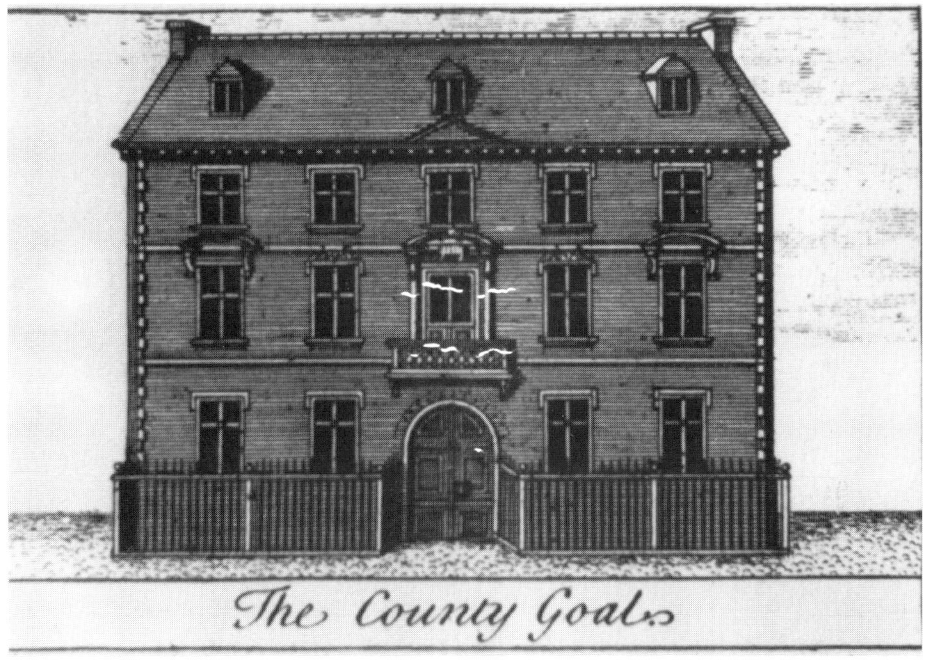


The old County gaol, next door to the Sessions House in George Row, Northampton. From a 1726 map of Northampton. (NRO)

The Judges' Lodgings, George Row, Northampton. Nestling between the Sessions House (on the right) and the gatehouse to the County gaol, the Lodgings were bought in 1819.

The two real gaols in the county were both in Northampton. One served the borough of Northampton, and the other the county of Northamptonshire.

Originally, prisoners were kept in the old Northampton castle, but it is not known for sure whether this was for just the borough prisoners, or the county's, or for both. But it is known that in the year 1584, the Northampton Corporation converted the ground floor of the old Town Hall into the Borough gaol for debtors and convicts. This was at the corner of Wood Hill and Abington Street.

Conditions and security here, apparently were none too good, but continued for 200 years, until in 1776, John Howard visited. He found that it was the only prison in the whole of England and Wales that did not have running water or an exercise yard. John Howard's agitation for prison reform resulted in an Act of Parliament of 1790, which virtually forced the country's prisons to modernise.

On the strength of this, a new Northampton Borough gaol was built in Fish Street (or Fish Lane as it was called then) in 1792. It was a small gaol, with a governor's house attached, but sufficiently large for the time being; in August 1801 there were two inmates, in September 1805, five, one of them a lunatic, in July 1807 three, in July 1808, four, and in August 1809, only one inmate, and he

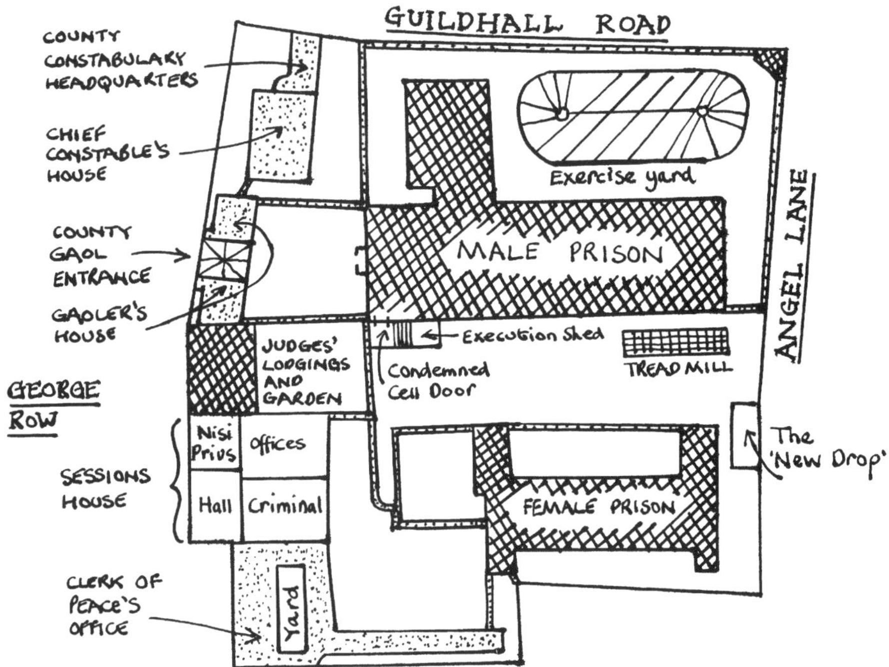


Map of the complex of county legal buildings, 1846-1881. The majority of these buildings still survive, mainly as offices for local government.

The front entrance to the County gaol, 1846-1881. This consisted of a gateway through to the rear, and the Gaoler's house. It has since been remodelled and is now a hotel and public house.

was a lunatic. The gaol was enlarged in 1823 and, in 1840, further enlarged to accommodate 40 prisoners.

But by the mid 1840s, even this was becoming too small, so in 1845 a new Borough gaol was built on The Mounts. This one had space for 100 prisoners, and cost £17,000 to build. The old gaol was immediately taken over as the headquarters for the Northampton Borough Police, with the Chief Constable, Henry Keenan, going to live in the old governor's house.

After 1880, the gaol on The Mounts became the only gaol in the town, as in that year the County gaol was closed down. But by 1922, even that was considered redundant by the Home Office, and was closed. It was demolished a few years later, and the site used for the new headquarters of the Northampton Borough Police, which is now Campbell Square police station of the present day Northamptonshire Police.

The story of the County gaol is more tangible, as the majority of the buildings can still be seen today. When the ruins of the old Northampton castle were finally pulled down in 1662, the County gaol moved farther into Northampton town

Northampton Borough gaol on The Mounts during the early 1890s. Replacing the old Borough gaol in Fish Street in 1845, it cost £17,000 to build. It was closed in 1922, and demolished in 1930. (Northamptonshire Libraries and Information service).

The demolition of the old Borough gaol in 1930. The new building to the rear was to become the Northampton Borough Police headquarters until the Borough and County police forces were amalgamated in 1966. It is now Campbell Square police station of the Northamptonshire Police. (Northamptonshire Libraries and Information Service)

centre, and a new gaol was built on the site of what is now the Sessions House in George Row.

But in 1675, this building, together with the majority of buildings in the town centre were destroyed in the great fire. This resulted in the new Sessions House being built, and next door to it on the western side, Sir William Haslewood built a house which he immediately leased out to the county magistrates as the new County gaol. This arrangement was far from satisfactory, and in 1691, the property was bought outright.

Because of the reforms of the prisons following the work of John Howard, in 1792, a new County gaol building was started, just to the rear of the existing one. It cost £16,000 and housed 140 criminals and 30 debtors. The old buildings were still kept on, but as the turnkey's lodge, and day rooms and exercise rooms and yards.

In 1819, the house immediately to the east of the Sessions House was bought. for use as the Judges' Lodgings every time the county Assizes were held. The total cost of buying and fitting up was £3,844.

Further prison reforms during the early 19th century required that another prison be built. Land was acquired on the eastern side of the Judges' Lodgings, and the new prison was built there, opening in 1846. The new building became the male block, and the old building became the female block.

The gateway to the new gaol was on St Giles Square, the site of which is now a public house and hotel, and previously a bank. The governor, John Grant, junior, moved into the new governor's house, which was a part of this gatehouse, and the house he had vacated, became the new central administrative headquarters for the Northamptonshire County Constabulary. It also doubled as the operational headquarters of the Northampton division of the County Constabulary, and it is important to appreciate the difference between these two functions.

The Chief Constable at the time, Henry Goddard, lived in his own house in Albion Place off Derngate, so did not need accommodation. But when he resigned in 1849, the new Chief Constable, Henry Bayly, had to take part of the police headquarters for his own personal residence.

In 1859, the Northampton divisional headquarters of the County Constabulary were moved to the old militia stores in Angel Lane, thus leaving the St Giles Square building just as the County Constabulary headquarters and Chief Constable's house. A new Northampton divisional headquarters was built in 1901 in Angel Lane, which is the building still there today.

The nationwide running of gaols became the sole responsibility of the Home Secretary in 1877, and not the local county magistrates. Consequently, Northamptonshire County gaol was considered redundant, and ceased to be used on New Year's Day 1880, with all the prisoners having to be moved up to the Borough gaol on The Mounts.

The exercise yard at the Northampton Gaol on The Mounts, 1890s. Note the policy of strict segregation. This photograph would have been illicitly taken, hence the poor quality. (NP)

Because of this, in 1881, all the gaol buildings, together with the governor's house, the Chief Constable's house, and the County Constabulary headquarters were sold. In a fit of pique the then Chief Constable, Thomas Lees, resigned. His successor, James Kellie-MacCallum on his arrival in the county rented Wootton Hall for a while, but then brought his own residence at Quinton.

The County Constabulary headquarters moved into George Row, on the site of the old 1675 Gaol, next door to the Sessions House, in a building which had been rebuilt with a new facade in 1846. These buildings remained the headquarters until May 1950 when the County Constabulary moved into its present home of Wootton Hall.

Today, all the old gaol complex is part of the Northamptonshire County Council offices. The old gaol entrance gate is a public house, and the old chief Constable's house and County Constabulary headquarters are the Northampton Tourist Information Office. And because a new court building has just been erected in Lady's Lane, the Sessions House no longer serves the purpose it was built for. It now stands forlornly empty, waiting for — who knows what?

# CHAPTER 8

## 'BECOME MUCH MORE THE BETTER': OTHER PUNISHMENTS USED IN NORTHAMPTONSHIRE

"They say best men are moulded out of faults
And for the most,
Become much more the better
for being a little bad."
*Measure for Measure:* William Shakespeare (1564-1616)

NUMEROUS other punishments for crimes have been given over the centuries, and Northamptonshire has used seven of them:

- i) **Branding**
- ii) **Cucking (or Ducking) Stool**
- iii) **Fines**
- iv) **Pillory**
- v) **Stocks**
- vi) **Transportation**
- vii) **Whipping and Birching**

### Branding

Only given as a punishment for theft (property or livestock) branding with a hot iron was always upon the left thumb and was always done there and then in open court. This punishment seems to have died out by the 1720s, but nevertheless the iron machine for carrying out the punishment was still bolted to the front of the dock in the criminal court of the Northampton Sessions House right up until the turn of this century. But because of alterations to the court, the instrument, which had on it the motto 'Come not here again', has long since been lost.

The punishment consisted of branding the letter 'T' (presumably meaning 'thief') onto the left thumb, was only given to men. But after 1623, it was given to women as well, for theft of goods worth more than one shilling.

The earliest surviving written record of branding in Northamptonshire was at the 1675 Assizes when Joseph Gilbey was found guilty of theft. At the Northamptonshire Assizes of 1720, five people were branded in open court: Silvester Green for sheep stealing; James Corby for pig stealing; and Jane Clarke and William and John Green for 'several petty thefts and larcenies'.

Possibly the last branding in Northamptonshire was at the July Assizes held on 26 July 1726 when Isabella Chapman and John Fielding were burnt on the hand and whipped and then transported for seven years. The crime? Stealing two sheep.

## Cucking (or Ducking) Stool

Consisting of a chair attached to a long pole which was pivoted on a pillar on the banks of a river or pond, the unfortunate who was strapped into the chair could be ducked into the water several times at will by men operating the machinery. And although it was mainly used for gossiping women, men were subjected to it as well. For instance, on Thursday 30 June 1735, John Kinsman, a Naseby shoemaker, was beaten up and ducked on the cucking stool at Kelmarsh on suspicion of being a wizard. And this incident surely gives us a clue about how the cucking stool was used.

For only on two occasions in Northamptonshire can written records be found that the cucking stool was a punishment of a court. At the Michaelmas Quarter Sessions of 1630, Jane Winter of Weldon, 'a woman of a turbulent spiritt and reviler of her honest neighbours in uncivill and unwomanly termes' was imprisoned until she found someone to stand surety for her, but on her return to Weldon, the parish constable was ordered to bring her 'with the cookinge stoole to some convenient place within the towne and there cause her to bee doused and ducked in the manner of scolds'. And at the Trinity Quarter Sessions of 1684, Frances Mason, a widow of Yardley Hastings, was bound over to be of good behaviour, and was ordered to be 'Douckt in ye ducking stoole in the town of Nor[thamp]ton, Saturday next between the hours of 11, 12, 1 and 2'.

These are the only two instances that can be found of the cucking stool being given as a punishment by order of a court. But it is obvious that the cucking stool was used far more than that, and although no cucking stool has survived in Northamptonshire, there is no doubt the majority, if not all, of the county villages had one. It is obvious that the cucking stool was given to dispense instant justice by an exasperated or outraged village populace acting as judge, jury and executioner right there and then. No need to bother with courts — that takes time — instant retribution is what the cucking stool stood for, as can be deduced from the Kelmarsh villagers' treatment of poor John Kinsman who no doubt had logical answers to everything he was accused of, but never had a chance to get his story across.

## Fines

This has always been a favourite punishment, and fines, either in money or kind, have been used since the year dot. The Kentish king Ethelbert (552?-616) in one of the earliest documents in the English language, drew up a code of laws where compensation in money was payable to the victim. A murderer had to pay 100s to the victim's family. Every part of the body had its price: 20s for the loss of a thumb; 50s for an eye, and so on, down to 6d for a toe-nail. Compensation was doubled for offences committed on Sundays, and was also on a sliding scale according to the class of person attacked, the higher the social class, the more money it cost.

But Ethelbert's system of fines went to the victim, fines in later times went into the court, and thence to the Crown, or in other words, straight into the pocket of the king himself. The medieval kings treated the criminal system as one vast money-making machine, and attempts to get money through the courts were blatant. As well as the Eyres (see Chapter 3), the Northamptonshire Assize roll for 1202 gives perfect examples of a medieval court fining people on the slightest pretext.

When Richard of Glendon was murdered at Glendon sometime during 1202, Sybil, his widow, had accused three men — the brothers Richard and William, sons of Henry of Glendon, and Roger of Oxhill — of his murder. The Rothwell Hundred jury had reported the murder to the Assize along with Sybil's accusations, as they were legally bound to do, even though it was obvious that Sybil was having second thoughts, and had not appeared in court herself to make her accusations in person, which, again, she was legally bound to do. She had already withdrawn her accusation against Richard, but the other two had been outlawed because of her accusations.

Both men, however, continued to live in Glendon without belonging to a frankpledge (see Chapter 5) and as the villagers of Glendon had failed to deliver up the two men for trial, the whole village of Glendon was fined. Sybil was also fined for failing to go to the Assize to follow up her accusations. But that was not all. The murdered Richard's brother, Stephen, continued to accuse the other Richard of the murder even though Sybil had withdrawn her accusation against him, and the Court accepted his innocence. So Stephen was also fined for false accusation.

For a piece of blatant money raising, this case is breathtaking, three people and a village fined before the actual case had even got into court.

Another trick of the medieval court for extracting money, is a real piece of 'heads I win, tails you lose' chicanery.

The jury of the Navisford Hundred (the Thrapston area) reported to the Assize that John the Smith's son had been murdered sometime during the year somewhere in the Navisford Hundred. The murder weapon was a stone. Because of the vagueness of the information, it was not known what frankpledge John was in, therefore fines could not be levied at any specific frankpledge of the hundred for not delivering the murderer to the Assize. So in this case, the Assize resorted to the system of 'Englishry'.

After the Norman Conquest, a 'murder fine' was levied on any hundred if a Norman was killed within that hundred. So after every death, an investigation was held to see whether the deceased was Norman or Saxon (English), with only direct evidence from next-of-kin being taken as good enough proof of the person being English. In the absence of any next-of-kin to prove his 'Englishry', the deceased was automatically assumed to be Norman, so making the whole hundred liable for the 'murder fine'.

The blatant use of the courts for money raising gradually tailed off, of course, but fining as a punishment continued up until the present day. There have been times however, when fining people for serious crimes appears inexplicable, although admittedly we do not know the full circumstances. For instance at the Northamptonshire Assizes held in July 1802, Mr Justice Thompson fined George Archer 1s for the killing of Jonathan Muddling at Chacombe. And a year later at the Assizes, Mr Justice Rooke fined William Smith 1s for the killing of Thomas Wilcox at Towcester, although this time he did get a three month spell in gaol as well.

**Pillory**

Like the stocks, the pillory goes back to Saxon times, but unlike the stocks, the pillory was also used to punish tradesmen, mainly brewers and bakers for selling incorrect measures and weights of their products. The pillory however, was not so widely used as the stocks, and not every village had one. It is possible that only Northampton, Weldon, Kettering and Towcester had them. The Northampton pillory stood alongside the stocks on the Market Square and apparently was last used at the start of the 19th century. No pillory, however, has survived in the whole of Northamptonshire.

The earliest Northamptonshire Quarter Sessions reference to the pillory is from the Michaelmas Quarter Sessions of 1689 when Thomas Smith of Kislingbury being convicted of counterfeiting was sentenced to 'stand in the pillory in the Publicke Markett place in the towne of Northampton for the space of one hour betwixt the houres of twelve and two in the afternoon with a writeing on his Breast declaring his crime and be from thence re-conveyed to prison ...'. In 1696, William Dawson was pilloried for two hours at Northampton for sedition, with his crime displayed on a notice above his head.

The pillory was discontinued by an Act of Parliament in 1816, except for perjury, but in 1837 even this was forbidden, and the pillory ceased to be used as a punishment.

**Stocks**

These implements have been used, certainly from Saxon times, and probably way before that as well. Every village had its stocks, as evidenced by the large number of Stocks Lanes and Stocks Hills there are in Northamptonshire villages, because in 1350 a statute made it compulsory for every village in the land to erect stocks, if they had not already got some.

Stocks secured the feet only, whilst pillories secured the head and wrists. Stocks were used as a punishment for the minor, and purely local, offences such as drunkenness, swearing, and that scourge of rural England, vagrancy, after sentencing at the manorial court or court leet. During the middle ages this was a common occurrence, and perhaps the medieval punishment philosophy was more sophisticated than we give it credit for.

When a person was in the stocks, the whole village could see. The person in the stocks could be (and obviously was) subjected to public ridicule. Ridicule is perhaps the ultimate and most hurtful experience that any person can be subjected to. The threat of a dose of public ridicule and embarrassment was arguably the most effective deterrent known to the criminal justice system. Medieval man knew that, and perhaps modern man, in spite of all his sophisticated technology, electronic 'tagging' and 'advanced' penal theories, has lost touch with that basic understanding of the human psyche, what makes people 'tick'.

Today in Northamptonshire there are seven villages where the stocks are still standing and intact, and some of them even have whipping posts attached as well. These stocks are not the medieval ones of Edward I — as being of wood,

Apethorpe stocks and whipping post. The stocks bench can just be seen behind.

Aynho stocks.

Eydon stocks and whipping post.

Kings Sutton stocks.

Little Houghton stocks and whipping post.

Sulgrave stocks and whipping post.

Gretton stocks and whipping post.

they have long since perished — but are of 18th and 19th century construction erected to replace the old ones in exactly the same spot, and it is therefore the site of the stocks that is medieval. Aynho and Kings Sutton have just the stocks, whilst Apethorpe, Eydon, Gretton, Little Houghton and Sulgrave have whipping posts as well.

Apethorpe stocks are a three seater affair, and are unique in the whole of England in that they still have the bench on which the miscreants sat. No other stocks in the country have a surviving bench. The whipping post is also unusual in that it is a separate post rather than an extension of the main stocks construction.

Aynho stocks are believed to be 18th century. The last recorded occupants are Richard Howes, a village labourer, for being drunk and disorderly on Queen Victoria's coronation day (Thursday 28 June 1838); and in 1846, an unknown person for bad language and swearing in the street.

Eydon stocks and whipping post are thought to be late 18th or early 19th century.

Gretton stocks, another three seater, and whipping post date from the late 18th century, but have just been restored. Joshua Pollard was placed in them for six hours in 1857, in default of paying a fine for a previous offence of drunkenness. A year later, Salathiel Warner was secured for exactly the same offence and for exactly the same amount of time, during the whole of which, the village constable PC John Cornish Bennett, who was only 21 at the time and had been in the force for less than a year, stood guard over him.

Kings Sutton stocks are probably of the late 18th century.

Little Houghton stocks and whipping post were erected in 1835 to replace the 18th century ones. They were last used in the 1830s by an unknown man for being drunk and disorderly at the Michaelmas village Feast.

Sulgrave stocks and whipping post are a 1933 reconstruction of earlier ones which stood on the same site.

**Transportation**

This punishment was first tried by Elizabeth I in 1597, but it was not until the early 1700s that transportation had really got into its swing, sending them to the American colonies. The transportation was carried out by private contractors, and those who survived were no doubt sold into slavery. But when the American Revolution came along, in the 1770s, America was no longer available, and so it was fortunate that in 1786, when Captain Cook claimed Australia for Britain, the convicts could be sent there instead. It was of course a further offence to return from transportation before the due time was up, and in Northamptonshire, two men have been hanged for doing precisely that, William Smart and Richard Dove, both in 1759.

Transportation to Australia started in 1787 and continued until 1868. Usually the men convicted for murder were given the choice between hanging or transportation for life. Not unnaturally, the majority, if not all, chose transportation, and in Northamptonshire we have an example of this.

At the 1841 Lent Assizes, Joseph Bedford (22) William Downing (31) and James Underwood (21) all Labourers, were transported to Australia for life for the extremely brutal and callous murder of John Dunkley, a gamekeeper, at Yardley Hastings, on Tuesday 6 October 1840.

Bedford, Downing and Underwood were all poaching on land belonging to the Marquis of Northampton, at New Hay Coppice, Yardley Hastings. After shooting a hare, they separated, but Bedford was caught by Dunkley, one of the estate gamekeepers, and heated words were exchanged. Suddenly both men levelled their shotguns at each other and fired.

Bedford missed with his shot, but Dunkley did not. Bedford was eventually to have 30 shotgun pellets taken out of his left shoulder as a result of Dunkley's shot, which had knocked him flat on his back. Hearing the shooting, Underwood and Downing came running up, and it was Underwood who immediately shot Dunkley in the head with his shotgun from a distance of 9 ft. Dunkley must have died immediately, but the three poachers were far from finished with him yet, and the attacks on the dead body of the gamekeeper continued in what can only be described as a fit of frenzied insanity.

Giving his opinion at the inquest, Dr Pell said that Dunkley had been shot once under the right ear, once in the top of the head, once in the back of the head, and once in the neck downwards when the deceased was lying face down on the

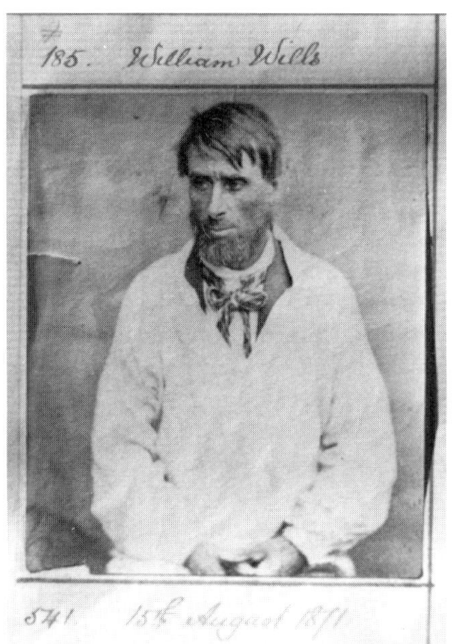


William Wills was sentenced to 15 years transportation at the 1850 Lent Assizes, for the highway robbery of 13s 6d from John Durham at Ashby St Ledgers, Such was the violence used towards the victim that 'he had probably injured his health for the rest of his life'. (NP)

ground. The back of the skull was also caved in, which could have been caused by his own gun being smashed down on his head (it had been found broken nearby) and on top of that, there were marks around the throat as though he had been strangled. Dunkley's body had then been dragged 50 ft to where it had been dumped.

Bedford, Downing and Underwood are the only Northamptonshire men to have been transported for murder. But transportation could be given for other crimes as well. It is not easy to know how many people, or for what offences, from the county's courts were transported. The registers, kept at the Public Record Office, are arranged by ship rather than by county, with each ship taking convicts on a 'first-come-first-served' basis, irrespective of where they had been sentenced.

### Whipping and birching

Without doubt the most widely used and ancient of punishments, whipping is even referred to in the Bible. In England, it has been used since ancient times, but because of a decree of the Star Chamber, was only used on the working class and never on 'gentlemen'.

Newspaper reports and the Quarter Sessions records for both the county and borough abound with cases of minor crimes (including the 'crimes' of having an illegitimate child and being insane) where whipping was doled out as a punishment. Sometimes the whipping was in private in the confines of the prison, such as at the Northamptonshire Quarter Sessions on Wednesday 2 October 1754 when Elizabeth Wormleighton 'convicted of stealing Beans and pease be privately whipt and then discharged on paying her fees'. And from the *Northampton Mercury* of Monday 21 August 1775, when 'three women who were detected in stealing (or what is commonly called shocking) Wheat from the Sheaves in the fields of Daventry ... received sentence to be privately whipped with some degree of severity which they suffered accordingly, and were discharged'.

But more often than not, the whipping was in public, which no doubt was thought to serve as some form of deterrent to others to commit crime, by introducing the public ridicule/embarrassment factor (presumably women, as well as men, were stripped to the waist) as well as inflicting bodily pain, the only common level on which every living person, rich or poor, meets. The public whippings took two forms, static and moving.

The static whippings were at whipping posts, and as we have seen when looking at stocks, the majority of village stocks had a whipping post attached or nearby. The earliest documented case of a public static whipping that can be found in Northamptonshire, is in 1673, when Elinor Child was 'sentenced to be whipt on Saturday next betwixt twelve and two of the cloke in the open mket in the Towne of Northt and then to be sent with a pass to ye place of her last settlemt'.

The last few words imply that Elinor was a vagrant who had wandered into Northampton in order to beg, but who had been caught and whipped for her pains and then sent back to where she had come from.

The moving whippings had the victim's wrists tied to the back of a horse drawn cart which then drove around the town, with the victim walking behind being whipped on the back as they went. In Northampton, there were two distances that the cart travelled whilst whipping was in progress: the 'Short Round' and the 'Long Round'.

The 'Short Round' was, for prisoners coming either from the Borough gaol in the cellar of the old Town Hall (corner of Wood Hill and Abington Street) or the County gaol in George Row — The Peacock Inn (on the Market Square, now replaced by the Peacock Shopping Arcade) — The Parade — The Drapery — Mercer's Row — and then back to their respective gaols. The 'Long Round' was from their respective gaols to the Peacock Inn — Sheep Street — Bearward Street — Horsemarket — Gold Street — George Row — Wood Hill — and back to their prison.

The 'Short Round' was recently paced out as approximately 440 yards, and the 'Long Round' at 1100 yards. It is not known how many lashes to the yard were given, but even if it was one lash for every ten yards travelled, then the 'Short Round' would give about 40 lashes, and the 'Long Round' an incredible 100 lashes.

All the mobile public whippings in Northampton were normally held on Saturdays. In 1690, the Northamptonshire Quarter Sessions sentenced 'John Mondes ... being this present Sessions convict of ffelony be severely whipt on Saturday next the Long Round in Northampton betwixt the hours of Eleavon in the fforenoon and one in the afternoon and be continued in prison till he gives good security for his being of the good behaviour'. At the Quarter Sessions of October 1753, Sarah Andrews of Corby was ordered to be whipped the 'Long Round' for stealing a cloth great coat, and then a week later, to be publicly whipped at Corby.

Presumably, the mobile whippings would be followed around the town by the usual rag, tag and bobtail that were attracted to spectacles like this, and no doubt copious intakes of beer would ensure a boisterous commotion accompanying the procession. In the early 1820s, a certain Miss Hoyland who kept a small school over a shop in The Drapery, always closed her shutters and suspended lessons whenever a flogging was coming down The Drapery, so as not to let her pupils see such an unedifying sight. It was said that at that time, the Official Town Flogger, a Mr Walker, wore a special uniform, and used to carry a red dye in his hand through which he used to draw the lash before every stroke, so that the punishment looked worse than it really was.

An Act of Parliament of 1817 had stopped the public flogging of women, and it is not known when the last public flogging of a man took place within the

Fifteen years old Charles Ashby was found guilty at the 1870 Michaelmas Quarter Sessions of stealing a gold sovereign at Little Houghton. For this he was given one month hard labour, plus ten strokes of the birch. A gold sovereign would be nearly a week and a half's wages — the equivalent today would be perhaps £200-£250. (NP)

county. But flogging and birching (with a bundle of twigs 40 ins long and 9 ozs in weight for those under 16, and 48 ins long and 12 ozs in weight for those over 16) continued inside gaols right through the 19th and into the 20th century.

Whatever the rights and wrongs of this form of punishment, and whether it was effective as a deterrent (there is evidence to show that it was not) and whether it should be retrieved, the fact remains that it was effectively abolished as a judicial punishment by the Criminal Justice Act of 1948, and in today's climate, is unlikely to return.

# CHAPTER 9

## 'DRAWING SUFFICIENT CONCLUSIONS' THE EPILOGUE

"Life is the art of drawing sufficient conclusions from insufficient premises"
*Notebooks: Life 9:* Samuel Butler (1835-1902)

SO what conclusion can be drawn from all this? The only concrete one is that mankind is innately criminal. Crime has always been with us, is with us now, and will always be with us. It is impossible to stamp it out. All we can do, therefore, is try and keep it down to some sort of 'acceptable level'.

Without having any other study of any other county to go on, we cannot say whether Northamptonshire is more criminal, or less criminal, then anywhere else. But it would be a good bet that when other counties are studied, they come up with the same amount of crime as we have in this county.

This has always concerned people, and the newspapers are often full of letters and leaders deploring the amount of crime, and asking what is to be done about it, or what are the police doing about it. In the 1850s there were long series of letters spread over many months, from correspondents sounding off about the level of crime in particular villages of the county. Morton Pinkney, Kilsby, Nassington and Grendon were all subjected to this. These diatribes were normally after the local crime statistics were published, and the usual rag-bag of armchair criminologists offered the usual crackbrain theories.

The statistics given in this book are rough and ready and unsophisticated, it is true, but they cannot be dismissed out of hand, surely, they must show something, or reveal certain trends. The summary is as follows.

**Rate of offences per 1,000 population**

| | Years | | | |
|---|---|---|---|---|
| | 1202 | 1657 | 1852 | 1993 |
| Murder | .4 | | | .01 |
| Damage | | | 1.17 | 16.02 |
| Assaults | .6 | | 1.59 | 4.81 |
| Assaults on Police | | | .21 | .30 |
| Burglary | | | .14 | 29.25 |
| Drunkenness* | | | .74 | .08 |

| | | | | |
|---|---|---|---|---|
| Poaching | | | 1.01 | .08 |
| Rape | .15 | | .02 | .10 |
| Breach of Peace | | .70 | .60 | .75 |
| Robbery | .35 | | .08 | .53 |
| Theft | | | 2.51 | 52.10 |
| Vagrancy* | | | .40 | .08 |

(*Because of different legal procedures, these yearly figures are not really comparable.)

The thing that immediately stands out is the colossal rise in the property crimes of damage, burglary and theft. What does this mean? Have there really been such serious increases in these crimes? Is it a sign of our affluence that we have more material things which are envied by others?

Or can it just be the result of easier reporting procedures? The above figures give the number of crimes reported, and not the number of crimes committed. These two are very different. Can it be that the ease of reporting nowadays is giving a far truer picture of the number of crimes being committed, which previously was hidden because some crimes were going unreported? Previously a petty crime may have been shrugged off because it meant going in person to the police station, but nowadays, we just have to pick up a telephone. So this begs the question, has the number of crimes committed actually increased, or has the number always been at this level, only appearing to have risen dramatically because we now know all the crime that is being committed, where previously we did not?

Certainly, we can also afford more insurance, and insurance companies insist on having every single crime reported. And no doubt, some insurance claims for compensation are made without there actually having been a crime committed, but which has to be reported as a crime in order to claim money (albeit dishonestly) from an insurance company. It has been known.

But there can be no glib explanation of the above figures. Crime is such a complex entity, that no trite theory about its causes can be given in a few words. However, every right thinking person must be concerned about crime, and if this book helps in some small way in the fight to get crime down to our 'acceptable level', then the research and compilation of it would have been worthwhile.

# APPENDIX 1

## GLOSSARY OF LEGAL TERMS USED

**Outlawry**

Everybody knows of Robin Hood's outlaw band, but few would know what an 'outlaw' actually was. In medieval times, it was a specific and well defined legal state.

Only the Assizes could declare anyone an outlaw. The accuser must present his or her allegations before the court, which would then summon the alleged offender to come and face the charges. If the offender failed to appear after being summoned three times, then he would be declared outside the law, an outlaw, or in the colourful legal Latin of the day 'quod gereretur Lupinum capud' — 'let him bear the wolf's head'.

**Sanctuary**

This system was used extensively in medieval times. A fugitive who gained the sanctuary of a church or other religious institution such as a monastery, could remain there for up to 40 days. During this time, the parish had to supply sufficient food to keep him alive, and the four neighbouring parishes had to supply men to keep a constant watch upon the church to see that the fugitive did not escape.

At any time during the 40 days, he could send for the local Coroner, confess his crime, and either give himself up for trial or swear to 'abjure the realm'. If he chose exile, then the Coroner assigned a specific port to him, and he had to walk there 'ungert, unshod, bare-headed in his bare shirt, as if he were to be hanged on the gallows'. He was given a fixed time for his journey, normally one day for each 25 miles distance.

Along the route, he was to carry a Cross as a means of recognition, and was forbidden to stray off the main highway, on which alone he was safe from any harm. He was passed from parish constable to parish constable along his journey, and each parish where he stopped for the night was legally bound to supply him with food.

When he arrived at his port he had to board the earliest available ship. If there were no ships ready to sail, he had to walk into the sea as though to demonstrate his readiness to leave the country, and had to do this every day until there was a ship sailing.

In 1540, the right of sanctuary was much curtailed by abolishing the need to leave the country. Instead all sanctuary seekers were to be kept in a kind of house arrest in any one of eight designated towns throughout the country, one of which was Northampton. This system was never popular and was never a success, despite several attempts at 'tinkering' with it. By an Act of Parliament in 1623, sanctuary was abolished entirely. Hereafter, 'no sanctuary, or privilege of sanctuary, shall be ... permitted or allowed in any case'.

# APPENDIX 2

## UNSOLVED MURDERS

AT this present time, there are several murders in Northamptonshire that are still unsolved, stretching back well into last century.

1 Wednesday 18 April 1838. 48 year old Ann Chown, a single shopkeeper from Braunston, was found horribly murdered and mutilated, with her head nearly separated from her body.

2 Friday 24 December 1886. 78 year old Samuel Osborn was found dead in a cottage in Newland Street, Kettering. His head and face had been smashed to a pulp with a heavy, blunt instrument of some kind.

3 Wednesday 21 January 1891. 72 year old Joseph Dickens, a farm labourer, was found in a ditch in a field in Bedford Road, Rushden. He had been shot, and also had had his head sliced open by his own axe.

4 Saturday 25 October 1952. 65 year old George Henry Peach, and his 70 year old wife, Lilian Rose, were found at their home of West Lodge, Ashton, near Oundle. Both had been bludgeoned to death, possibly by a coal hammer.

5 Thursday 29 June 1972. 20 year old Paul Smith was found dead in a shallow brook in Kings Cliffe.

6 Sunday 29 February 1976. Avis Mary West, an 82 year old lady who was crippled with arthritis, was found battered to death at her home in Northampton.

7 Tuesday 17 April 1979. 15 year old Sean McGann was found dumped in a Northampton alley after he had been asphyxiated.

8 Monday 23 November 1981. Three gypsies, Dolphus Smith aged 57, Siddie Hickling aged 27, and his 27 year old common law wife Susan Ovens, were all found shot in their caravans in Ditchford Lane near to Wellingborough,

9 Saturday 26 March 1988. Despite being charged with the stabbing of 13 year old Carol Baldwin in Lings Wood Park, Northampton, two youths were later acquitted, leaving the murderer still to be found.

10 Saturday 2 January 1988. Plumber Cyril Fensome and his fiancee Florence Pennell were burned to death after ignited petrol was squirted through their letter box, at their home in Rushden.

11 Tuesday 2 August 1988. 70 year old Percy Francis was found battered to death at his home in Rushden.

# APPENDIX 3

## THE NORTHAMPTONSHIRE PRIVATE PROSECUTION ASSOCIATIONS

AS far as is known, there were 33 separate associations in Northamptonshire. This list may not be complete, there may have been more:

| | | |
|---|---|---|
| 1 | Wellingborough | established 1781 |
| 2 | Corby, Huxloe and Rothwell Hundreds (possibly renamed Kettering Commercial and Agricultural in 1818?) and | 1783 |
| 3 | Thrapston | 1783 |
| 4 | Oundle 'Original' | 1783 |
| 5 | Daventry 'Town' | 1783 |
| 6 | Towcester and Brackley (separated later) | 1783 |
| 7 | Barby | 1783 |
| 8 | Crick | 1783 |
| 9 | Northampton | 1783 |
| 10 | Kettering 'Original' | 1783 |
| 11 | Rushton | 1797 |
| 12 | Spratton | 1798 |
| 13 | Harlestone | 1798 |
| 14 | Higham Ferrers | 1810 |
| 15 | Kingsthorpe 'Original' | 1814 |
| 16 | Weekley | 1816 |
| 17 | Warkton (Weekley and Warkton combined in 1869) | 1816 |
| 18 | Northamptonshire, Warwickshire and Oxfordshire (centred on Charwelton) | 1816 |
| 19 | Daventry 'District' | 1817 |
| 20 | Cranford | 1818 |
| 21 | Rothwell | 1818 |

| | | |
|---|---|---|
| 22 | Walgrave | 1819 |
| 23 | Broughton and Cransley | 1823 |
| 24 | Gretton | 1826 |
| 25 | Burton Latimer | 1834 |
| 26 | Oundle 'New' | 1837 |
| 27 | Weldon | ? |
| 28 | Kingsthorpe and Weston Favell Union | ? |
| 29 | Wymersley Hundred | ? |
| 30 | Welford | ? |
| 31 | Clipston | ? |
| 32 | Geddington | ? |
| 33 | Brixworth | ? |

# APPENDIX 4

## CHIEF CONSTABLES

**Northampton Borough Police**

1 1836-1851 Joseph Ball
2 1851-1887 Henry Keenan
3 1887-1923 Frederick Henry Mardlin
4 1924-1955 John Williamson
5 1955-1966 Dennis Roy Baker

**Northamptonshire County Constabulary**

1 1840-1849 Henry Goddard
2 1849-1875 Henry Lambart Bayly
3 1875- Charles Pearson
4 1875-1881 Thomas Orde Hastings Lees
5 1881-1931 James Dalgleish Kellie-MacCallum
6 1931-1941 Angus Arthur Ferguson
7 1941-1960 Robert Henry Dundas Bolton
8 1960- John Aidan Hastings Gott

**Northampton and County Constabulary**
*(Formed 1966 by the amalgamation of the Northampton Borough Police and the Northamptonshire County Constabulary)*

1 -1972 John Aidan Hastings Gott
2 1972- Frederick Arthur Cutting

**Northamptonshire Police**
(Renamed in 1974)

1 -1980 Frederick Arthur Cutting
2 1980-1986 Maurice Buck
3 1986-1991 David John O'Dowd
4 1991-1996 Edward Crew
5 1996- Christopher Fox

# APPENDIX 5

## GAOL GOVERNORS

**Northamptonshire County Gaol**

| | | |
|---|---|---|
| 1 | 1660s | John Snart |
| 2 | 1670s | Valentine Chadwick |
| 3 | 1681-1689 | Thomas Chadwick |
| 4 | 1689-1698 | John King |
| 5 | 1698-1726 | Thomas Chadwick |
| 6 | 1726-1743 | Michael Warwick |
| 7 | 1743-1744 | Joseph Warwick |
| 8 | 1744-1752 | Guy Warwick |
| 9 | 1752-1767 | William Warwick |
| 10 | 1767-1773 | Philip Warwick |
| 11 | 1773-1800 | John Scofield |
| 12 | 1800-1818 | John Wright |
| 13 | 1818-1845 | John Grant, Senior |
| 14 | 1845-1857 | John Grant, Junior |
| 15 | 1857-1876 | Benjamin Rust |
| 16 | 1876-1879 | Charles Farquerson |

**Northampton Borough Gaol**

| | | |
|---|---|---|
| 1 | 1842-1878 | George Arkesden |
| 2 | 1878-? | John Howe |

# APPENDIX 6

## JUDGES BORN IN NORTHAMPTONSHIRE (UP TO 1900)

**Abbreviations:**
**B of=Bishop of**
**b=born at**
**br=brother**
**bur=buried at**
**d=died**
**dis=dismissed**
**CJ=Chief Justice**
**ChEx=Chancellor of the Exchequer**
**(C)JE=(Chief) Judge in the Court of Exchequer**
**(C)JCP=(Chief) Judge in the Court of Common Pleas**
**(C)JK/QB=(Chief) Judge of the Court of King's/Queen's Bench**
**cr=created**
**gs=grand son of**
**imp=imprisoned**
**J=Judge in an unknown Court**
**LdCh=Lord Chancellor**
**LdTr=Lord Treasurer**
**MI=monumental inscription at**
**MP=Member of Parliament for**
**res=resigned**
**s=son of**

BASSET, Ralph. Of Weldon. CJ to William II
BASSET, Richard. s of Ralph. CJ to Henry I. d c1154 bur Abingdon
BILLING, Thomas. b Ashwell. MP City of London 1448. CJ of King's Bench 1469-1481. MI Wappenham
BLENCOWE, John. b Marston St. Lawrence 1642. MP Brackley 1690. JE 1696. JCP 1697-1726. d 1726. bur and MI Brackley
BOUDON, William de. 'Of Northamptonshire'. JE 1327
BRAYBROOKE, Robert of. Possibly J 1199-1207.
BRAYBROOKE, Henry of. s of Robert. Possibly J 1224.

## *Appendix 6*

BRAYBROOKE, Robert de. B of London. CJ 1382-1383. d 1404. bur St. Paul's Cathedral
BROWNE, Samuel. b Polebrook. MP Dartmouth 1640. JKB 1648-1649 res when refused to try king. JCP 1661-1668. d 1668. bur Arlesley, Beds
BRUDENELL, Robert. b Deene. JKB 1507. CJ 1521. bur Deene
CATESBY, John. b Whiston. JCP 1481. bur St. James, Northampton
CAVE, Lewis William. b Desborough. JCP 1881-1897. d 1897 Epsom
DE CAVE, John. b Stanford. J 1254-1261
DOLBEN, William. b Stanwick. JKB 1678-1683 dis. JKB again 1689-1694. d 1694. bur Temple Church
EVERDON, Silvester of. B of Carlisle 1246. J 1251.
GREEN, Henry. b Brigstock. JCP 1354. CJKB 1361. d 1369
HATTON, Christopher. b Holdenby. MP Northamptonshire 1572. LdCh 1587. d 1591. bur St Paul's Cathedral
HOLT, John. 'Of Northamptonshire'. JCP 1383. d 1418
LANE, Richard. b Courteenhall. CJE 1644. d 1650 France
MONTAGU, Edward. b Brigstock. CJKB 1539. CJCP 1545-1553 imp in Tower but released. d 1557. bur Kettering
MONTAGU, Henry. gs of Edward. b Broughton. MP for Higham Ferrers 1601. CJKB 1616. LdTr 1620. cr Earl of Manchester 1626. d 1642. bur Kimbolton
MONTAGU, William. br of Henry. b Broughton. CJE 1676-1686 dis. d 1707
MONTAGU, James. gs of Henry. JE 1714. CJE 1722. d 1723
MORGAN, Francis. b Kingsthorpe. JQB 1558. d 1558. bur Nether Heyford
NICHOLS, Augustine. b Ecton. JCP 1612. d 1616. bur Kendal. MI Foxton
NORTHAMPTON, Henry of. Vicar of St Peter's, Northampton. Canon of St Paul's. J 1188-1202
PAGITT, James. b Barton Seagrave. JE 1631. d 1638. bur and MI Tottenham
PATTISHALL, Simon of. J 1193. d c1217
PATTISHALL, Hugh of. s of Simon. B of Lichfield and Coventry. ChEx 1230. d 1241
PATTISHALL, Martin of. J 1217
PATTISHALL, Walter of. J 1219
PINKENI, Gilbert of. b Moreton Pinkeney? 1170
PRESTON, Gilbert de. 'Of Northamptonshire'. J 1242. CJ 1269?
QUINCY, Saherus de. b Long Buckby. J 1214. cr Earl of Winchester 1210
RAINSFORD, Richard. b Staverton. MP Northampton 1653, 1661. JE 1663. JKB 1669. CJKB 1676. d 1679. bur and MI Dallington
SAUCEY, Robert de la. 'Of Northamptonshire'. J 1234?
SAUNDERS, Edward. b Harrington. MP. JCP 1553. CJCP 1557. d 1576
TANFIELD, Laurence. b Gayton. JKB 1606. CJE 1607. d 1625. bur Burford, Oxon
THORPE, Simon of. 'Of Northamptonshire'. J 1252-1256. d 1259

WARD, Edward. b Stoke Doyle. CJE 1695. d 1714

YELVERTON, Christopher. b Easton Maudit. MP Brackley and Northamptonshire. JQB 1602. d 1612. bur Easton Maudit

YELVERTON, Henry. s of Christopher. b Easton Maudit. MP Northampton. Attorney-General 1617. JCP 1625-1629. d 1629

# APPENDIX 7

## NORTHAMPTONSHIRE EXECUTIONS

HISTORICALLY, Northampton has always been important, and in the olden days there must have been numerous executions within the town, and within the county also, because some of the Lords of the Manor had the power of dispensing the death penalty at their manorial courts. But of these early executions scant trace remains. As we come nearer to our own times, however, written records made at the time have been preserved. It is from these sources that the following list was compiled, although it is not claimed as complete, there may be some more. Every execution for an offence which occurred within the Borough and County of Northampton (not including the Liberty of Peterborough), and for which there is documentary evidence, is included. All executions were held in Northampton unless stated otherwise, and all were executed by hanging unless stated otherwise.

| | | |
|---|---|---|
| 1 | 1202 | Godfrey of Warkton for Murder |
| 2 | 1296(?) | William de Havering for Murder |
| 3 | 1316 | Henry of Killingworth |
| 4 | | William, son of Peter Gosse |
| 5 | | William the Miller<br>all for Murder |
| 6 | 1316 | Julianne de Murdak. — Burnt for Murder of Husband |
| 7 | 1316 | John Cicaying for Murder |
| 8 | 1317 Wednesday 20 July | John Poydras for Treason |
| 9 | 1469 Thursday 27 July | Earl of Pembroke; and |
| 10 | | Sir Richard Herbert — Beheaded for 'Treason' |
| 11 | 1557 September | John Kurde — Burnt for Heresy |
| 12 | 1587 Sunday 8 February | Mary Stuart, Queen of Scots — Beheaded (at Fotheringhay) |
| 13 | 1607 | Enclosure rioters (at Newton) |
| 14 | 1611 Wednesday 23 February | Thomas Sparrowe (at Abington) |
| 15 | 1611 Friday 8 April | Stephen Preston (at Kingsthorpe) |
| 16 | 1612 Sunday 22 July | Agnes Brown; |
| 17 | | Joan Vaughan; |
| 18 | | Arthur Bill; |

| | | |
|---|---|---|
| 19 | | Hellen Jenkinson; and |
| 20 | | Mary Barber — all for Witchcraft (at Abington) |
| 21 | 1622 Monday 7 March | Alice Chadwick |
| 22 | 1623 Wednesday 19 July | John Hilliar |
| 23 | 1630 | 'A malefactor pressed to death' |
| 24 | 1631 | Mrs Lucas — Burnt for Murder of Husband (on Hunsbury Hill) |
| 25 | 1636 | John Barker; |
| 26 | | his 'Kinswoman'; and |
| 27 | | his Servant for child murder (at Abington) |
| 28 | 1638 Friday 5 March | Arthur Bett (at Abington) |
| 29 | 1645 | An unknown woman — Burnt for Murder of Husband |
| 30 | 1651 | Leonard Bland for Theft |
| 31 | 1655 | An unknown woman — Burnt for Murder of Husband (on Boughton Green) |
| 32 | 1674 | Ann Foster for Witchcraft |
| 33 | 1685 Sunday 11 March | 'An unknown malefactor' |
| 34 | 1685 Sunday 27 May | George Tarry for Murder |
| 35 | 1705 Tuesday 17 March | Elinor Shaw; |
| 36 | | Mary Phillips — both for Witchcraft (the last execution for Witchcraft in England) |
| 37 | 1714 Monday 9 April | 'Mr Knighton' for Murder |
| 38 | 1715 | Elizabeth Trasler — Burnt for Murder of Husband |
| 39 | 1724 Monday 20 March | Richard Snarey for Murder |
| 40 | 1729 Monday 21 March | Samuel Adams for Murder |
| 41 | 1730 Monday 24 July | Benjamin Frier for Robbery |
| 42 | 1731 Monday 26 March | William Walker for Murder; and |
| 43 | | John Woodroff for Burglary |
| 44 | 1732 Monday 10 March | John Cuthbert for Robbery; and |
| 45 | | Samuel Bayley for Burglary |
| 46 | 1733 Monday 9 March | William Allcock for Murder |
| 47 | 1735 Monday 8 August | Elizabeth Wilkinson — for pickpocketing; and |
| 48 | | Elizabeth Fawson — Burnt for Murder of Husband |
| 49 | 1736 Monday 20 August | May Hadon for Murder |

| | | |
|---|---|---|
| 50 | 1737 Tuesday 6 August | Henry Doggs and |
| 51 | | Jacob Medlicouts — both for Highway Robbery |
| 52 | 1738 Tuesday 29 July | Henry Clark for Murder |
| 53 | 1739 Sunday 22 March | John Cotton for Murder (at Paulerspury) |
| 54 | 1740 Monday 25 April | William Welford for Burglary |
| 55 | 1741 Monday 3 April | Bryan Connell for Murder (at Weedon Common) |
| 56 | 1743 Monday 11 March | William Porter for Murder |
| 57 | 1743 Tuesday 26 March | William Attenborough for Murder |
| 58 | 1745 Monday 9 August | Joseph Goodman for Robbery |
| 59 | 1747 Monday 14 August | William Curtis for Murder |
| 60 | 1749 Monday 17 March | Joseph Elliott and |
| 61 | | William Lamb — both for Highway Robbery |
| 62 | 1750 Monday 23 March | Thomas Wakelin for Robbery |
| 63 | 1750 Monday 24 August | Joseph Dobbs for Burglary; and |
| 64 | | John Lavendar (17) for Arson |
| 65 | 1754 August | William Love (16) for Robbery |
| 66 | 1755 Thursday 24 July | John Brown for Burglary |
| 67 | 1759 Saturday 31 March | Ann Loale for Murder |
| 68 | 1759 Friday 6 April | John Forward for Forgery; and |
| 69 | | Richard Alcock for Horse theft |
| 70 | 1759 Saturday 28 April | William Smart — for Returning from Transportation |
| 71 | 1759 Saturday 11 August | Richard Dove — for Returning from Transportation |
| 72 | 1764 Monday 23 April | Thomas Seamark for Robbery |
| 73 | 1764 Saturday 5 May | Russell Rowledge for Robbery |
| 74 | 1764 Saturday 4 August | Benjamin Deacon; |
| 75 | | John Croxford; and |
| 76 | | Richard Butlin — all for Murder |
| 77 | 1764 Friday 10 August | John Kilsby for Robbery |
| 78 | 1770 Tuesday 14 August | Anthony Harwood and |
| 79 | | William Craddock — both for Highway Robbery |
| 80 | 1775 Tuesday 11 April | Samuel Paine for Burglary |
| 81 | 1775 Friday 11 August | William Barker for Forgery |
| 82 | 1784 Monday 8 March | Elizabeth Nokes for Murder |
| 83 | 1784 Friday 26 March | John Wilson for Wounding |
| 84 | 1785 Monday 7 March | John Roberts for Robbery (at |

| | | |
|---|---|---|
| | | Boughton) |
| 85 | 1785 Friday 18 March | Thomas Skelcher and |
| 86 | | John Bull — both for Horse Theft |
| 87 | 1785 Friday 22 July | James Tarry for 'Robbery' |
| 88 | 1785 Friday 5 August | John Smith and |
| 89 | | Richard Kelly — both for Robbery |
| 90 | 1786 Saturday 11 March | William Howell for Murder |
| 91 | 1786 Friday 24 March | Thomas Allen for Horse Theft |
| 92 | 1787 Friday 3 August | John Smith; |
| 93 | | William Bowers; |
| 94 | | Richard Law; and |
| 95 | | William Pettifer (The Culworth Gang) —all for Robberies |
| 96 | | David Coe and |
| 97 | | John Hulbert — both for Robbery |
| 98 | 1788 Saturday 22 March | John Bateman for Sheep Theft |
| 99 | 1789 Tuesday 18 August | Thomas Gordon for Murder |
| 100 | 1789 Friday 27 March | ? Underwood for Burglary |
| 101 | 1790 Sunday 28 March | ? Higgins for Horse Theft; and |
| 102 | | ? Brawn for Robbery |
| 103 | 1792 Monday 23 March | James Cross and |
| 104 | | Thomas Smith for Robbery |
| 105 | 1794 Friday 21 March | Benjamin Pearce for Theft |
| 106 | 1799 Friday 19 July | Thomas Hanger for Horse Theft |
| 107 | 1801 Friday 31 July | William Walters for Horse Theft; and |
| 108 | | William Higgerson for Sheep Theft |
| 109 | 1807 Friday 20 March | Robert Stafford for Attempted Murder |
| 110 | 1812 Monday 9 March | William Jones for Murder |
| 111 | 1813 Friday 13 August | Huffham White and |
| 112 | | Robert Kendal for Theft |
| 113 | 1814 Saturday 23 July | Thomas Morris for Murder |
| 114 | 1815 Friday 28 July | Thomas Bayson for Sheep Theft |
| 115 | 1818 Friday 27 March | James Cobbett and |
| 116 | | George Wilkin both for Forgery (the last execution on Northampton Racecourse) |
| 117 | 1819 Friday 19 March | William Minards; |
| 118 | | William George; |

| | | |
|---|---|---|
| 119 | | Benjamin Panther; |
| 120 | | John Taffs; and |
| 121 | | Edward Porter — all for Burglary |
| 122 | 1819 Friday 6 August | Richard Lilleyman for Arson |
| 123 | 1821 Thursday 8 March | Philip Haynes and |
| 124 | | Mary Clark — both for Murder |
| 125 | 1821 Friday 23 March | James King for Rape |
| 126 | 1822 Friday 22 March | George Julyan alias Jennings for Sheep Theft |
| 127 | 1822 Friday 2 August | William Meadows; |
| 128 | | William Gent; and |
| 129 | | Redmond Gent — all for Rape |
| 130 | 1825 Friday 29 July | William Longslow for Sheep Theft |
| 131 | 1826 Friday 21 July | George Catherell for Robbery |
| 132 | 1830 Friday 19 March | Thomas White for Rape |
| 133 | 1831 Friday 18 March | James Linnell for Arson |
| 134 | 1832 Monday 5 March | William Grant for Murder |
| 135 | 1834 Monday 31 March | Thomas Gee for arson — the last execution for a non-homicide offence |
| 136 | 1852 Tuesday 16 March | Elizabeth Pinckard for Murder — the last public execution in Northamptonshire |
| 137 | 1871 Monday 31 July | Richard Addington for Murder |
| 138 | 1874 Monday 30 March | Thomas Chamberlain for Murder |
| 139 | 1878 Tuesday 12 November | Patrick Byrne for Murder |
| 140 | 1893 Tuesday 10 January | Andrew MacRae for Murder |
| 141 | 1893 Wednesday 18 July | Richard Sabey for Murder |
| 142 | 1899 Tuesday 11 July | Joseph Parker for Murder |
| 143 | 1901 Sunday 7 July | Alex Claydon for Murder |
| 144 | 1904 Wednesday 13 July | Samuel Rowledge for Murder |
| 145 | 1914 Tuesday 10 November | John Eayrs for Murder — the last execution ever in Northamptonshire. |

# SOURCES

## BOOKS, ARTICLES AND THESES


Anonymous *Executions in Northampton 1277-1893* (1886)

Charlesworth, Andrew (ed) *An Atlas of Rural Protest in Britain 1548-1900* (1983)

Christian, Garth (ed) *James Hawker's Journal. A Victorian Poacher* (1961)

Cowley, Richard *Policing Northamptonshire 1836-1986* (1986)

Cowley, Richard *The Inspectors of Constabulary: Their influence on the policing policy of England and Wales 1856-1919* Unpublished MA thesis, University of Leicester (1990)

Critchley, T. A. *A History of Police in England and Wales* (1979)

Emsley, Clive *The English Police: A Political and Social History* (1991)

Gatrell, V. A. C. 'The decline of theft and violence in Victorian and Edwardian England' in *Crime and the Law. The Social History of Crime in Western Europe since 1500* (1980)

Greenall, R. L. 'Parson as a Man of Affairs: The Rev Francis Litchfield of Farthinghoe, (1792-1876)' in *Northamptonshire Past and Present* (1990-1991) Volume VIII, 2, p.121

Hanawalt, Barbara A. 'Violent Death in Fourteenth- and early Fifteenth-Century England' in *History* (1976) Vol 18, No 3

Hatley, Victor A. 'Some aspects of Northampton's History' in *Northamptonshire Past and Present* (1965-1966), number 6

Hawkings, David T. *Criminal Ancestors: A guide to Historical Criminal Records in England and Wales* (1992)

Hay, Douglas and Snyder, Francis 'Using the Criminal Law 1750-1850' in *Policing and Prosecution in Britain 1750-1850* (1989)

Hibbert, Christopher *The Roots of Evil. A Social History of Crime and Punishment* (1966)

Manchester, A. H. *A Modern Legal History of England and Wales 1750-1950* (1980)

Markham, Christopher *History of the County Buildings of Northamptonshire* (1885)

Markham, Christopher *Ancient Punishments in Northamptonshire* (1886)

Mather, F. C. *Public Order in the Age of the Chartists* (1959)

Pearson, Geoffrey *Hooligan, a History of respectable fears* (1983)

Pringle, Patrick (ed) *Memoirs of a Bow Street Runner* (1956)
Savill, Stanley *The Police Service of England Wales* (undated, 1901?)
Serjeantson, Rev R. M. *Sanctuary Seekers in Northamptonshire* (1913)
Shorthouse, R. W. 'Justices of the Peace in Northamptonshire 1830-1845' in *Northamptonshire Past and Present* (1974) Volume V
Smith, Constance I. 'Northamptonshire in the History of Witchcraft' in *Northamptonshire Past and Present* (1966-1971) Volume IV, pp341-347
Steedman, Carolyn *Policing the Victorian Community. The formation of English Provincial Police Forces 1856-1880* (1984)
Stenton, D. M. (ed) *The Earliest Northamptonshire Assize Rolls AD 1202 and 1203* (1930) Northamptonshire Record Society, Vol V
Stephen, Sir James *A History of the Criminal Law in England* (1883)
Stone's *Justices' Manual* (1919)
Storch, Robert D. 'The plague of Blue Locusts. Police Reform and Popular Resistance in Northern England, 1840-57' in *International Review of Social History* (1975) 20, pp61-90
Storch, Robert D. 'The Policeman as Domestic Missionary: Urban Discipline and Popular Culture in Northern England, 1850-1880' in *Journal of Social History* (1976) ix, 1976, pp481-509
Thompson, F. M. L. *English Landed Society in the Nineteenth Century* (1963)
Wake, Joan (ed) *Quarter Sessions Records of the County of Northampton 1630, 1657, 1657-8* (1924) Northamptonshire Record Society Vol I
Wilson, Colin *A Criminal History of Mankind* (1984)

# NEWSPAPERS AND MAGAZINES

*The Northampton Mercury*
*The Northampton Herald*
*The Kettering Evening Telegraph*
*Northamptonshire Notes and Queries*
*The Northampton County Magazine*
The Chief Constable's Annual Reports
Printed Parliamentary Papers

Original photographs and various Registers kept at the Northamptonshire Police force museum at Wootton Hall.

# *Guilty M'Lud!*

# Index

# Index

# *Index*